D1569063

By the same author

Pick Up Your Couch and Walk:
How To Take Back Control of Your Life

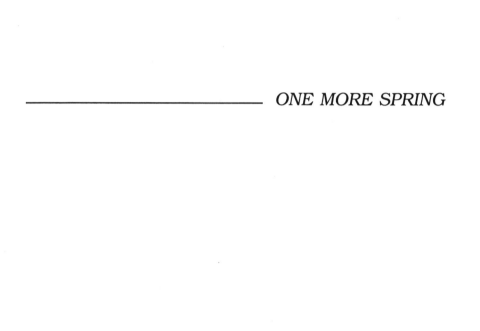

ONE MORE SPRING

PETER M. KALELLIS

ONE MORE SPRING

A Story of Hope and Friendship

Crossroad • New York

1995

The Crossroad Publishing Company
370 Lexington Avenue, New York, NY 10017

Copyright © 1995 by Peter M. Kalellis

Printed in the United States of America

Library of Congress Cataloging-in-Publication Data

Kalellis, Peter M.
    One more spring : a story of hope and friendship / by Peter M.
Kalellis.
        p.   cm.
    ISBN 0-8245-1524-2 (hardcover)
    1. Kalellis, Peter M.   2. World War, 1939–1945—Personal
narratives, American.   3. World War, 1939–1945—Greece—Mytilēnē.
4. Youth—Greece—Biography.   5. Psychotherapists—United States—
Biography.   6. Mytilēnē (Lesbos Island, Greece)—History, Military.
I. Title.
D811.5.K2987   1995
940.54'8173—dc20   95-34098
                                                        CIP

My Gratitude

to my friends and coworkers,
Dr. Wendell Shackelford and Margery Hueston,
who enthusiastically edited the original draft.

The characters in this book are real.
With the exception of the four friends,
who stood united and survived the Nazi invasion,
most names are fictitious to protect the innocent
and their relatives from painful reminders.
The historical circumstances that determined
their actions are authentic. The life of Takis
during those dark days is a synthesis of the lives
of a number of young men who were victims
of the Nazi oppression. Several of them
were personally known to the author.
This book is reverently dedicated to their memory.

Beseiged by land and sea,
starved, tormented, haunted by daily executions,
our hearts yearned for justice and freedom.

In blessed memory of
two dedicated Greek Americans
who were trapped in the Nazi plan
of human destruction,
my father, Asimakis,
and his friend Lefteris.
Memory Eternal!

To my loving wife, Pat,
who never tires of listening
to my war experiences.

And
to my children,
Mercene
Michael
Basil
Katina,
in fervent hope that someday
they will tell the story of
One More Spring
to their children.

Contents

Prologue

I am a therapist. A half-dozen diplomas and a state license hang on the walls of my office where I practice in Westfield, New Jersey.

Young and old with all sorts of psychological problems come to me searching for a cure. A cure for what? I haven't cured anyone yet, but as they talk to me, many get better, or feel better.

On a Tuesday afternoon in late October, David Holstein shuffled into my office for his weekly session. This was his third appointment. Hair hanging over his eyes, pimpled face, blue windbreaker, torn jeans, and sneakers untied, he flopped into the leather chair opposite mine. As his anxious brown eyes looked at me, he kept biting off the skin at the edge of his thumb until the raw flesh showed. He sucked at the wound and agonized. Stretching toward him, I gently took his large hand in mine and said, "This needs a Band-Aid."

"No-o-o," he sneered, shaking his hand free and returning the injured thumb to his lips.

The sun streamed through the window to my left. I felt its warmth, took off my glasses, and rested my back. Even with blurred vision, I could see anxiety in David's eyes.

Therapy don't do me no good," he said, licking his thumb. "Prozac, the miracle drug—that didn't do much either."

"It seems pretty hopeless to you," I said.

"Yeah."

"What would you like to see happen?"

"I don't know." He shrugged his shoulders sadly.

"That is not an answer. You must have some notion . . ."

"Sure," he interrupted. And clenching his fist he placed his index finger to his temple and pulled an imaginary trigger.

"What are you not telling me?" I asked, ignoring his pantomime.

1

"Don't play shrink with me, Doc," he said, raising his voice. "You know what I'm telling you. I know where to get the money, and I know where to buy a gun, and I know what to do with it."

"Use it?"

"You guessed right! Use it! But before I use it on myself, a few others have got to go . . . you know—a holocaust. I can see the headlines: Holstein's Holocaust!" Now his trigger finger was pointed at me.

"Am I one of the 'few others'?" I asked, concealing my concern.

"Oh no, Doc, not you!" he protested.

"Why not?"

"You're a good man—a silly old shrink—but at least you listen when I talk."

"I try," I said, and kept processing my thoughts as I looked at this tormented youth who was threatening to end his life. I needed a strategic effort. I rolled my tongue over my dry mouth.

David, in the sixteenth year of his life, a former A student, tall, handsome, and very bright, was caught in the dilemma of his parents' explosive divorce. He had recently lost his girlfriend to a popular senior, failed in most subjects, and totally lost motivation. He spent his free time watching television and was late for school every morning. He repressed his feelings about such a life and became destructive of his personal possessions—stereo, VCR, computer—and he burglarized houses.

David was the grandson of Dr. Herbert Holstein, who had died in Germany in a concentration camp. He had never met his grandfather, but he had seen photographs of him and read some of his published articles, written prior to World War II. David's father, Dr. Bernard Holstein, always talked with pride about "Grandfather Herbie," the wise physician, whose valuable contributions to the field of medicine ended with his execution by the Nazis. Bernard had escaped the Holocaust, thanks to his uncle, who had taken him to America and supported him through medical school. Now a prominent physician, Bernard had aspirations for his son. He wanted him to follow in his and Herbert Holstein's footsteps. The boy's failing school grades disappointed him deeply.

Although I perceived some difference in his posture and interaction with me, his unexpected statement burst my bubble of optimism, and there I was with a sixteen-year-old who threatened suicide.

"Life is lousy," he said. "It stinks."

"It's unfair, too," I said.

"Others have all the luck."

"What do you have?" I asked.

"Pain." He sighed.

I believed him.

The following week, David walked into my office with an air of grandiosity. He held a violin case, which he rested by his feet as he sat across from me. It appeared to be heavy. He smirked.

"Are you taking violin lessons?"

"Sure." He laughed as he lifted the case and laid it open on his lap.

I looked at the gun, complete with silencer, and managed to force a casual smile. "That's quite some violin. May I see it?" I was hoping my voice did not betray my anxiety and fear.

"Sure." He placed the case on my lap.

I could hear my heart pounding, and it took all my strength to pull myself together. "I know a lot about these babies," I said, with a great show of confidence. Carefully I lifted up the gun, and as I examined it, I had an instant recollection of the day when Alexis, the tavern keeper in my hometown on the Greek island of Lesbos, took me and my friends to a hiding place where stacks of guns were stored. It was during the Nazi occupation of Greece. American marines had smuggled the guns onto the island, and Alexis was one of the few people who knew about the episode, for he had helped the marines in the operation.

"How did you get it?" I asked.

"I told you last week I can lay my hands on anything I want."

"I see you're a man of your word."

"You bet."

I replaced the gun and snapped the case closed. "David, for safety purposes," I said, pointing to the storage closet under my bookcase, "why don't you leave the gun with me. Nobody can touch it here. We need to figure things out."

"I have my own plans."

"I know that, but it would be a good idea to leave the gun here until you have thought things through."

"How do I know I can trust you?"

"David, if you didn't trust me, would you have shown me the gun in the first place?"

"I suppose not." He exhaled with what sounded like a sigh of relief.

He began talking with great feeling about the adults in his life and seeing the world—his world—for the first time. He had repressed a whole segment of feelings: the unjust death of his grandfather, the unexplained divorce of his parents, his demanding and unreasonable teachers, and the losses he experienced. He felt no motivation to live.

If he felt there was at least one person he could trust, he said, life would look different. I took the key chain out of my pocket, removed a key, and gave it to David.

"What's this for?"

I handed over the case. "You can lock this in my closet, and anytime you need it, you are free to come in and get it."

"And how do I get into your office if you're not here?"

"I didn't think about that. Here's the spare door key," I said, as I retrieved it from the corner of my desk.

"I can't believe you trust me with the key to your office!"

"You trusted me with serious secrets," I said.

He locked up the violin case, and on his way out, he tested the door key.

"You're a good guy, Doc. A bit crazy, but good."

During the fifth session, David checked the closet. Satisfied that the gun was where he had left it, he was willing to reveal more information about his life. He belonged to a secret organization, the NNC, Neo-Nazi Club, whose purpose was to clean up the scum of the town, certain teachers, some parents, and a number of yuppies. He took the list out of an envelope and showed it to me.

"You should keep the list with your gun."

"Why?"

"For safety," I said. I suspected he was still testing me.

He followed the suggestion and seemed pleased with himself. He shook my hand, saying, "No games."

"No games, David."

The possession of a weapon and his membership in the Neo-Nazi Club enabled David to display an air of superiority, but beneath the display was an enraged boy who hurt deeply. I wanted him to learn that he was not the only sixteen-year-old who had suffered at the hands of adults.

At the next weekly session, I said, "When you handed your gun to me, you shot me back fifty years ago to the time when I was sixteen. A Nazi soldier pointed his gun at me and scared the pants off me."

"But you told me you were Greek."

"When you asked me about my accent, I told you I was *born* in America. But I grew up in Greece."

"What was a Nazi soldier doing in Greece?"

David suddenly realized that I had not always been a silly shrink and that at one time I was a boy.

"It's a long story. Like the rest of Europe, Greece was invaded by thousands of Hitler's soldiers."

"Did you fight back?" Now I could see curiosity in his eyes.

"Indirectly," I replied.

"Did they hurt you?"

"A great deal."

"How?"

"The first day they landed on my island, they ransacked my home, took my bike away from me, and burned the little American flag I had fastened to the handlebars. They killed my father's best friend, and eighteen months later they killed my father."

"How terrible!" he said, his voice sad and low. "Did they kill many?"

"Too many."

"Weren't you afraid they'd kill you?"

"All the time."

"How long did the Germans stay?"

"Four years," I said. "Four gruesome years of famine, illness, and death. I saw people dying of starvation; hundreds of others were executed."

"How did you manage to survive?"

"It was not easy. I always had hope that I would live to see my country free."

"Just hoping . . . that's what kept you going for four years?"

"Yes, hope was my motive."

"You should write a book about this." His eyes brightened with sincere interest.

"If I do, will you read it?" I smiled.

"I know I will. I do some writing myself."

Here, I thought, I had the eye of the needle to his soul. I had read two excellent poems on death that he had written and a maudlin story about Diane, a girl in prison. (Indeed, I wondered if Diane were not a symbol of David's imprisoned psyche.)

"I like your poems. You have a flair for imagery."

"I'm better with prose," he responded.

"Will you ever finish Diane's story?"

"I don't know." He thought for a few seconds. "I don't know how to finish it."

"Well, will you leave Diane in prison?" I was pretty sure that David really was writing about himself—feeling completely trapped.

"I don't know how to get her out," he said.

"Maybe if I tell you how I survived the Nazi occupation, you may get some ideas." I smiled at him, and he, in turn, gave me a genuine smile.

The urge to tell David what had happened to me kept me awake that night. Early the next morning, I was at my typewriter and once again started the story of the Nazi occupation. I say "once again" because I had started the story some thirty years before and was unable to bring myself to finish it; the recollections were too painful. Now my typing clicked along, trying to keep up with my thoughts, as I sang the song "One More Spring," written by my friend Pantsaris. I wanted to tell my story just as it had happened.

On each of the five weekly visits that followed, I sent David home with a chapter describing what had happened to me and my three boyhood friends back in Greece. He brought each chapter back, and we discussed various incidents. It was evident that my experiences evoked feelings in him about his own life.

"I don't know how you lived through such horrors."

"I don't know either. Would you have survived?"

"If a Nazi soldier slapped me like that, I'd have attacked him and choked the life out of him."

"That's how I felt—but he had a gun!"

"Why didn't you get yourself a gun?"

"If the Nazis discovered anyone with a gun, they not only killed the owner but the whole family."

David was stunned. His face was a mixture of empathy and confusion. He looked at me almost in disbelief. Perhaps it was curiosity, but the look caused me to have some doubts about involving David in my experiences. I could hear the conflicting voices of my two supervisors when I was in training: Dr. Fred Tate said, "Your patients pay you to listen to their stories. They don't want to hear yours." On the other hand, Dr. Thomas Adams claimed, "In relating your experiences to your patient, when appropriate, you invite him to come out of his own neurotic cocoon and see that there are people in this world who have similar or even worse experiences."

"Well, do you think you would like to read any more chapters?" I asked.

"You said you'd give me a chapter a week. I'd rather read your stuff than take Prozac every day."

So I gave David a chapter a week. By the end of the fifth week he brought me a rough draft of a revised version of his story of Diane.

It is fascinating what symbolic material the unconscious can produce. David's Diane finds herself prisoner in a concentration camp, tortured by SS soldiers, raped by Hitler himself, and pregnant. Again and again she throws a thick burlap bag over the barbed wire fence and attempts to escape, but she is dragged back. Her father visits her unexpectedly, but he is not her father—he is Hitler. Her mother becomes a whore, dresses in sleazy clothes, and is patronized by Nazi soldiers. Both parents blame Diane for her imprisonment: "It's your own fault; you disobeyed us." Their treatment leads her to believe that being in prison is preferable to living at home.

"Diane prefers the security of misery in the prison," I remarked.

"She has no choice," David blurted out.

"From what you have read of my story so far, did I have any choice?"

"You had friends."

"Right! In your story, can Diane have friends?"

"I guess she could be a friend to some of the prisoners in the camp."

"Suffering shared may not be as painful as suffering in isolation," I suggested.

"Did having friends help you?" he asked.

"You'll see when you read the next chapter."

Over the following weeks, I saw new vitality in David's face. He kept coming back to me, and we shared our stories with each other. His story of Diane contained self-discovery, and by the following spring, David had survived the descent of the Furies upon his psyche. He no longer considered the gun. He was healing.

This book is the story that helped David recover his hope and his will. I tell it as I lived it with my friends and my family on the island of Lesbos more than fifty years ago.

CHAPTER 1

Nazis Invade
the Land of Colors

Lesbos, May 4, 1941

"A swastika! What happened to the blue and white cross of the Greek flag?" His heart fell to the pit of his stomach. The broken cross of the swastika flapped fiercely over the castle tower. As he reached the bottom of the hill, the old castle of the city of Mytilene came into view, and Takis pulled on his brakes, skidding to a halt. The sky-blue flag that had waved every day over the castle was gone. In its place, a swastika snapped in the stiff wind. Takis blinked in shock. *It's true,* he thought sadly, *the Nazis have invaded Lesbos.* He got off his bike and walked slowly the rest of the way to school.

The flag with a white cross in the center symbolizing faith in religion and homeland had been ripped down. The Nazis had erected in its place their flag of horror: a crooked cross to defy religion, red to signify bloodshed and rage, and the black of death—to those who disobeyed the Führer. As if to reflect this threatening presence, a cloud hung over the eastern horizon, casting gloom on Mytilene, the capital city of Lesbos.

Takis, a tall, thin teenager with wavy hair and deep-set brown eyes, rode his bike daily from his little town of Moria to Mytilene. He felt older than sixteen, and his behavior was more mature than that of his peers, so he tended to choose friends older than himself. He had a special fondness for seventeen-year-old Stratis Bouras, who had a beautiful sister, Eleni, with whom Takis was in love; and he also enjoyed the company of Alexis, the staunch tavern keeper, who was twelve years his senior.

The morning tide of the Aegean sea was high, and waves of blue broke into foamy masses on the rocky shore below the road. He felt the spring breeze cool his sweat, and the rapid beating of his heart slowed as he descended the hill. The town of Mytilene, where he went to school, was spread out before him.

Mytilene, an ageless town established about 3000 B.C., is tucked away in the foothills of the mountains that sprawl out into the distance. Like a flock of white sheep, whitewashed houses stud the slopes down to the harbor. A cement walkway in the shape of a horseshoe marks the shoreline, a haven for colorful boats, both large and small. The marketplace, a kilometer long, maintains its own identity. Takis always enjoyed this part of his ride to school, for he was fascinated by all the stores with their big window displays and mirrors.

He had the best bike on the island. He had always dreamed of owning a bike, and then, one day, his stepmother, Katerina, received a registered letter that answered his prayers. His father sent money from America and gave him permission to make his precious purchase. Every night, Takis polished his bike with passion, so that it shone a deep metal blue. On his way to school every morning, he would ride past Eleni's house, ringing his bell, hoping that she would look out of the top window and see him. It was easy to recognize his bike by the Stars and Stripes mounted between the handlebars. His father had sent him the small American flag, which, Takis knew, was his father's way of saying "Son, you're an American."

As he went through the streets of Moria, the villagers smiled, calling out as they always did, "Here comes the *Americanaki*—the little American." Takis was as proud of being an American as his father was. He would return to the New World in five-years time, he knew, for there was not much future for men on the island. Takis, like his dad, would seek his fortune in America.

Takis had been born in Philadelphia, Pennsylvania. His mother died when he was three years old, and Takis and his father, Asimakis, journeyed from America to Lesbos. Soon his father remarried and within a few years had returned to America to make more money, leaving Takis and a younger brother and sister with his stepmother, Katerina. World War II, however, propelled Asimakis back to his homeland to protect his family. He did well in America, but now his family needed him at home.

* * * * *

There is a changeless quality about the island of Lesbos. Nearly every morning the sun bathes the whitewashed houses lavishly, and the stucco walls in turn reflect this blinding brilliance. Every day, older folks frequent the olive groves or orchards to trim and prune trees and to harvest ripening fruit. Wives and younger women tend to domestic matters. Young men shepherd the goats and sheep to the hillsides. Children walk to school.

With its two thousand inhabitants, Moria, one of the many little villages on the island, rests on the slope of a hill, among a forest of olive trees, pomegranates, and pine stretching to the blue Aegean sea. The white sand of the shores melts into the sea where motorboats and ships with open sails, built to withstand the storms, set out for distant lands. The old harbor glitters in anticipation of a friend or in dread of a foe.

Always near the sea, boys who are to become men are taught by elders to breathe toward that place where the shadow of a sea gull vanishes, that they may be strong. Along the shore, the rocks assume the shapes of the saints, for it is here that their spirits dwell. They do not move. They do not speak. They do not feel. They communicate on deeper levels, and this is the reason they understand only one another. The sea breeze blends gently with the fragrance of the trees and caresses the swarthy faces of the islanders. An aura of peace and harmony, not to be found on the mainland, pervades.

It was not until 1939, when the people of Lesbos began to hear about the ill fate of distant European countries, that they began to feel uneasy. It was hard for them to imagine that the tranquility of their remote island could be disturbed by a world war.

*****

Cycling through the side streets and narrow alleys on the bumpy cobblestones, Takis felt sick with fear and was unaware of the perfume of jasmine and roses that garlanded the walls. He heard church bells clanging vehemently. People, half-dressed and barefoot, rushed in panic from their homes, and slamming the doors behind them they raced in the direction of his school. Terror stiffened the muscles in his legs, and to avoid cramps in his calves, huffing and puffing, he pedaled faster.

He sensed that tragedy was coming. He had heard the news on the radio the previous night: the two major cities of Salonika and Athens were in the hands of the conqueror. Would the Germans take over his island? This thought tormented him as, in his panic and confusion, he sped to school to find out what was happening.

When he finally arrived, the playground was filled with students as well as men and women and children of the village who had come to hear the latest news.

On a marble dais at the top of the steps near the main entrance he saw Mr. Lainos, the one-armed teacher of history, who paced up and down, his temples throbbing, waiting for a quiet moment. *He's my teacher,* Takis thought, recollecting the stories of war Mr. Lainos told in class—how he had fought the previous year in the Albanian war and lost his right arm.

Takis weaved through the crowd, making his way to the steps across from Mr. Lainos. The teacher's dark eyes flashed, and Takis could see he was adamant. A moment of silence prevailed, and Lainos began to speak.

The throngs surrounded the dais to listen to the speaker, who paced firmly right and left, his words forging their spirit with pride.

"The book of Genesis begins with the creation of man and woman and God empowering them with dominion over creation. Genesis was written by inspired men, not by monkeys."

A nervous laugh rippled through the audience.

"We're not absolutely sure that God did actually grant humans dominion over other creatures." Mr. Lainos lowered his voice so that it rolled like thunder. "When Hitler read the book of Genesis, he decided that God spoke about him, and he set himself up to rule over nations, large and small, even our little island of Lesbos." He paused, and with compassion in his eyes, surveyed the crowd that continued to swell as waves of people joined it.

"The Nazis have invaded the land of colors. Lesbos, the Bride of the Aegean, succumbed to the enemy forces last night. Our whole nation will be under Hitler's yoke, but only for a while. The Greek spirit cannot be conquered, for we have given the world much: the ideal of democracy, the importance of human life, art, drama, culture, science, and philosophy. Our destiny as a nation is to be plagued by enemies: Persians, Romans, Turks, and now Nazis. But it is also our destiny to fight for our freedom. Our soldiers and sailors have taken their weapons and retreated to the mountains and seas to prepare themselves for the fight."

Takis saw the glitter in his teacher's eyes. Again his voice thundered: "There will be long, dark days ahead, but remember, of all the virtues we honor in our fathers, mothers, and glorious ancestors, the most noble is the love of one's country."

Suddenly the people, young and old, began to sing, raising their voices in the old patriotic song:

> *Greece will never die,*
> *She is afraid of no foe,*
> *A few days she needs to revive*
> *To continue her glorious role.*

Kozyris, the gray-haired mayor, shook the hand of the speaker and advised the crowd to return home quietly and to begin cultivating the soil carefully that the island might be self-sufficient as far as food was concerned.

Takis pushed his bike back home, not having the heart to ride it. Heavy, black clouds covered the blue sky. The news was threatening to everyone, and bad news traveled quickly. The territory of the Third Reich had expanded rapidly. Hitler's gigantic army shattered Europe, and, having overthrown Yugoslavia, next attacked Greece. On their way to Athens, the Nazis burned two thousand villages and killed the inhabitants.

This information was confirmed in the evening by the radio station in Athens. Takis and his friends Bouras, Pantsaris, and Tsakiris had joined the older folks in Alexis's tavern. Enveloped in cigarette smoke and tavern noise, the villagers huddled together and listened to the bulletin, which filled their hearts with defiance.

Earlier this evening, the enemy destroyed the entire monastery complex of Agia Lavra in Kalavryta and killed all the monks. A firing squad executed thirteen hundred men who protested.

An uproar broke out in the tavern as the customers, wild with rage, cursed Hitler and his army. Alexis pounded his fist on a table and told everyone to shut up or get out. Takis and his friends stayed beside the radio, and Alexis stood near them so that he could listen to the rest of the news.

After a few seconds of silence, the station began to play the Greek national anthem. Suddenly, the listeners could hear the sound of men in the background shouting in the German language. The announcer came on the air again. "We have been invaded. This is the our final broadcast. People of Greece, swear on the holy gospel never to heed the tyrant's words, neither work for him nor be beguiled by bribes." His voice was choked with emotion.

That night, Takis tossed and turned and was unable to rest. He visualized the Germans taking over the island. What would the enemy do to his family? He was tormented.

In the morning as he cycled past St. Basil's Church, he slowed down. The words of the announcer echoed in his mind. He gazed at the cross and, placing his hand on his turbulent heart, swore eternal revenge against those who had conquered his island. He wanted to climb the walls of the castle and tear down the swastika. He wanted to burn down the German quarters. He wanted to poison the Nazis and kick every one of them into the Aegean. He looked up at the darkened sky and decided that someday he would burn the Nazi flag.

Within three days, the German soldiers were taking over houses, harassing the villagers, and throwing them out of their homes. Everywhere children were wailing. Takis gnashed his teeth as he watched a woman, her children in her arms, escaping by the back window of her house to avoid the invaders' attack. Men and women dragged bundles of belongings as they sought refuge in the fields. As he passed the house of his father's friend Lefteris, he saw Merope, Lefteris's wife, and Niko, their ten-year-old son, at the windowsill, weeping.

In her desolate house, Merope sat close to her son; a mother next door squeezed her babe in her embrace and shuddered. Apostolos, the butcher, his shoulders drooping, passed by and blasphemed at his barking dog. And in the village square, the Nazi boots pounded the cobblestone streets with the sound of rolling thunder, and the spurs, echoing "tran, tran," chilled Takis's heart.

"Mrs. Merope, what's the matter?"

A flood of tears was the only response. Merope, her face buried in her black mantle, held on to her son. Takis's knees trembled, and he felt the despair of helplessness. Something terrible must have happened. Would the Germans treat our hometown of Moria as the Turks had for four hundred years—killing the men, enslaving the women, filling their harems with our young girls, raising our boys as Turks? How many times had his teacher, Mr. Lainos, told the gruesome stories!

Takis cycled past the chaos of horrified, innocent folk and arrived at his own home to find that the place had been ransacked. A tall, slender German lieutenant was in charge, his face expressionless under his helmet. He obviously felt important in his well-pressed green uniform and shining officer's stripes. Beside him stood Cara Beis, the town leech, who acted as interpreter. The lieutenant barked out orders to Cara Beis, and they both carried out boxes piled with dishes, silverware, and blankets, and placed them in a military jeep. The lieutenant's extended index finger cut through the air with menacing gesture, which Takis would soon come to know as particularly German. The sight and smell of the Germans, and the untimely absence of his father, who would have defended his family, increased Takis's apprehension.

He took a deep breath and held it for as long as he could. He could not recall any consoling words from his teacher's patriotic speech. His mind was paralyzed with anger and fear, and he held on to his bike for security. Seeing the American flag, the lieutenant frowned and approached, mumbling biting German words at Takis, who instinctively knew he was being cursed. Then, pulling a cigarette lighter from his pocket, the helmeted invader set fire to the American flag between the handlebars and laughed boisterously as the silk cloth turned to ashes.

"Please, please, don't take my bike," Takis cried. "It's my only . . ." His heart rose into his throat, and he was unable to finish his plea.

The lieutenant unclenched the boy's fingers and freed the bike, and Takis lost his balance and fell backwards. From the rear of the yard his stepmother hurried to his side, wrapping her arms around him. It was a warm embrace that conveyed strength, comfort, and love. Her tender face was framed with abundant black hair, and her gracious smile, the most powerful of her characteristics, could melt steel—but could not change the will of the Nazis.

Takis, from the safety of her embrace, cried out, "Leave my bike alone, you lizard-faced monster!"

Katerina touched Takis's lips. "Sh. . . ." Her penetrating eyes stared at the enemy. "My son needs his bike to go to school. Seven kilometers each way, six days a week, is too far to walk."

"He's young and strong. He can walk," the lieutenant replied through the interpreter as he tested the saddle of the bike.

Through his tears, Takis saw the lieutenant riding away on the bike behind the jeep. The boy was brokenhearted, but his tears dried with the thought of revenge. *Bouras, Pantsaris, and Tsakiris, they will understand. They are my friends, and together we'll blow the Nazis to pieces,* he told himself. He rushed off to the White Dove, the sweet shop of Moria, in the hope that he would find some of his friends there.

Katerina's sadness over the loss of her son's bike was now added to her distress at the loss of her household belongings confiscated by the Germans. Having been born into a poor family, she could deal with deprivations, but how would her husband react, she wondered. She stood before a mirror in the foyer, twining her hair into a big chignon before cleaning up in the Nazis' wake. She could scarcely hold back her tears, for her son's shouting still echoed in her ears. The face in the mirror looked sad and helpless.

She was worried, too, about her husband, Asimakis. He was a stable and mature figure in her life, but he could not deal with emotional elements in his own. He frequently admonished Takis not to waste his time with friends. He advised his son to work hard, succeed, surpass all his classmates, and stay out of trouble. Takis was twelve when his father went back to America, and during his four years there, Asimakis had no emotional contact with his son. Therefore, he had no rapport with his son; yet he expected Takis to behave like a mature adult. Instead, the two argued—about Takis's friends, his school reports, and his general lack of industry.

Katerina fully accepted her husband as an equal mate, but an equal who ought to be obeyed. She never called him by his first name but addressed him as "Lord," or "Good One." "Your lord will be upset if you come home late," she would say to Takis. Now she could hear him say to Takis, "You didn't listen to me. I told you to hide your bike from those infidels."

By dusk, the high spirits and easy laughter of the Moriani were no more. Eight hundred soldiers were temporarily billeted in their houses, and Moria, a village that had shed so much blood fighting Romans, Persians, and Turks, that village whose people would drink ouzo, glass after glass, for any festive occasion, that village once as fierce as an aroused lioness, was now silent and sad. Now Moria, with her whitewashed houses and elegant landscape, lay in the sunset like a bereft widow. Her children, speechless and frowning, sat in the coffee shops, arms dangling listlessly over the sides of the straw chairs, heads bent forward in shock. Their eyes had no spark, no desire, no joy. Only pain.

CHAPTER 2

Moria's First Victim, An American

When Takis's father, Asimakis, returned from America to the island of Lesbos, the Nazis had already invaded Yugoslavia. Six weeks passed before they landed in Lesbos. What his American friends had told him in the States again and again about Hitler—that he would not last six months—had proven false. Every day the Führer moved more forcefully toward his goal—to conquer the world. After fifty-two days of war, though men, women, and children had fought for their freedom, the entire nation of Greece had been subjugated.

When Asimakis had first seen the swastika flying over the castle of Lesbos, his heart was heavy with sorrow. A glance at the red and black symbol sent him to the nearest tavern, where he drank alone, with each glass questioning his decision to leave America. He definitely resented having to return to Greece because war endangered his family. His sense of reason and justice could not tolerate the fact that the Germans had already invaded Lesbos.

The weight of sorrow soon subsided, however, when he began to think of the possibility of escape. *Maybe Lefteris and I could find a way,* he thought. *At least, we could organize some sort of resistance to undermine the enemy.* Several days later he sought out his childhood friend Lefteris, who had also spent a number of years in Brooklyn. He found Lefteris on the outskirts of Moria, under an olive tree. He was with his ten-year-old son Niko, resting while they grazed their goats.

"What kind of Americans are we?" Asimakis asked.

"Shush . . . are you crazy? The trees have ears."

Niko was climbing an olive tree pretending to look for a nest, but he actually wanted to listen in to the conversation between his father and Asimakis.

Asimakis, a fine, stately, if rather corpulent man, sat down beside Lefteris, pulled out a jackknife and carved himself a cane out of an olive-tree shoot. He had great respect for his friend and shared with him a bond of pride and good fortune—they had both sought and gained American citizenship.

"I should have listened to my friends and stayed in the U.S.A.," he told his friend, "but I thought of my son Takis and his future. Who would have thought that these green dinosaurs would come to Lesbos and occupy our little town of Moria!"

Asimakis trimmed the olive branch skillfully and cursed under his breath. His stick seemed ferociously straight as he raised it against the cloudy sky. Lefteris elbowed him gently and whispered, "Asimakis, we are at the mercy of these accursed creatures. Only God knows if we'll ever escape their fury."

But in his memory hid a shadow that Lefteris had never revealed to anyone, not even Asimakis. While he was in America, he had met a German girl, hardly seventeen years old, who, like him, had gone to America to study. They both worked in a Greek restaurant on Flatbush Avenue in Brooklyn, he as a chef, and she as a waitress. Nature took its familiar course; they fell in love, and Ute became pregnant. When Lefteris found out, he disappeared. He left Ute with his child growing in her belly—and a dozen snapshots of themselves in bathing suits, taken at Coney Island.

Lefteris was thirty-four, small boned, and usually wore a kindly expression. He preserved a tender and beautiful memory of Ute, the seventeen-year-old blond in Brooklyn. Merope, his wife, was also of light complexion and blue eyes, but she had more Mediterranean contours. He had returned from America, two years before World War II had been declared, to be with his young wife and son.

In Lesbos, he tried to live a peaceful life with Merope, but he could not be content. A lingering fear that his sin of abandonment might catch up with him some day caused him to remain in a perpetual state of unhappiness. Now, with eight hundred German soldiers in Moria, Lefteris avoided any possible confrontation. Even the sight of a Nazi uniform caused his stomach to churn.

Lately, Asimakis, with his staff in one hand and pulling a goat with the other, had taken to meeting Lefteris every day under the same olive tree to share stories and dreams. When the whistle of the olive-oil factory signaled noon, they ate stale corn bread with salty black olives and drank fresh water from the well.

May 12, 1941

The sun's rays came down upon them and warmed their bodies, but a devastating loneliness had fallen upon the two friends.

Asimakis thought fondly of a breakfast of ham and eggs with hashbrown potatoes and a cup of American coffee. Lefteris smacked his lips over a vision of apple pie and ice cream.

When the clock in the belfry rang five, they prepared to leave.

"It's time to go home. I'll see you tomorrow, eh?"

Asimakis rubbed his long nose and pinched it. "Okay," he whispered.

In silence, the two men crossed the Camela river and slowly ascended the hill of Moria. At the top of the slope they parted ways, for their homes lay on opposite sides of the village. As Lefteris turned the shoemaker's corner, he saw a crowd of women and children whose eyes were filled with fear. He did not understand what was going on, but his heart beat rapidly. At the entrance to his house, two German shepherds were chained to the doorknob, and a short man, Cara Beis, known in Moria for his scams, was acting as interpreter. Upon seeing him, Lefteris felt sick. "Cara Beis, what's the meaning of this?" he asked.

"I'm only an interpreter." Cara Beis shrugged his shoulders. Lefteris grabbed him by the shirt and looked him in the eye. "I asked you a question."

Cara Beis's eyes shifted left and right, and Lefteris knew he had been betrayed. But why? He turned toward his house. *What do they know about me?* he wondered.

Inside, the lieutenant and a soldier who were searching through the drawers and closets had found documents, savings certificates, pictures of Lefteris dressed in a Masonic uniform, and a rifle, all of which he had brought from America.

At the sight of the invaders in his home, Lefteris hesitated, but the thought of what might be happening to his wife and son propelled him forward. Cara Beis pulled him by the sleeve of his jacket and said, "Don't go in—that is, if you're smart."

"This is my house."

"Not any more." Cara Beis laughed.

The lieutenant and his escort emerged from the house carrying photographs, a mason's pot, and the hunting rifle. Lefteris's face lost its color, and his knees trembled.

"I am a loyal citizen. I have harmed no one." Lefteris addressed these words to Cara Beis, but before any attempt to interpret was made, the lieutenant barked a command to his soldier and to the interpreter. The soldier, assisted by Cara Beis, handcuffed Lefteris and escorted him roughly to the jeep.

"I want my daddy," screamed Niko.

"My husband hasn't done anything wrong, Mr. Cara Beis. Please, please tell the officer," begged Merope. But the jeep roared away, leaving behind a cloud of dust and confusion.

* * * * *

"Where's our son?" Asimakis asked before greeting his wife with the familiar "*Kalispera*—good evening."

Katerina, with fingertips over her mouth and fearful eyes, replied that she had not seen him since noon.

"Going to Alexis's tavern with his friends and visiting girlfriends at night is no longer allowed. The army of occupation is adamant about the 6:00 P.M. curfew."

Takis and his friends Stratis Bouras, Yioryo Tsakiris, and Patroklos Pantsaris were not at Alexis's tavern or visiting girlfriends, as his father feared they might be. They were indeed violating the curfew, but if Asimakis had known what rebellious thoughts they were entertaining, he would have been infuriated and frightened.

These four friends sang in the church choir, and in the evenings they serenaded the village girls. They attained fame as the Moria quartet; Takis's voice seemed to excel over the other three, and perhaps that was why he became their leader. He had persistent organizing skills and had the distinction of owning a soccer ball, which enabled him to become captain of the team. As goalkeeper, he was excellent and had aspirations of playing on the Greek national soccer team. His friends called him "Spider," for he caught the ball as cleverly as a spider catches flies. The Nazi invasion disrupted their teenage activities. Although Nazi soldiers patrolled every inch of the island, they did not dampen Takis's hope to escape to freedom. It was his spirit that breathed solidarity into the quartet. "Look!" he would say, pointing across the sea to Turkey. "All we need is a small boat to row ourselves to freedom."

The risks involved in escaping were intimidating, but Bouras appeared to be brave and was enthusiastic about making escape plans. He knew an old craftsman in a village by the sea who could build them a boat. It was at this point that Takis renamed Bouras, "Bull."

Pantsaris was of a shy disposition and appeared troubled. He grew up in a home where the father was absent most of the time. His father, a professional thief, was in jail during his son's schooling years. Pantsaris's mother was determined to make her son a professor. However, his friends paid little attention to her idea, for they had decided on his career and had dubbed him "the Poet."

Tsakiris was a school dropout. He believed he had better things to do with his life. He enjoyed improvising meals, developing recipes out of existing herbs and vegetables. The joy of freedom was wrapped up in the discovery of food. He could not tolerate the tragedy of children starving to death. His prize meal, a sort of meatless meatballs, a composite of ground roots, flour, spices, and eggs, won him the title "Chef." Although in love with his teacher's daughter, Nepheli, he could not be persuaded to return to school. When he became aware that the Poet was also enraptured with Nepheli, he became enraged. The situation was resolved when the Poet said, "We're friends. It's not worthy of us to fight over girlfriends." Tsakiris replied, "Whoever touches my girl, my gun, and whatever I love, will turn me into a criminal." His friends, who disapproved of him for dropping out of school, called him "Boudala," an endearment meaning "stupid jerk," but he did not mind. He loved his friends and would even kill for them if necessary. He was the first of the four to learn how to fire a gun, and eventually, he owned one, in spite of the Nazi law that "natives caught possessing weapons or radios will be sentenced to death instantly." Boudala defied the rule, for he was determined to kill the enemy before the enemy killed him.

While Asimakis was worrying about his son's whereabouts, the four friends were involved in their own trials and tribulations. Long before sunset, they had gone to the cemetery on the outskirts of Moria. After wandering among the crosses and monuments and noting the dates of the deceased, they went into a cement repository under the chapel. Surrounding a pile of bones of unclaimed corpses were neatly painted boxes containing the remains of identified persons who had died a few years ago. The friends sat on the boxes, and in the dusk they held each other's hands in fear and anguish and swore secretly to fight the Nazis. "Sabotage," they whispered, looking at each other earnestly. "Sabotage!" Together they sang softly their national anthem:

> Out of the sacred bones of our ancestors
> rises hope, rises freedom . . .

Tears streaming down their faces and voices rough with emotion, they could not finish the verse. But as they shook hands, they solemnly pledged freedom or death together.

Later that night, Takis removed the sign with the name of his village, Moria, written in large German script. Having committed his first act of sabotage, he took the sign home; and exhausted with fear and exultation, he burst headlong into the kitchen, holding the sign for all to see. His father stopped what he was doing and looked in disbelief at his son. "I tore down that marker. I hate the Nazis and their bold black letters," he told his father.

Katerina and her children were frying pancakes made of broomseed flour. In the total absence of bread, these crunchy pancakes were to be divided equally among the whole family. Takis noticed that his stepmother favored eight-year-old Kiki and six-year-old Jimmy with the largest pancakes.

When Takis was finishing his last bite, Katerina excused herself and took the little ones to their bedroom. Father informed Takis that they must talk, and Takis felt his body shake with a wintry chill when he looked into his father's eyes; in one sharp, quick blast, Takis was so cold and dry that his cheeks felt scorched and turned red, burning like the flames under the frying pan.

In the next room Katerina moved as quietly as she could in order to hear the conversation between father and son. She could hear their low, controlled, angry voices.

"Little devil. Why did you do that? The Nazis would have burned us alive if they had seen you carrying that sign. We are Americans; you know what they would do to the rest of the Americans on the island if they had caught you."

"If they took your bike away, wouldn't you do the same?"

"Son, they emptied our house."

"And you intend to do nothing about it?"

"No, I intend to keep my mouth shut until the day the Americans liberate us."

Their voices grew less and less audible to Katerina as they were drowned in the crackling flames that burned the sign in the fireplace.

Asimakis's face was wrathful as he hacked the plywood sign into pieces. Each time he cut through the board, his forehead contorted; each piece he threw on the fire symbolized another Nazi burning. Takis watched his father's movements and envied his strength. *He could kill them all if he wanted to,* he thought. But his gratification ended in disappointment. He had planned to make a table out of the plywood and paint it blue, but his father had insisted that if the Nazis should ever find out, they would shoot him instantly and burn down their house.

Watching the flames dancing, he asked, "Why are you so afraid, Father?"

"I might be the next," his father said simply, his eyes veiled in sorrow. The news of Lefteris's arrest had already reached him, scaring him out of his skin.

"Is there a way for us to escape these infidels?" Takis asked, interrupting his father's worrying.

Asimakis, watching the last sparks among the ashes, shook his head in silence.

Takis could not sleep that night; he felt angry with his father for breaking the sign into pieces and burning them. He had hoped to make the sign into a table that he would eventually place in Alexis's tavern where it would be a piece of Greek history.

Whenever he closed his eyes, Takis saw scenes from that cruel encounter with the lieutenant—the flick of the cigarette lighter, the burning little American flag between the handlebars. He could smell the burning cloth and see that sneering face. The enemy rode the bike down the street, and Takis's eyes brimmed with tears. It was then that he decided to fight.

What occurred at the Gestapo headquarters that night was a mystery. The following morning, Lefteris—his face and hands swollen from a beating—was delivered to his family, dead. The entire village lamented the loss; Niko and his mother were inconsolable. Merope's dirge and the screaming of her son echoed through the village of Moria from dawn on that dreadful day of Lefteris's funeral. Tears trickling down his cheeks, Takis had tried to keep his ears covered to avoid hearing the heart-rending lamentation that hovered in the air.

Without a word to his parents, he left the house.

A fine drizzle fell all morning from the lowering sky. All along the street he saw the villagers, dressed in black, emerge from their houses and head silently for St. Basil's. The columns under the dome of the church were veiled in black drapes, and purple ribbons were fastened to the flaming tapers on the altar.

The open coffin lay in the center of the church, directly under the dome, and hundreds of tearful eyes looked upon the bloated, bluish face and swollen, scratched hands, still bearing the marks of chains, crossed over the chest of Lefteris's body. The boys' choir, which included Takis and his friends in black shirts made from old drapes, solemnly began to sing the funeral hymn: "What an ordeal the body suffers when it is separated from the soul. . . ."

At the foot of the coffin, the widow and her child cried inconsolably, and the other mourners, too, wiped their tears. As he chanted, Takis's eyes remained fixed on the corpse of his father's friend. At the sight of Niko falling into his mother's arms, he wept. Pantsaris's voice cracked. Takis could sing no longer. Wiping his tears, he thought, *I'll make Niko my friend. It doesn't matter that he's younger. I'll teach him things—how to make a kite. I'll be his big brother.*

Papavasile, the priest, burned incense as he chanted: "Number him among your saints, O Lord," and his eyes moved from Lefteris's bruised face to the serene countenance of Jesus, peaceful and loving, in the vaulted dome above St. Basil's Church, and then to the pensive faces around the coffin. *Why, Lord, do you allow such tragedies to occur among your innocents? As with all tragedies, the human mind will find a purpose*, he thought, shaking his head.

As he looked out over the people he witnessed sadness, shock, bafflement in their eyes. That this could happen, a death so suddenly in their midst—and for what reason? Was Lefteris guilty of some crime? Was he one of those smuggling weapons to the island, weapons which the priest knew to exist—Alexis had told him about them? His eyes sought Asimakis. Perhaps it was Lefteris's American citizenship, a once-proud badge of success that now marked its wearer as an enemy of the new and unforgiving tyrants who had taken over their island. He saw pain and grief and all the signs of worry on Asimakis's face. If the Germans got wind that Asimakis was an American, he might meet the same fate as his dead friend.

Papavasile continued with the prayers, the hymns, and the burial service which followed, knowing things would never be the same. It was as if some unseen hand had the village in its grip, and with each small, unpredictable event, the tension leapt up a notch.

As the Moria quartet brought the chanting down to a hushed diminuendo, ending "Memory eternal . . . " on a perfect cadence, Takis's teary eyes perused the grieving faces. Eleni was not there. He felt her absence. Merope, striding toward the coffin, reached for her husband's hand, her facial expression changed from affection to horror. The screams of her son could not bring her husband back to life. She felt as if a sword had been driven into her soul; her man was dead, and nothing would ever be the same. The muscles in Merope's face relaxed, her jaw grew slack, and grief spread along her face like a rash. It was like watching a second death.

Thus, Moria mourned its first victim.

CHAPTER 3

Houses Empty,
Ghosts Huddled in Corners

Nine days before their appearance on Takis's island, the Germans had suffered hundreds of casualties in a bloody battle on the island of Crete. Men, women, and children fought them with bayonets, knives, scythes, and stones. Their valiant little island held off the enemy longer than did France and some other European countries. But, eventually, the mechanized forces of Hitler leveled their land, leaving behind a vast cemetery, charred earth, ruined homes, and desolation.

Since dawn, Takis had been listening to the distant goose steps of the soldiers, who were steadily advancing. He stood at the top window of his home watching the German battalion that had survived the bloody onslaught in Crete and was now occupying Moria. Eight hundred strong, the SS soldiers flowed through the village in waves of armored jeeps and military trucks, on horseback, motorcycle, and on foot. The iron-shod hoofs of the great horses clattered on Moria's cobblestone streets. The heavy odor of sulphur and soap permeated the air as each phalanx passed by. This was the unrelenting swarm that would live, side by side, with the people of Lesbos. After the thunderous parade through the marketplace, the men were dismissed. By twos and fours the SS entered the houses of their choice, forcing out the inhabitants.

The population being by nature peaceful, the Nazi invaders met with little resistance in Lesbos. General Otto Mueller had learned from classic literature—and had shared the knowledge with his troops—that Lesbos, unlike the warriors of Crete, produced philosophers, teachers, poets, and olive pickers. "Men of the Third Reich, you who are destined to redesign the Mediterranean world, and eventually to rule the world," he announced. "Lesbos will give you rest, Aegean breezes, and a cup of mountain tea."

By the second week of May, the occupation of Moria was complete.

At dusk, the besieged Moriani appeared lifeless and sad. Even the sea breeze that wafts from the Aegean every evening had taken its relief elsewhere.

From the shores of the island to the Turkish mountains, the Aegean sea unfolded, sad and calm as a lake. Takis wished he had the wings of Daedalus or the fins of a dolphin to flee across the eighteen miles of water to Turkey. He lowered his eyes in despair and withdrew from the window to the edge of his bed, where he sat in meditation. He felt numb. The thought of enslavement, especially of his own little village of Moria, was intolerable to him. In school, he had just finished a history course on the four hundred years of slavery under the Turks, who had inflicted brutal tortures on the Greek nation during those four centuries. What if this should happen again? His spine tingled with harrowing feelings of hate and helplessness.

Takis returned to the window. Rain was falling on the deserted streets of Moria, and like tears, it drenched the trees, flowers, and earth, releasing a sweet-smelling fragrance into the cool air. The shower became a downpour, lashing the roof of his house.

He gazed at his room, its bleak walls holding only a mirror and, above his bed, an icon of St. George, patron of the fighters, a present which Papavasile, his priest, had given him when he first began to sing in the choir. On his night table was a gift his father had brought from America—a clock, his fine companion, the singer of passing time. Evenly, it seemed to tick out a dirge: "O how long, how long will the invaders stay?" He opened the window a crack, and the scent of musk crept in, flooding his little room. Then, something phantom, hazy and intangible, seemed to touch the clock, answering the ticking dirge: "One more spring—maybe one more summer—enslaved, enslaved." Takis lay on his bed and buried his head in his pillow, attempting to sleep.

The next morning, fog blocked the sky, an unusual condition during spring in Lesbos. The sun retired behind the gray folds. Olive trees dripped dew on the grass; and in the faces of the few students on their way to school, the day was reflected in somber looks and gloomy expressions. Most of the students were barefooted. They wore faded blue pants and a white blouse. Under one arm they carried three or four books, and their other hand clasped a paper bag containing cured olives for lunch. Food was becoming scarce because the army of occupation had confiscated most of the supplies.

The familiar laughter of the young was absent, and their parents on their way to work showed none of the blind human optimism to help them hope that today would be better than yesterday. The reality of the invasion had sunk in, and the enslaved islanders began to think that their yesterdays were better than their todays.

In Alexis's tavern there was a back room used as a meeting place by a few young men of Moria. It was a white stucco room furnished sparsely with a table and six chairs, separated from the main part of the tavern to allow for privacy. In one corner, a ladder led to the attic above. From the plaster ceiling hung a cage in which the owner's parrot, Plato, resided.

"I talk to Plato," said Alexis. "He's my philosopher, and he gives me advice."

"Has he learned any new words?" Takis asked.

"A few."

About three o'clock in the afternoon, Alexis placed on the table a dish of black olives, a bowl of okra stew, four empty dishes, and a bottle of ouzo.

* * * * *

The boys were devoted to Alexis, for out of the kindness of his heart he had taken them into his life, told them his dreams and disappointments, and shared his intimate ambitions, one of which was to organize the best soccer team on the island. He bared his soul before them. They felt that no other man of his age understood that teenagers needed support and acceptance. They were part of his life, and this became important to the story of Moria as events unfolded and circumstances shifted. How many times during the war did the four friends recall how Alexis used to come through the tavern door to the back room, greeting them in his rasping voice, "Little pricks, be careful of the three evils: war, wine, and whores."

Takis touched his friends on the arm as he glanced around the low-ceilinged room which they considered their hideout. When Alexis joined them, sitting on one of his straw-woven chairs, Takis saw an expression of fear in his eyes. Alexis dished out the okra and poured the ouzo, a quarter of a glass for each of them.

"You mean you'll allow us to drink ouzo?" said Takis.

"Why not?" said Bouras.

"Yeah, why not?"

"Guys, you know we're not of age," Takis protested.

"Listen, sperms of the devil, this is my little kingdom, and when I say you can drink ouzo, then you drink ouzo. No excuses." Alexis demonstrated, adding a little water to his glass. "Drink it slowly and eat something along with it. In that way, you'll never get drunk."

Looking askance at Alexis, the four friends lifted their glasses, saluted each other, and drank. Sipping it slowly, Takis felt the silky, soothing drink numbing his intestines. Alexis took another shot, cleared his throat, and squinted.

"You're no longer boys. You're men with balls," he said in his guttural voice.

"We are men," Tsakiris added.

"Alexis, you're drinking it too fast."

"Shut up, Bouras. Don't insult a veteran drinker," said Takis. "Let Alexis talk."

"We're enslaved, but we're free. Free to fight these vultures that have taken over our land." A glow surfaced in Alexis's face, and courage glittered in his eyes. "This part of my tavern is going to be your inner sanctum, your sacred and secret place."

"Why such an honor?" Pantsaris asked.

"For two reasons," replied Alexis.

With each sip of ouzo, Alexis appeared more daringly patriotic. Takis and his friends took his reasons to heart. Alexis was trusting them with a mission that stirred their youthful minds. They were to become members of the underground movement to overthrow the enemy, and their job included taking supplies of food and weapons to the fighters for freedom.

"Weapons?" Takis gulped his ouzo and coughed. "Where are we going to get the weapons?"

"Leave that to Alexis," said Tsakiris with a laugh. The ouzo made him feel a little muddled.

"Trust me," Alexis said.

"Will you serve us ouzo from now on?" asked Takis, his speech a little slurred.

"Didn't I say that you are now men?" The glasses and dishes jumped as he pounded his fist on the table.

"Alexis means what he says," Bouras said, pleased with his license to drink.

"Okay, little pricks, easy on the ouzo, and don't tease my bird." He pointed to Plato.

"We're not little pricks," Bouras said.

"I know you have a big one," Alexis said with a teasing laugh. "All of you have big ones, so take good care of them. No whores or nonsense." Picking up the empty dishes, Alexis said, "I've got work to do," and he returned to the main area of the tavern.

Takis and Bouras were tall for their age and as thin as beanstalks. Tsakiris and Pantsaris were short and chubby, and both of them claimed that their mothers always made them clean their plates. Pantsaris's mother would say, "Eat, my son, eat, and you'll grow up to be big and strong." Tsakiris needed no urging; he ate everything in sight and was always hungry.

The four friends saw Alexis as a hero, a dedicated patriot who would do anything for his homeland. They saw his wily eyes, but they could not imagine what machinations lurked behind them. Someday he would make men out of them. He would even take them to Despina's house, where the *good girls* resided.

"Alexis can't fool around with us," Takis said as he looked each friend in the eye. They all agreed that Alexis's only purpose in their lives was to make his back room available for fun, serious thought, and shelter. "He can be trusted," added Takis. He felt a sudden sadness moving like a fever from his moistened eyes to his chest to his stomach, causing a strange tightness. He poked his belly a few times and sensed some relief. Then, touching his friends on the arm, he suggested that since it was a lovely May day and the milk was now thick, they should make their customary rice pudding.

After the third round of drinks they were relaxed. Takis began to talk more freely. He told them that during the morning lesson his teacher had ridiculed him in front of the class for misspelling the word *antistasi*, "resistance." "You know how much *iota* sounds like *eta*—well, I used *e* instead of *i*—big shit."

"And what did Zianos say?" Pantsaris asked.

"Mr. Kalellis, you are completely illiterate."

"Big shit . . . and that upset you?" Tsakiris lifted his glass. "Let's drink and celebrate. Resistance is resistance, and you are not completely illiterate just because you can't spell it."

"Thanks, Tsakiris, you're a friend." Takis took another sip. With a sigh, he said, "I hope I live to prove to that pig Zianos that resistance means action."

"Did you tell him that?" Tsakiris asked.

"You bet. I stood on top of my desk and said, 'Mr. Zianos, resistance doesn't have to be spelled in any particular way; it has to be acted.'"

Takis mimicked his teacher's voice: "Oh, you want to be a hero? Class, Takis Kalellis of Moria wants to be a hero, he said, yanking me by the ear and turning me around to face the class. What a beautiful youth you are. Tell your mother to hang a head of garlic and a string of beads around your neck to rid you of the evil. Then she must take you to a studio and have you photographed. Every window in the marketplace of every town on the island should have your picture displayed.

Of course, your classmates and I will pass by every day to admire you and exclaim, 'What a beautiful youth he was!'"

"He's a master of sarcasm." Pantsaris laughed, and the others joined in. "I tell you guys," Takis interrupted, "you may think it's funny, but I felt miserable. I wanted to kill him."

"I would have punched him," Tsakiris said, clenching his fist.

"I'm not going back."

"Takis, it's stupid to drop out now at the end of the year. Another month and school is over," Pantsaris said.

"I want to join the resistance movement. Mountains! Freedom!" Takis said, his eyes shining.

Alexis came back to their table with pieces of octopus sizzling in a ceramic dish. "Right out of the coals," he said. "Eat while it's hot. It'll make your pricks stronger."

"What we need is guns."

"Guns? I have no guns."

"We want to join the mountaineers and fight for freedom."

Alexis bent over them and whispered, "It's not time yet, but I'll keep you in mind, okay? Now, eat and drink."

Alexis went off again and later returned with half a loaf of bread wrapped in a linen napkin.

"Where did you get the bread?" Tsakiris asked.

"That's German bread, I can tell," Bouras said.

"Eat it and shut up." Alexis pretended annoyance, but Takis saw mischief in those sunken eyes.

"Tell us, Alexis, where did you get the bread?" Takis was anxious to find out, for he wanted to discover a source for his own family.

"You may not like to hear how I got it," Alexis said.

"We don't mind how you got it since you're sharing it with us," Bouras said with a grateful smile.

"Before the curfew last night, two young soldiers came into the tavern. 'Cognac, cognac,' they ordered. I was scared. I took two glasses and filled them with Metaxa and gave it to them. Both saluted me and emptied their glasses in one gulp. They wanted refills, and I served them up. Then one of them passed out. The other one unbuckled his belt and motioned me to come closer. I realized what he wanted, so I gave it to him. Early this morning he brought me the bread and wanted me to do him again."

"You mean?"

"Yes, Bouras, I did it again. But believe me, it was no pleasure. It was revenge. The bastards killed one of our good men in Moria. I'll fuck them all, one at a time."

"Revenge is what I want, too," Takis said. "But we can't take revenge with our pricks, Alexis. We need guns."

Alexis shook his head, his eyes full of intrigue. "Guns?" He pondered, and with raised eyebrows, he said, "Come, little American," and he beckoned Takis to follow as he ascended the narrow ladder to the attic. "You, too, Big Prick Bouras. Tsakiris and Pantsaris, follow me, if you really have balls."

They all entered the musty attic. A small skylight illuminated the cobwebbed walls and closets. On the floor lay an old mattress covered with a blanket.

"Sit here." His serious tone was gentle. They sat at the fringe of the blanket. "I may tease and call you names, but I want you to know that your help is needed. The number of mountain guerrillas increases every day, but we need young blood. We want commitment, not empty promises. What do you say?"

"I'll fight," said Tsakiris.

The other three asked in unison, "What are you suggesting we do?"

"Can you keep a secret?" Alexis's eyes looked formidable. "I want to train you to fire a rifle, a revolver, a machine gun—if we can get one." He spoke with confidence and determination. "That was my job when I was in the army. I trained soldiers to attack and kill."

"You'll have us all killed by the Germans once they hear us firing a gun," Takis said.

"Am I a fool? I'll teach you how to handle weapons, how to aim, and when to fire. But of course we won't use live ammunition."

The boys stared at him, their mouths agape.

"When and where do we start?" said Takis.

"Trust me," said Alexis. "I've thought this through. Monday afternoon, Kakourgos, the musician, comes here to practice on his *santouri*. As he strums those thick wires, they make a deafening noise, and that is when you and I will pull the triggers."

"You should be renamed Odysseus," Pantsaris said.

"Can I trust you?"

"You can trust us," Takis volunteered.

"Okay, stand up!"

All four got to their feet, and Alexis pulled the mattress aside while he observed their reaction. In the floor was an opening fitted with a hinged door. He opened the creaking panel to reveal an array of colors; a quilt was neatly spread out. Tsakiris knelt and caressed it; he felt something hard and lumpy under it. Delicately, he lifted the edge, and his eyes widened as they fell upon a shiny revolver and rifle. Alexis turned back another corner of the quilt and revealed a rectangular radio. Takis and his friends were stunned. They knew that possession of a gun or radio spelled an instant sentence of death.

"Alexis, do you want to enter holy immortality?" Pantsaris asked. Tsakiris picked up the gun and held it to his breast.

"Put it down. Don't touch anything."

"I'm just feeling this baby. Wow!"

"Where did you get these?" Takis asked.

"Never mind, *Americanaki.*" Alexis was one of the few villagers in contact with the American marines who had stopped off at Lesbos about two months previously, but he felt that at this point there was no reason to tell the boys the details of that encounter. "The time will come when we'll overthrow the enemy."

"When?"

"When?"

"When?"

"You'll be told when in good time," Alexis reassured them. "Now, make the sign of the cross and promise me that you saw and heard nothing."

"We promise."

Silently, they tiptoed down the stairs and sat at their table. Last to descend was Alexis. He looked taller; his well-combed hair was still neat, his twisted mustache gave him an air of importance, and his face was glowing.

They saw the town of Moria and the whole island through the eyes of Alexis. In the early morning while the boys were on their way to school, Alexis would sit in his favorite chair in front of his tavern, sipping coffee and talking about the town. He was one of those men who were gifted storytellers, who could capture the spirit of a place or event by recounting forgotten incidents, or by digging up skeletons the town might have preferred to leave buried and untouched. Alexis knew them all and could sketch an accurate biography of everyone—the olive pickers, the merchants, the cheaters, the hypocrites, the religious, the insane, the generous. He could list every theft, where the stolen goods went, the infidelities, who slept with whom. He knew the wealthy, too, with all their weaknesses and pretentiousness.

The women of Moria were busy knitting sweaters and preparing meals. Surreptitiously, the four friends took these to the liberators in the mountains, along with personal messages from sweethearts and loved ones in the village. Each Monday at dawn, when the Nazis were out on maneuvers, Alexis loaded his donkey and the boys with bags of ammunition and guns and carefully crept up the mountains to the hideouts. Since hope and weapons came from American marines, Alexis called his assistants *Americanakia.*

Over this secret unveiling of weapons the four friends learned to trust Alexis and his mission, and their love for him grew.

"It's the time of year when young men make rice pudding," he said one evening.

"That's a good idea," said Takis.

"We need to borrow a cup of sugar," said Pantsaris.

"I'll give you a cup," offered Alexis.

"I'll steal some milk from my neighbor's goat." Bouras giggled.

"I'll supply the rice," Tsakiris said.

"Are we meeting at our usual hideout?" Takis asked.

As they talked, Alexis sensed a change in their voices. An incipient fuzz appeared on their upper lips. Curiously, he pursed his lips and went into the main part of the tavern. In that devilish gleam of his eyes, one could suspect what he thought: "Youth coupled with vitality in this quartet; we have an asset for the resistance."

Alexis returned from the front of his tavern with a cup of sugar for Pantsaris. "Go to St. John's Chapel," he said, winking at the four friends. St. John's, at the top of the mountain, was their shelter, their sanctuary.

It took an hour for the friends to reach St. John's through the pastures, then up the rocky trail to the mountaintop. From the chapel belfry, Takis and his friends cherished a panoramic view of Moria, veiled in sadness. Lefteris's death left echoes of tragedy and fear, an atmosphere of silent gloom.

Beneath the chapel was a hidden entrance to a fifty-foot-long tunnel which led into a large cave. Patches of light penetrated cracks in the rocks, giving the cave an eerie atmosphere. Who built it and why had always been a puzzle to the villagers, though the old men said it dated from sometime during the four-hundred-year occupation of Greece by the Turks. It could easily hide a hundred people or more. Since the Nazi invasion, Takis and his friends had met several times in the cave to discuss plans for resistance.

It took a few minutes to build a fire. Tsakiris had brought a few handfuls of rice; Bouras had stolen milk from a neighbor's goat; and Pantsaris had the sugar which Alexis had given him. Takis brought a pot.

The fire of olive-tree branches filled the cave with a soothing smell, and it didn't take long for the rice pudding to thicken. Each one took his turn mixing it with an olive stick. When Takis pronounced it ready, Bouras pulled out a small bottle of cognac, but he had forgotten the glasses. Tsakiris made his way along the tunnel and out of the cave, returning a few minutes later with four long scoops of wood which he quickly carved into flat spoons. "I don't know what you'd do without me," he said.

"Now that you've carved the spoons, why don't you make us some cups for the cognac?"

Hungrily, they ate the rice pudding, savoring its creamy sweetness. Taking a deep breath," Takis said. "We'll drink from the bottle."

"Sure! We're all friends, aren't we?" said Pantsaris.

While the rice pudding was fast dwindling, each took a sip from the bottle—a ceremony, Takis said, to seal their friendship. Then he sang a verse from an old song, "A friend will tell his friend your secrets," which reflected what was in their minds: friends are not always loyal to each other. Their eyes, mirroring flames and fear, focused on Takis.

"If we are not united in soul, mind, and body," Takis said, clenching his fist, "we don't belong together." He thought of how Alexis trusted them with his secret. Then the reality of Lefteris's death and the feeling that such a fate could also befall his father made him shudder. He shifted his position.

"Takis is right," Bouras said. "We've got to stay united."

"Under all circumstances," Pantsaris added.

"We've got to trust our friendship, in life and death. No lies, no excuses."

"Takis, when you talk like that, I don't think you trust me," Tsakiris said. He offered him the bottle. "Here! Each of you can drink first, and then I will take my turn. I trust each one of you and love each one of you, and I hope you all can say the same."

Each one took a sip from the bottle, assuring the others as they did that from that moment on, whatever life brought, joy or sorrow, they would share it equally.

"Tsakiris, I may sound like chicken shit. I want to fight the enemy, but since Lefteris's death, I'm scared."

"How do you think I feel?" Bouras blurted. "I'm seventeen, a year older than you guys. I should join the resistance force and blow some Nazi brains out, but I'm just as frightened as you are."

"Those vultures have taken our homes, our food, my bike, and God knows what's next," said Takis.

"Soon they'll be taking the women and children, just like the Turks did," Pantsaris said.

"I've thought about that, too." Takis smiled, but under that smile he sensed a flood of emotions. Takis saw Bouras as more than a friend; he was the brother of Eleni, the girl he had grown to love with all his heart. In this part of the world, demonstrations of love were unacceptable unless the marriage date had been established. Although trapped on the island, he was determined to do something heroic. His adolescent innocence had no limits. Besides, he had to protect Eleni; he planned to marry her eventually and take her to America. Takis longed for her, and his temples throbbed at the thought of the enemy taking her away. To diffuse his fear, he said, "The history teacher was right when he said that this is a senseless and meaningless war. Hitler's intention is to conquer the whole world. And then, once he conquers the world, he will probably start a war against the celestial world, against God and his angels."

They all laughed. "Crazy man! What a lunatic!"

"What about us?" Bouras's eyes glittered. "Suppose that the Germans drafted us and sent us to Germany for training?"

"Bull, that's a hell of a thought!" Pantsaris shivered. "Can't you think of anything nice to talk about?"

"I'd die before I'd succumb to . . ."

"Spider, dying is easy; we can all blow our brains out, but isn't that cowardly?" Tsakiris asked.

"Okay, Boudala, what do you suggest? Become traitors or accomplices?" Bouras was silent for a while, and then his face lit up. "Even if they send us to Germany or put us in a concentration camp, as long as we're together we'll sabotage the bastards."

They agreed.

The cognac was disappearing quickly.

Takis grabbed the bottle and brought it to his lips, casting a benevolent look on his friends. His fear that one of them might betray their friendship was gone, and now, with the last guzzle of cognac, the clutter in his mind had cleared.

Tsakiris pulled a revolver from his waist and placed it on the ground. "There are six bullets. If any one of you doubts my friendship, comrades, I'm ready to blow out my brains."

"Hey! Where did you get that toy?" Pantsaris asked.

"Poet, it's not a toy! I can tell," said Bouras, "and I know where you got it. Alexis told you not to touch the guns."

"I had to, Bouras; I need one."

"You'd better hide that thing. You could get us all killed."

"Stick to your poetry, Pantsaris," Tsakiris said, returning his revolver to his belt. "Trust me."

"I'd like to borrow it for one night," Takis said quietly, and the other boys fell silent at the venom in his voice.

Puzzled, Bouras and Tsakiris looked at each other. Pantsaris scraped the last grains of rice pudding from the pot.

"Okay, the gun is ours," Bouras said, "but we can't do crazy things with it. When the right time comes, we'll use it."

"We need to get some lessons, remember?" Pantsaris said.

Takis piled more wood on the fire. The burning olive logs yielded a fragrant smoke, and the flames were reflected in the eyes of the four friends. Takis's cheeks were flushed, not from the heat of the fire, but from his own thoughts. He had plans, and he wanted his friends to join him. Killing the lieutenant, ripping the swastika from the castle top, and building a boat to cross the Aegean to Turkey and freedom—these thoughts raced through his mind—they should be making plans instead of sitting immobile in a cave drinking and eating like furtive children. He was sixteen, yet he yearned to be older so that he could join the army of liberation.

Fire, cognac, and rice pudding had kindled passionate spirits in their youthful hearts. Bouras stretched his legs, and winking at Pantsaris, he pulled a pair of panties from his pocket, caressed his face with them, and then attached them to a stick which he waved over the fire.

"Are you going to wear them?" Pantsaris laughed. "Where did you get them?"

"I stole them from my neighbor's clothesline. You want a sniff?"

"A good weapon to fight the enemy with," Tsakiris said. "Like Alexis with his penis."

"Bouras, your enemy is in your pants, too." Takis's annoyance showed in his voice. They all laughed nervously.

Bouras's nose wrinkled a little, like a dog's. He sat back in a quiet reverie. "I'm going to take a stroll, my friends. I'll be back shortly, so don't leave without me."

They watched as Bouras folded the panties and put them in his pocket. As he trudged away, they smiled at each other in a knowing way. "He's going to polish his scepter," said Takis.

When Bouras came back, his friends teased him. "You look exhausted," Tsakiris said.

"Will you be able to walk back?" Takis asked.

"Friends, we are going nowhere. It's already dark outside." There was a penitent look on his face.

Takis cast his eyes to the ground and tried to think clearly, but his thoughts grew gray. He felt only a profound helplessness. Through his blurred eyes, he looked at his friends. "Guys, I'm afraid for my father," he said. "They killed that good man Lefteris, and I'm afraid they might take my father away. The thought haunts me night and day."

"Why did they kill Lefteris?"

"Maybe he had guns," Bouras said as he cast a frightened glance at Tsakiris.

"It was said that Lefteris owned a rifle," explained Tsakiris.

"Takis, your father wouldn't kill a fly. There's no need to worry about him, okay?" Pantsaris said to comfort his friend.

"He's an American and proud of it. But now he may pay a price."

The fire gradually died down. Occasional sparks jumped out of the ashes, shedding a glow over the young faces. Pantsaris lit an oil lantern he had found in the chapel above them. The cave was now filled with light and warmth, inviting slumber. It was too late for the four friends to return to Moria, for a 6:00 P.M. curfew was in effect.

"We'll have to spend the night here," said Bouras.

"Our parents will wonder where we are, and you know how they worry," said Takis. "But if we're caught outdoors after the curfew, we'll be shot on the spot. We haven't much choice."

Takis knew that the Germans would show no mercy. The previous week, a German patrol had fired on one of the villagers who was out after curfew in search of a doctor for his wife. They left him dying in the street, and his wife gave birth alone.

Early the following morning, the four friends, pretending to gather oregano and sage, descended the mountain. To all appearances, it was an ordinary morning for them and for Moria. The sun, on its lazy climb over the eastern mountains, was ushering in another spring day.

Suddenly the olive-oil factory in the center of Moria exploded, sending scraps of wood and metal ripping through the town as a blazing cloud spiraled to the sky. The boys heard screaming and saw the villagers scattering in all directions. Just as the frightened crowd began to flee, the German soldiers blockaded the village with their jeeps. Clouds of smoke hovered over the houses, and the stench of burning oil and gunpowder filled the air. He was only five minutes away from home, but Takis did not dare take the chance of continuing in that direction. In silent agreement, the quartet fled, scurrying back to St. John's Chapel to seek refuge in the cave. Takis was terrified and wanted to call out for his father, but that was too risky. He could only scream silently in his heart. Thick clouds of smoke blanketed the village, and the olive-oil factory lay in smoldering ruins.

Word reached the resistance that the Germans had confiscated a thousand barrels of olive oil, which they planned to ship to Germany. Through their connections in the factory, the resistance fighters had managed to sabotage the entire transaction. They had lived up to their slogan: "We'll burn the quilt so the fleas won't survive." The general feeling was that the less the Germans got out of Greece, the sooner they'd leave.

The next day, Takis and his friends headed back to Moria, trudging along the primitive paths and scavenging wild roots and berries to feed their ravenous hunger. Shafts of sunlight streaming through the trees warmed their bodies. They were cautious, afraid of being seen by the Germans. As they were crossing the Camares river on the south side of Moria, two soldiers blocked their way. The four boys cowered together, supporting each other in their fear.

"*Poie iste kai apo pou erheste*—who are you, and where have you been?" Takis's fierce eyes scrutinized the German soldier who had spoken in flawless Greek. He noticed his faded green uniform, but it was his swarthy face that attracted Takis's attention. Where had he seen that face before—the pulpy nose, stiff gray hair, cunning bluish eyes, and the shovel of a mouth with yellow uneven teeth? There was not a trace of doubt that he was Cara Beis, the Greek turned accomplice. It took Takis a few seconds to control his feelings. He remained silent and motioned to his friends not to speak. Without any outward sign of fear, although he felt it in his heart, he walked up to the Greek-speaking soldier and spat in his face. While Cara Beis was wiping off the spittle, Takis punched him in the gut, knocking him flat on his back.

"*Prodoti*—traitor!" screamed Takis. "Shame on you, dirty Judas." The other three boys jumped on the traitor, beating him with their fists, and stopped only when other soldiers suddenly appeared on the scene and fired a volley of shots in the air. Within minutes came two motorcycles on patrol, splashing along the mud path. The engines coughed and spluttered and then died out.

Their knees trembling, the four friends stood side by side facing a machine gun and the booted officers, well over six feet tall, who displayed a neat little row of decorations on the left side of their chests. One of them held the machine gun; the other had a swagger stick which he occasionally slapped against his left palm, providing punctuation marks for the thoughts that crowded and strutted invisibly within him. Finally, he spoke to the Greek accomplice, who bowed and replied, "*Jawohl.*"

The accomplice, his uniform wet and muddy, approached the boys. He raised his hand, and Takis felt the blow across the left side of his face, followed by another across his right cheek. The other three were spared punishment, for, without apparent reason, the patrol gave the order to stop. Tsakiris searched under his belt and discovered that his gun was missing. For a few horrifying moments he thought he must have dropped it in the scuffle and was relieved when he remembered it was still in the cave.

As Cara Beis surveyed the boys from head to toe, he spoke to the officers, who repeated "*Jawohl*" several times and then attacked the boys, kicking and beating them mercilessly with their clubs. The traitor joined in, punching with his fists. There were no tears. The boys stood their ground, obstinate and openly defiant of the enemy, and they remained silent, for they knew it would be foolish to further antagonize Cara Beis, a man who had sold himself and his countrymen.

Plagued by uncertainty and pain, the courageous quartet was prodded on a long march to Cara Tepe, the Black Hill prison camp. Behind them was Cara Beis, now armed with a gun, and one soldier, the officers having driven off on their motorcycles.

"Friends, don't be lulled to sleep," said Takis, and winking at Pantsaris, he added, "Hey, Poet, start us a song."

"Is that okay with you, Mr. Interpreter?" Pantsaris asked.

"I have a name," shouted Cara Beis.

"Of course you do, but I have forgotten it," Pantsaris replied. The boys had secretly agreed to ignore him, for they perceived those who worked for the Nazis as traitors who should remain nameless.

"My name is Cara Beis," he said angrily.

Bouras fell back a few steps and in a soft voice asked Cara Beis for permission for his poet friend to sing. He nodded.

"Sing, Pantsaris, sing," said Bouras.

"I'm not saying this to make you mad, " said Pantsaris, "but the song I want to sing is unfinished."

"Sing it anyway. We have a long way ahead of us. Maybe you can complete it on the journey, " Tsakiris said.

"Just one more spring . . . one more summer . . ." Pantsaris sang softly like a girl.

"Louder," said Takis.

"Just one more spring . . . one more summer,

"Just one more spring . . . enslaved, enslaved. . . ."

The three joined in, and instantly Cara Beis clicked open a switchblade which he pointed at Pantsaris. "You want your balls cut off?"

"No, sir."

"Then shut up, all of you, chicken shit. Walk."

Boisterously, the other three continued the song.

"Shut up, I said," shouted Cara Beis. "You'll treat me with respect and obey my orders; otherwise I'll be forced to perform radical surgery on your asses."

Takis saw the rage in Cara Beis's face and mumbled, "Traitor!" as he tramped along. To his left, he could see Moria in the distance, like a mother bitterly bemoaning her enslaved children. A sudden thought caused an electrifying shiver in his spine: What if Cara Beis fabricates a lie and gets Asimakis in trouble with the Nazis? Avoiding any eye contact with his escorts, he walked silently. Masses of black clouds hovered over the houses, and from the ravine below the road, the river roared over stones and gorges.

In the front of a grey rectangular building, a door opened with a crash, and the four were thrown into an empty room. They were exhausted, and there was no place to sit. The cement floor was covered with brown slime from a faucet that dripped rusty water. They stood waiting, thinking that something terrible would happen. Time passed slowly, and there was no sign of action.

Takis wondered what he should say if they asked him where he had been at the time of the explosion. None of them could come up with a suitable reply. Bouras suggested that they change their names, but Pantsaris thought that idea was foolish because it would make them look guilty.

"We haven't done anything wrong," Tsakiris said.

"What if they blame us for the fire?"

"Takis, they can't pin that on us," Pantsaris said.

"What's wrong with saying that we were at the aqueduct; it's ten minutes away from Moria," Takis said.

"That's it. After school, we took a hike." The others agreed to Takis's suggestion.

Bouras looked at the dripping faucet, thirsty but knowing that the water wasn't fit to drink. Time passed, drop by drop.

The door opened and a German officer entered, a tall man smoking a pipe. His hazel eyes seemed angry, framed between thick eyebrows and protruding cheekbones. He was followed by Cara Beis. The boys feared for their lives. The officer made a short speech, looking at them coldly and accentuating each word. Cara Beis interpreted. They had to take off their clothes and give them to the interpreter who would return them once they had been thoroughly searched.

"We haven't done anything wrong. They can't do anything to us," Bouras whispered. He felt the chill air on his naked body.

"As Alexis said, you have a big one," Pantsaris said to Bouras.

Takis nodded. "Strong in genitals and in courage."

Bouras was cold; he shivered, hugging himself. He winked at the others, and with pursed lips, he controlled thoughts of pride and fear. He certainly had the biggest penis. Alexis was right in calling him Big Prick. At the sight of Bouras in his bare skin, the German officer bit on the stem of his pipe, exhaled smoke, and mumbled a few words. The interpreter gave Bouras back his clothes and told him to dress quickly. The others were ordered to put on their clothes. Lost in a daydream, Takis took his time in dressing. He felt his body, firm, broad shouldered, muscular, and strong, the body of a swimmer. He played soccer, but his love affair was with the sea. Soon the swimming season would start. If his muscles could stand the test, he wanted to cross the Aegean to Turkey.

As they dressed, questions were asked: "Name? Age? Parents' occupation? Their occupation?" These were the easy questions.

"What do you know about the explosion?"

"Nothing."

"Who could have caused it?"

"I don't know."

"Could you have caused it?"

"No."

Later in the afternoon, the door opened and a second German officer entered. Takis recognized him at once, and his knees almost buckled. It was the lieutenant who had confiscated his bike. *What if he remembers me*, thought Takis. Anger replaced his fear, but he was determined to show no emotion. Katerina's voice echoed in his mind: "My son needs his bike to go to school." He lowered his eyes, and again, as in a haze, the picture came back to him—the rapacious hands, cold and hard as steel, unclenching his own fingers and taking the bike; the burning of the little American flag between the handlebars. Now, this could be the end. He visualized himself and his friends lying dead in one huge coffin in St. Basil's, and Papavasile chanting: "Memory Eternal!" Never before had he felt such fear.

The interrogator interrupted Takis's reverie with the same questions, and the officer replied, "*Jawohl*," again and again. Now, with a simulated smile, the lieutenant changed his tone. "Should any one of you provide information about the explosion or any other acts of sabotage, I will personally reward you with bread, food, or money."

The lieutenant motioned Takis to follow him to the next room, and the interpreter advised him to obey. Pantsaris and Tsakiris were ordered to remain put. After an interval, Bouras was summoned by another soldier who led him through a narrow corridor to the infirmary, a small room containing a cot and a table on which was arrayed medicine bottles of all sizes and shapes. The soldier motioned Bouras to lie down and then untied the boy's belt. Puzzled and fearful of what torture was planned, Bouras's heart thumped with terror—*What if he castrates me!*—and his face became flushed. But the soldier, with a suave glance, only fondled Bouras's genitals, and then, noticing the anxiety in his eyes, buckled the boy's belt and helped him to get up. "*Jawohl, jawohl*," he said, touching his head, and he pulled two German bills out of his wallet and pushed them into Bouras's pocket.

Takis was more fortunate. The lieutenant took him gently by the arm and guided him into a kitchen furnished with a table, four chairs, and a counter on which sat a bowl of cherries. Takis followed the lieutenant's movement as he took a handful of cherries, washed them, and placed them in a dish in front of him. He put one in his mouth and indicated that Takis should do likewise. The cherries were sweet and disappeared quickly. From a cupboard, the lieutenant fetched a loaf of bread—enough to feed a family for three days—wrapped it in wax paper and then in newspaper, and handed it to Takis. Takis, incredulous, bowed his head and said, "*Efharisto*—thank you." The lieutenant repeated, "F-Harry-Stow."

Takis did not see the broad grin on the lieutenant's face.

Takis, with the loaf under his arm and the lieutenant behind him, met Bouras and his escort in the corridor, and together they walked out of the barracks. Bouras looked shaken, as if he had been hit over the head. The four friends were reunited in front of the building. They eyed each other warily, wondering if the incident was closed. Then they noticed Takis's package and could not believe what they saw. He had faced the enemy and had come out smiling and holding a present? What had happened to the brave words about fighting the enemy? No one uttered a word.

Interpreting the wishes of the German officers, Cara Beis told the four to stay out of trouble and to cooperate with the army of occupation. Sensing that they were free to go, they smiled at the lieutenant with gratitude and set out for Moria. When they were a safe distance from the barracks, Takis produced the loaf and divided it into quarters. Bouras brought out two folded bills, one hundred marks. Tsakiris, calculating quickly, said, "Opa, opa! That's ten thousand drachmas. We can buy two bottles of ouzo."

"That son of a whore—I thought he was going to fuck me," said Bouras.

"Maybe it's the other way around; he looked like a butterfly to me." Tsakiris, seeing the dismay on Bouras's face, tried to soothe him.

"You could be right, but who do you take me for—Alexis?"

Though the days are longer in spring, the boys felt this day in May was the longest they had known. Silently, they devoured the bread as they walked, and soon the village came into view.

Five minutes before the curfew, Takis reached home. His father grabbed him by the arms and said angrily, "Where in the devil's name have you been?"

"Thank God you're alive," shouted Katerina, running out of the kitchen and wrapping her arms around him. "My son, are you all right?" Her eyes were brimming with tears of joy.

"I'm just fine. I'm okay; why do you worry so much about me?"

His mother went back to the kitchen and returned with a big oval plate of fried eggplant smothered in tomato sauce and oregano. A strong, pleasant fragrance filled the room. The first to sit at the table were Takis's younger brother, Jimmy, and sister, Kiki.

As dinner was served, Takis saw that although his father was relieved, he was still angry.

"I want to know where you were before and after the explosion."

Katerina, knowing how distraught her husband was, tried to divert his attention; she produced one slice of bread and cut it into four pieces, denying herself a share. Takis offered his piece to her, but she refused it. "You eat it," she said. She cherished the look on her children's faces when there was sufficient food on the table. As soon as the two younger ones had finished, they slipped away from the table and went to their rooms.

"Young man,"—that is what he called Takis every time he was annoyed—"I haven't heard your answer."

"*Baba*—Dad—me and my friends got together two days ago and went to St. John's to make rice pudding. All the kids my age do that."

"You've been away three days."

"The first night, we lost track of time and it got too late to start home. There's the curfew, you know, and with all the machine guns around . . . we didn't want buttonholes in our bodies, so we slept at St. John's."

"You expect me to believe that?"

"It's true." Takis then told his family about the Cara Tepe camp incident.

The death of Lefteris had left Asimakis in gnawing uncertainty, and gruesome thoughts lurked in his mind. What if the Germans found out he was an American citizen, arrested him, and put him through an interrogation? Had someone seen Takis carrying home the German street sign? And worse still, what if they took Takis away and sent him to a concentration camp in Germany?

This thought contorted his sun-darkened face to such an extent that Katerina's heart palpitated faster. Takis, still unsettled after the ordeal he and his friends had endured, sensed a resurgence of peace. Although the early years with his stepmother had been turbulent, now in his teens he had grown to like her a great deal, to the point of trusting her even with personal secrets of his meetings with Eleni and his love for her. Such a secret was totally unacceptable to his father, who deemed family reputation as one of the Ten Commandments. Takis kept his eyes on Katerina. Tonight she looked exceptionally beautiful. Her freshly washed hair exuded the fragrance of the leaves of a walnut tree, which she used frequently. She smiled, and the gleam in her eye brought him comfort. She was an expert at hiding her fears, and no one guessed that she worried about the Germans hurting her family, too. What if her husband should follow the fate of Lefteris? Then, she would never forgive herself for asking him to return from America. She moved closer to him and gently combed his hair with her delicate fingers.

Referring to her husband in the manner which she used in front of the family, she spoke to her son. "Our *kyrios*—our lord was worried about you, Takis."

"About me?" protested Takis, looking at his mother.

"Don't play with fire; you know what I mean." Asimakis's tone showed both annoyance and fear. "Stay as far away as you can from those . . . you know who I mean."

"Baba, I'll be careful. You don't need to worry about me."

Katerina looked from one to the other, hoping to head off any conflict. "Our *kyrios* will tell you our story. You won't believe what happened to us!"

"You mean the panic?"

"Just tell Takis what happened to us after the explosion."

"I snatched up your brother and sister and followed the crowd that sought refuge at the Roman aqueduct. We made that ten-minute walk in five. Your mother followed."

"I was frightened because, in the commotion, you were nowhere to be found, and the jeeps and gunfire made me think we were being pursued by the Germans," Katerina said.

"We spent two nights without sleep in the bushes with scarcely anything to eat, and then we crept back to the village along with the others."

"Thank God we are together," Katerina said.

"Mom, when are we going to get more bread and vegetables?" Takis asked.

"Not for a while," she replied.

"I'll be setting out at midnight," said Asimakis. "I'm going to visit the Paleologos family in Kalloni. Paraskevas Paleologos was my classmate in high school. He'll help us with food, I'm sure. And his father has corn for sale, so we can buy a few bags."

"I'll come with you; you may need help," Takis said.

"Forty kilometers?"

"I can walk."

"We'll talk later." His father felt apprehensive; there was danger in setting off at midnight, going through forests and crossing mountains. Who knew what waited in the darkness.

CHAPTER 4

Friends Become Angels

On his way home with the week's supply of food—simply a burlap sack of cabbage heads—Bouras met Takis trudging up St. Basil's hill. Bouras couldn't believe how ill his friend looked. He appeared weak and frail and seemed to have difficulty in walking.

"Little Brother, you look as if Death is casting his shadow on you. Your eyes, forehead, nose—in fact your whole face is like an El Greco painting—you know, the one of the betrayal that Alexis has hanging on his wall."

"Bouras, that's not funny. I haven't eaten anything since yesterday— except about two hundred green olives."

"No wonder your face is green."

"As I was leaving for school this morning, my mother said, 'I've nothing to give you for lunch.' I knew there was nothing, for last night we ate the last of the potatoes. So I filled a bag with salted olives."

"And you ate two hundred olives!"

"Yes. I was looking out of the window at the castle and counted the pits one by one as I spat them at the swastika."

"I've a few dry figs at home," Bouras offered.

They walked side by side, making small talk as they passed the marketplace.

* * * * *

Three months after Lefteris's death, the Moriani were in despair. It was as if their island had been devastated by a plague of locusts. There was no food—no eggs or chickens, no goats or sheep. A few emaciated donkeys roamed the streets munching on anything in sight. Many villagers died of starvation, and disease spread. The vegetable peddlers, fishmongers, shoemakers, grocers, and bakers had to close their businesses. The milkman ceased his rounds. The beautiful market of Moria, famous throughout the island for its plenty, seemed in deep mourning. The few stores that remained open sold salted olives and hot sage—a sort of coffee made from roasted chickpeas.

Theodore's tavern, the joy of the town, closed down, as Theodore, along with others of the village, fell victim to malnutrition and was hospitalized in a warehouse that served as the infirmary. The people then took their custom to Alexis's tavern, an enterprise consisting of a large room with a high ceiling, two ancient pictures hanging on the wall, three leather sofas, and straw chairs around wooden tables.

Before the invasion, the marketplace had been noisy and bustling with energy as customers went from store to store, shopping and perusing, and using idle moments to gather under the oak tree of the town square to discuss politics and gossip. Peddlers of all sorts had roamed through the streets and alleys of Moria, shouting in praise of their goods.

Now, the faithful mailman, who could be counted on to deliver letters and packages three days a week, no longer appeared. Communications and travel by sea were completely under Nazi control. The death of Lefteris was remembered as the first of the many happenings that propelled the town into a state of cruel uncertainty.

Explosions awakened the villagers the following morning. Windows and doors were blown out, the houses shook in their foundations, and debris flew through the air, littering the streets. The terrified inhabitants jumped out of bed and scurried through the shattered glass to their basements and cellars where they awaited the end. The Nazis were on their first maneuver; the nine cannons facing Asia Minor fired in unison for thirty minutes. Then the "All Clear" siren howled, signaling the end of the operation.

That night, a group of seven young men stole a small boat, and, under the ruse of fishing, attempted to escape to Turkey. At daybreak, a Turkish surveillance ship caught them and immediately returned them to Lesbos. At sunrise, without trial or sentence, the German authorities tied them to the little pine trees bordering the statue of liberty of the island and shot them.

These losses were only the beginning. Not only were the Germans stepping up their campaign of cruelty, but the scarcity of food added to the misery of the villagers. Fear prevailed, and as each day unfolded, hunger and malnutrition showed in the haggard faces. Takis and his father brought back a bag of corn and a bag of broom seeds that Paraskevas Paleologos had given them. The broom seeds were to be used as feed for their two animals, a donkey and a goat, but Katerina suggested that since the animals could survive on grass, the seeds be put aside for the family.

One evening after her husband and two younger children had gone to bed, she and Takis stone-ground the corn and the broom seeds, mixing the two together. "This will make good pancakes, and it should last us two months if I use it sparingly," Katerina said. The next day, she proudly announced this new ingredient to her family, and then began to experiment. She made about two dozen pancakes. Takis and his brother and sister gobbled them while they were still hot. "They are good," Takis said. Katerina placed what remained on a large, flat dish, pointing out that two should be plenty for each person. She added another one to her husband's portion. "Your father needs more than the rest of you; he's bigger."

"What about the last six?" Takis pointed to the frying pan.

"I want you to rush over to Merope's with those while they're still hot. I'm sure she and Niko are hungry."

Merope Kontogianni, Lefteris's widow, and her child lived in a corner house in the center of Moria. She was in her mid-thirties, had a good figure, and, unlike most of the women of her village, was of light complexion. Her sixty-year-old father was one of the few men of Moria who still dressed like a Turk, with puffed up breeches and turban, a costume dating back to the time of the Turkish occupation of Greece.

Griefstricken, Merope covered her blondish hair with a black shawl tied under her chin and, as was the custom, prepared to dress completely in black for at least three years; after that, if she were to be sought in marriage, she could wear gray or dark-brown colors. She gave little thought to her appearance, for her cares centered on taking care of Niko and harvesting the olive grove that her husband left her.

Takis saw the sympathetic smile on his mother's face and felt happy that she cared about the welfare of the family of her husband's dead friend. Hurrying through the back alleys, he reached Merope's back door. He pushed it gently, and as he entered the kitchen he saw Merope sitting on the sofa, holding Niko in her arms. Niko was too tired to be excited over Takis's visit but grabbed a pancake and stuffed it into his mouth while still clinging to his mother. The room looked bare, and there were no smells of cooking in the air. On the wall beside the window hung Lefteris's portrait, the upper half of his face covered by a black veil attached to the top of the frame.

"Please thank your mother for me."

"Tomorrow is Saturday—there's no school. May I take Niko for a hike?" Takis blurted out. He was embarrassed and could not think of anything else to say.

"That would be very nice," Merope said, placing her arm around her son, who smiled and nodded.

"Tomorrow, then," Takis said. Outside the kitchen door, he hesitated, for he could hear Niko whimpering. He was not sure if he should go back to comfort him or return home. Merope must have given Niko another pancake, Takis thought, for the plaintive cries ceased. A sadness overwhelmed him, and he lingered to listen to the conversation between mother and son.

"I want my daddy. I want my daddy now!"

"Your father has gone away, far away, to live among the stars of heaven." Her voice was gentle and soft.

"The Germans killed my daddy. How could he go to heaven?"

"Souls have wings and can fly."

"Then why don't our souls fly to daddy so he won't be alone in heaven?" Niko persisted.

"He's not alone. Angels flap their wings all around him."

Takis listened attentively. Merope's explanation was reassuring.

"Mommy, when can we visit daddy?"

"Niko, my son, without an invitation from God, no one can go to heaven. Rest, rest now, my little angel."

"Mommy, who is going to play with me now?"

"I will, my little son, and your friend Takis—I know he loves you."

"But you weep. Daddy never wept."

"Yes, I know. Close your eyes now. Lean on me. May your sleep be sweet as sugar."

"I am sleepy, Mommy. Give me your hand. I'm afraid you may fly away, too!"

Takis ran back home with tears in his eyes.

Asimakis and his family waited in silence around the table. As soon as Takis joined them, Katerina served small portions of boiled black-eyed beans, which smelled of the earth. In the center of the table she placed a dish of radishes. She poured olive oil on each plate, and the fragrance filled the air. The children were each given two pancakes, her husband three, and for herself she kept just one.

"Why are the beans so crunchy?" asked Takis. He well knew that they must be filled with grubs, but he wanted to forestall any questions from the younger ones, who were eating heartily.

"Have some radishes with the beans, and you won't hear the crunch," Asimakis said with a dispassionate look. Every waking moment, it seemed, he worried. How could he provide food for his family? Katerina maintained a gracious attitude and always managed to improvise with what was available. And when she sensed a complaint forthcoming, she would say: "Our bellies have no windows— just eat, and no one will know what you ate. Think of poor Merope and her little boy and all the other starving people."

* * * * *

In the middle of September, the Red Cross sent a ship laden with supplies of flour to Lesbos, and for a while, bakeries functioned again. Albanis reopened his bakery; he managed to get a mill where he ground all sorts of seed, which he mixed with the Red Cross flour. The smell of the baking bread attracted a crowd of people to Albanis's shop nearly every day. When the Nazis first arrived in Lesbos, the bread ration was three ounces per person per day; a month later, it was reduced to two ounces every other day; and three months after that, it was further reduced to one ounce every other day. Into the bargain, the bread became darker in color and the taste changed. Although death diminished the starving population, the supply of Red Cross flour was still not sufficient to provide for everyone.

The fat Albanis, in his white shirt and pants, came out of his shop holding up a large cardboard sign which read: BREAD WILL BE DISTRIBUTED TODAY, TUESDAY, OCTOBER 2, 1941 AT 11:00 A.M.

This was cause for commotion. Doors, windows, and cellars opened, people climbed walls and balconies, women uncombed, men unshaven, young barefooted boys and girls in their tattered clothes swarmed to the store and waited in line half a kilometer long.

At the head of the queue stood Apostolos, the butcher, wrapped in a thick brownish coat lined with lambs' wool. The forty-year-old considered himself lucky to receive a portion of the bread supply; it was irresistible, warm and soft, and he was tempted to finish it off in one bite. If only he could have a chunk of boiled meat with it! But his store was empty. Munching and prolonging the last bite of his bread, Apostolos entered Alexis's tavern to get a drink. It was noon, and because there were no customers, Alexis in his white apron busied himself cleaning his marble counter. Serene and quiet, Apostolos sat in a corner, thinking about the state of life when a person has to stand for an hour in line to get a quarter ration of bread. And now, he had to await Alexis's pleasure for a glass of wine. Meanwhile, the line at Albanis's was increasing in length.

"Are you going to stand in line?" he asked.

"No." Alexis didn't even raise his head. "Did you get your ration?" he asked, when he eventually brought the butcher a glass of wine.

"Enough for a bird. I've eaten it already." He took a sip, savored it, and looked out of the window at the breadline. "That leech, Albanis, adulterates the flour; my teeth are still crunching on something—I think it's sand. That makes the bread heavier, and of course, he makes more money on it, the bastard."

"Oh, stop bitching!" Alexis said, sitting down next to him. "Thank God we can still get a bite of bread."

"Sure! One ounce a day! It's not even bread—he mixes it with donkey bran. Soon we'll begin to bray."

Alexis looked down the street, and the sight of the two familiar SS soldiers approaching made him anxious.

Alexis leaned toward Apostolos and whispered, "Drink up quickly and disappear. There are two soldiers coming up the street, and I know they're going to want their cognac, if not something else. You must go."

* * * * *

After lessons, Takis and his friends left their school in Mytilene and returned to Moria where they saw Niko in the breadline.

"How would you like to come home with me?" said Takis.

"Mother sent me to get bread."

"Okay, I'll wait."

The line was still long when the baker stepped out and announced, "No more bread until Thursday." The crowd groaned and blasphemed, but he ignored them.

"Takis, what'll I tell my mother?"

"Just wait here."

The line dispersed, grumbling. Takis slipped into the bakery through the back door.

A German jeep whisking through the marketplace of Moria slowed down as it rounded the corner by Albanis's bakery. The pedestrians pulled back against the buildings.

Two SS soldiers occupied the front seats, and behind them sat a young girl of about fifteen, who was crying and struggling with the officer beside her.

At the bakery, Takis begged Albanis for a few ounces of bread. "I don't want it for myself, Mr. Albanis; Lefteris's family is hungry."

"I don't have any. I sold it all. Come back on Thursday."

"I see a big loaf on the top shelf."

"That's a special order."

"What's more special than a starving family who needs just a small piece?"

"Listen, boy, I work hard to make bread available for others. That loaf is for my needs."

"Can't you spare about six ounces of it? I'll do anything you ask to pay you for it."

Round-faced, big-bellied, well-fed Albanis changed his expression from pleasant to calculating. He sized up Takis in the way a cat looks at a mouse. Rumor had it that he was a pederast. He pulled the bread off the shelf, placed it under Takis's nose, and said, "I could give you a quarter of it if you let me. . . ."

Takis smelled the freshly baked bread, looked at the baker, and sensed that his offer was one of seduction. At the same time, he visualized Niko and his mother enjoying their meal, filling their empty stomachs. But the loaf was costly. *So he's after my . . .* he thought. *I have to trade my body to this pig for a piece of bread!*

"Okay, I'll give you half a loaf, not just six ounces, but sixteen. It'll be our secret, of course."

"The whole loaf," insisted Takis.

"And what am I going to eat?"

"The whole loaf, I said."

"Okay, okay. Let's go upstairs first. I have a good bed and it's nice and clean."

"You must give me the bread first. The child is waiting outside."

"Let him wait."

"Hunger can't wait. You wait, Mr. Albanis; I'll be back."

"How can I trust you?" His eyes gleamed with desire.

Takis searched his pocket and pulled out the jackknife his father had brought him from America. "I wouldn't lie. I'll come back, I promise. Here, hold the knife; it's very precious to me."

"It's a deal." He wrapped the bread in newspaper, and the knife and bread changed hands.

Under an archway beside the bakery, the little boy was still waiting. Takis handed the loaf to Niko, saying, "Keep it under your coat and hurry home." Takis returned to the bakery, banged the door closed behind him, and then reopened it silently.

"Takis, come on up. Don't be afraid."

A wooden stairway led to the upper room where the seducer awaited in high anticipation. The steps creaked as Takis ascended slowly, and as he stood on the last stair, he could see the baker fondling his genitals. Never before had he seen the penis of an adult. Either a momentary impulse of the flesh or naive curiosity prompted excitement, in spite of the contempt he felt. He collected a mouthful of saliva, leaned over the baker, and spat fiercely in his face. "You dirty pig," he said scornfully as he retraced his steps to the staircase.

"I didn't mean any harm, boy. Come back! I won't hurt you. What about your knife?" shouted the baker, controlling his rage.

"Stick it in your ass, you filthy worm." Takis had no desire to touch anything that had been handled by the baker. He ran all the way to Alexis's tavern, arriving distraught and perturbed.

"You must have heard the news," said Alexis.

"What news, Alexis?"

"They took your girlfriend, Eleni—Bouras's sister."

"The Germans?"

"It happened within the past few minutes. Where were you?"

"It's complicated. Does Bouras know?"

"I haven't seen him, but Apostolos has gone to tell the priest about it."

"What can a priest do?"

"Papavasile is a powerful man."

Takis nodded his head, but doubt showed in his eyes. "If Bouras or any of my friends show up, tell them to stay here until I get back."

"And where are you going?"

"I'm going to talk to the priest also," Takis said with a twinkle in his anxious eyes. "Cara Beis had been Papavasile's gardener, not too long ago. He may accept to act as interpreter for the priest to free Eleni."

"With a big bribe that snake will sell his mother," Alexis said.

Takis searched his pockets. "I only have a thousand . . ."

"We need at least five thousand drachmas," Alexis said and went behind the counter to his drawer. He gave Takis four new bills and said, "Give Papavasile the money and let him handle Cara Beis."

Half an hour's walk from Moria lay the Cara Tepe camp, but it took Cara Beis and Papavasile only twenty minutes to get there. They stood at the barbed-wire fence exchanging a few timid words and throwing frightened glances at the two armed men guarding the gate. With bittersweet smiles they spoke to the austere, boyish faces beneath their green helmets and produced their identification cards. Cara Beis asked to see the captain, and the guard in charge of the cards pointed to the building on the right.

The tall, well-groomed officer in his sharp uniform stood at attention listening to the request. He appeared surprised that his soldiers would kidnap a woman without reason.

The priest spoke with patience, and Cara Beis explained that the girl, who was not more than fifteen, was a poor orphan who lived with her aunt at the far end of the village.

The captain was irritated, but he retained a stiff, artificial smile. "I shall investigate the matter and let you know. There may be some mistake."

The priest and Cara Beis looked at each other. The visit seemed to have been futile.

* * * * *

On two occasions, Niko was sent home from school because he seemed to have a fever. His face was yellow as if he had jaundice, and Merope kept him in bed and fed him warm sage tea. After an examination by a doctor, it was found that he had anemia. Feeling upset at his decline in health, Merope acknowledged that she fed him boiled cabbage sprinkled with olive oil. "They need real food—bread and milk." The doctor's words reverberated in her mind all night long, and at dawn, Merope climbed the hill of the Virgin Mary and entered the chapel. She lit three candles, burned an abundance of incense, and fell on her knees before the icon of the Virgin and prayed.

"My husband has been taken away from me forever. Please, Virgin Mother of Jesus, protect my child."

The news of Niko's illness spread quickly through Moria; Takis and his friends found out from Alexis.

In their hideout, Bouras silently sipped ouzo to drown his pain. He could not tolerate the feelings of shame that his sister's abduction was causing. He was barely aware of his friends' conversation.

"We'll all die of starvation," Takis said. "Like a plague of locusts, they'll eat all our vegetation."

"They'll devour us alive," said Pantsaris, looking at Tsakiris, who had lost a few pounds.

Niko's illness distressed them. As they drank more ouzo, Takis said, "We can't let Lefteris's child starve."

"And I must find my sister," said Bouras. He was up and gone, shouting for the others to follow before they had a chance to ask him what he was planning.

An hour later, during the afternoon siesta, the four friends carried out a quick raid on the fruit trees in Kapsimalis's garden. Bouras prepared a basket of pomegranates and quinces and went off in search of the German that had given him money. He had no fear this time; his gesture was genuine, and a theft for a good cause brought him no guilt. At the Cara Tepe camp, the German recognized him and took him to his room. He assured Bouras that no girl had ever set foot in the camp, but he offered to make inquiries and help find her. To convince the tormented brother of his good intentions, the German wrapped half a loaf of bread in wax paper and gave it to him. An hour before curfew, Bouras arrived breathless at Merope's house. He handed her the bread, and before she had a chance to thank him, he left.

Several days later, Takis managed to "acquire" two gallons of olive oil. This time, Alexis mounted his donkey and carried the oil to Mytilene where he bartered it for two kilos of beans. Merope was delighted when she calculated how many meals she could make out of them.

Yet, for all the boys' efforts, there was an emptiness in Merope's house, and Takis felt sorry for both mother and son, living without Lefteris in the midst of such violence and hunger. He could not help but feel the need to discuss Merope's situation with his friends each time they met.

"We've got to tighten our belts," he said to Bouras, "and save some food for the widow and her son."

"You should have seen the gleam in her eye last night when I took her some bread!" said Bouras. But he did not reveal his growing fascination with the widow's breasts.

The four friends agreed to take food to Merope and Niko at least twice a week. Bouras suggested they take turns in visiting, but Takis saw the familiar glint in Bouras's eye and insisted that they go two at a time.

"I'll go with you, Bouras," said Takis with a smile.

"And I'll go with Pantsaris," added Tsakiris.

"Don't get any ideas. She's too deep in her grief," Bouras said sadly.

"You're probably the only one with such ideas," remarked Takis.

"Well, I'm bigger and I'm older than you guys."

"Bouras, keep your pants on," said Pantsaris, shaking his head. "You have a one-track mind."

Merope saw Takis and his friends as angels. However, she knew the busy tongues of Moria were wondering how she was feeding herself and her son, and her neighbors now looked at her with raised eyebrows. "I don't want you boys to get into trouble," she said as she escorted them to the door. "I don't want to embarrass you, but I'm concerned you might get hurt by . . . you know who."

"No, no," they responded in unison, convinced that they were invincible.

"Niko does not look well," said Takis. "He looks as if he has malaria. When I was ten, I had it and I turned the same color as he is now."

"Is there something we can do for him?" asked Bouras.

"He is ailing. He has a touch of malaria, but I think he'll be all right," Merope replied. "He needs meat, something to sustain him. And quinine for his malaria."

The friends knew what had to be done, in spite of her warning, and they held a conference at Alexis's tavern. Not a hint must be given to others; otherwise they might end up in prison.

The next night, four dark silhouettes moved softly as shadows through Moria to Kapsimalis's garden where, during their first visit, they had seen a goat nursing her two kids. It was time for Kapsimalis to share his meat with a sick boy. The capture did not take long, and carrying the kids in two burlap bags, the four shapes, huffing and puffing, slipped over the wall to safety.

As the village belfry struck two o'clock in the morning, Merope was awakened by a knocking on her back window.

"Who's there?" she whispered.

"Open the back door quickly," replied Bouras, his voice shrill with excitement.

She lit a lantern and opened the door. Barefooted, they marched into the kitchen with their two heavy sacks.

"You could get killed for being out at this hour of the morning," she said.

Merope squatted and felt the moving sacks.

"Baby goats? A miracle!" she cried.

"Oh, what a wretched sinner I am," she moaned. "Virgin Mother of Jesus, protect my providers." And wiping away her tears of gratitude, she said to them, "Please don't get yourselves into trouble."

The four friends felt an unusual attraction to the widow, a gentle unsullied attraction, and they wished there was a chance of making love to her that night. She held together the neck of her nightdress, for she probably noticed a curious fascination in their eyes as they looked at her slightly exposed bosom. They felt acute discomfort, an absurd and impotent mixture of desire and disillusionment as they admitted to themselves that Merope was older and in mourning.

That afternoon, the four friends enjoyed their reverie at Alexis's tavern. What a sensation it would be to touch those swollen breasts or get under Merope's covers. Then Takis changed the subject. "We need quinine for Niko." Bouras was sure his German friend could get him Atabrines, a sure cure for malaria. They clinked their glasses for joy, for their mission was complete.

Merope soon discovered a method of browning the chunks of meat in order to preserve it so that it would last longer. As she boiled the heads of the animals to make broth, she thought, *These four friends are angels, but if they are caught, may God have mercy.*

CHAPTER 5

Eleni's Cruel Fate

October days are short, but to the enslaved who awaited that *one more spring* of liberation they seemed to drag on in slow motion. The mystery of the kidnapping and the whereabouts of Eleni, Bouras's sister, remained unsolved. Around the neighborhood well, busy tongues gossiped: they shipped her to Germany, and perhaps she is better off living there than trapped in Lesbos where famine plagues and depletes our people daily.

Carrying a burlap bag of dandelions he had picked in the nearby fields, Takis was ascending the hill of St. Basil. The thought that tonight the meal would consist of boiled dandelions and olives was promising. It was around four o'clock in the afternoon, and the marketplace was quiet. Soothed by the smell of the trees, most of the inhabitants were still in their olive groves, harvesting the crop. Some of the older folk gravitated to the coffee shops, which had nothing but mountain tea to offer.

Outside Alexis's tavern sat Alexis and Papavasile the priest, sipping their evening tea and whispering—not an uncommon sight in village life. Papavasile had the most heart-grabbing presence. His thick, salt-and-pepper mustache, blending with his prematurely gray beard, nearly covered his lips, which registered a most articulate narrative of unspoken compassion. Every wound and grievance of his priestly life had signed its name on his face, offering proof of twenty-two years of dedicated service in God's vineyard. There were four deep wrinkles in his forehead, which moved in harmony as he spoke to Alexis.

Takis rested his bag on one of Alexis's chairs and greeted the two men. He noticed the frown on the priest's face and wondered if another serious event had taken place.

"Takis, before curfew tonight," the priest said, "could you come and sing at a service?"

"A service?" Takis was sure this was not a holy day.

"A memorial service, my son." The priest signed.

"Who died?"

"Many, many innocent people." The priest grabbed his beard and tugged it.

"Innocent people," repeated Takis. He shook his head, sensing the priest's agony and feeling a wave of nausea. "I'll be at St. Basil's by five."

"Bring your friends," said the priest.

Takis lifted his bag and, looking at Alexis, said, "Boiled dandelions. Care to join us for dinner?"

"I'll bring the wine." Alexis simulated a smile.

When Takis was at a safe distance, the priest continued to inform Alexis of the news he had heard on his hidden radio. The Voice of America issued the report: a million Greeks were homeless; the Nazis had burned two thousand villages. The country at large was ruined and in disorder. The harbors, ships, railroads, bridges, and telephone lines were destroyed.

"The vultures will destroy our souls," Alexis said, as the priest prepared to leave. "Father, what's very frightening to me is that they're drafting the men between seventeen and thirty-five. They'll send all these young men to Germany to work in the munition factories."

"Let's hope not," the priest said. "I have a son. He'll soon be eighteen."

Pantsaris and Tsakiris were still searching for Bouras, who also had disappeared. Even Alexis, who seemed to be now at the center of the events that shaped the destiny of the Moriani, was unable to provide news of Bouras.

"Before it gets too dark, I'm going over to Merope's to help Niko make a kite. Then, around five, I'll meet you at St. Basil's. Papavasile wants us to sing at some service," said Takis to his two friends.

"Who's getting married?" Tsakiris asked.

"I don't know. Just be there."

Meanwhile, in the hope of getting some information about Bouras and Eleni, Pantsaris and Tsakiris went off to visit Pelagia, Bouras's aunt, who lived in a hut beyond St. George's cemetery.

Takis was glad to see Niko's smile as they tied three thinly spliced canes together in the middle to make a hexagon. Niko got his mother's scissors, and Takis skillfully cut the pieces of blue paper symmetrically. The boys were alone in the house, Merope having gone to arrange flowers on her husband's grave. Takis folded the paper and pasted it over the string joining the ends of the cane sticks, and Niko held the kite in the middle while it dried. His ten-year-old fingers held fast the folded paper; his face filled with joyful anticipation. He could already see the kite climbing high and reaching the sky.

"Takis, why do you hold your breath when you do things?"

"I want to be able to endure under water," Takis answered.

"Why?"

"In the summer I swim, and I love to stay under water."

"Aren't you afraid you might die?"

"Not when I develop strong lungs."

"Will you teach me to swim?"

"Sure, next summer. But now let's fly the kite." Takis held the kite high, concealing strong feelings he had for the little fatherless boy. His hope was that by next summer or next spring, he and his three friends would not be around. He could not stand the sight, sound, and smell of the Nazis.

As the breeze momentarily caught the kite, Takis recollected the time when he had constructed his first kite. His father was so pleased. Then the thought crossed his mind that Niko's father would have been proud to see his son's beautiful blue kite. He sighed deeply, so much so that Niko shouted, "That's the longest breath ever."

Merope returned as they were attaching the tails. Dressed all in black, she looked elegant, with full breast, rosy cheeks, and sparkling eyes, all framed in a black shawl. Her smile was joyous, but the joy was fringed with grief. In her face, hardening experiences were registered in soft places. She had the kind of face a son could love and a husband could worship.

"Now all you need is a stronger breeze," she said, admiring the craftsmanship. After a brief pause, she gave Niko a hug. "Son, you have a good friend.

"I know," said Niko, nodding.

"Takis, I saw your friend."

"Bouras?"

"He was almost unrecognizable in his dark glasses."

"We haven't seen him for three days! Where is he? We've all been looking for him."

"This morning at daybreak, he brought me a basket of wild chicory— said he'd gathered it yesterday and it would be good for Niko. And then he left. He looked despondent."

"The loss of his sister will kill him," Takis said. He couldn't stand the thought of Bouras doing something crazy and getting himself killed. He, too, was suffering over Eleni; he loved her so much, and now she was in the hands of the enemy. Since there had been no discussion of marriage, let alone a wedding date, his feelings toward her had always been carefully camouflaged; otherwise the family reputation would have been at stake. The local gossip tended to ruin whatever was good.

Meanwhile, Bouras found comfort in the fields. He made a slingshot for himself and had gone hunting, hitting anything in motion, particularly lizards. Each time he traumatized a lizard, he would perform a ritual of torture, and then he would dissect the serpent, envisioning the cruel soldier who had kidnapped his sister, and he would crush its remains with a big stone. For a little while his nagging rage would subside.

When Bouras first learned of his sister's abduction, he had followed his impulse to run all the way to Cara Tepe camp to seek help from the soldier friend who had given him money. The soldier was polishing his boots and claimed he had neither seen nor heard of the incident, but he volunteered to drive Bouras to Mytilene and inquire at the German headquarters.

The arrogant SS soldiers laughed at Bouras when he pulled his sister's picture out of his wallet. They returned to Cara Tepe and the soldier insisted that Bouras come into his quarters. The smells from the kitchen signaled supper, and the soldier filled an aluminum porringer with soup and gave it to Bouras. Food is food, and his emaciated Aunt Pelagia needed it; as for his own stomach, he felt no hunger, for anger darkened his mind. He took the soup and ran home.

He found his aging aunt crouched on the hearth in front of the fire, her head touching her knees, her hands supporting her face. Neither of them had any news to exchange, but Pelagia offered her faith. "I went to St. George's chapel at the cemetery and lit a couple of candles, one for our Eleni and the other for your peace of mind."

Bouras poured some soup into a bowl and offered it to Pelagia, the only living relative he had apart from his sister. *Neither God nor demon can help us,* he thought. His capacity to turn inward, to build around himself an invisible wall of defense, was astonishing, a mystery to his aunt and a challenge to his friends. Bouras felt an energy emanating from his psyche, propelling him to roam in the fields and collect chicory or run through the woods and kill serpents. He avoided contact with people, lest they ask him questions about his sister. He even stayed away from his friends so as not to burden them with his affliction.

"Your friends were here earlier. They wanted to see you," his aunt said.

"What about?" His abrupt tone cut sharply into her heart.

Pelagia, knowing her nephew's pain, yet not knowing what to say for comfort, shrugged her shoulders and whispered, "They care."

The fire was dying, and Bouras went toward the loft where his bed was. His sister's cot was there too, hidden behind a curtain, and he felt her absence sorely. Pelagia put the rest of the soup in a closet; she, too, had no appetite. Bouras kicked off his shoes and submerged himself under the covers.

He tossed and turned in despair, and when slumber slowly conquered, he jumped up with fear in his eyes, a haunting nightmare disrupting his sleep. He had seen himself in chains before the Nazi authorities. Next to him stood Lefteris, Niko's father, dressed in a German uniform. "Where is my sister?" Bouras asked. Lefteris laughed and answered in German, a language Bouras had grown to loathe. Still, it was only a dream. Shaken and cold, he shivered and drew the covers over his head.

* * * * *

"I'm dirty . . . ," she murmured. "Who would want me? Who would marry me now?" She cried, running through the olive groves and vineyards in her torn blouse, faded skirt, no panties, and bare feet, feeling the weight of her body for the first time. "Bouras, my brother, Aunt Pelagia, will you ever understand? They defiled my body!" There was not a soul around, just endless waves of rocks and trees. "*Panagia mou,* Most Holy Mother!" she screamed in a frenzy, the sound dying away to a shattered echo.

Like a gazelle, Eleni wandered, hiding in mountain caverns each time she needed rest. By early afternoon of the third day, she passed by an old fountain. The water trickled clean in a curved stone tub where peasants watered their animals. She plunged her face into the water and drank, filling an empty stomach. How much she wanted to drown herself! Put an end to her shame! But the water was shallow. She bent down, scooped some water in both palms, and watched it fall like tears from her fingertips, drop by drop, multicolored against the setting sun.

"*Panton prostatevis agathi*—you protect all of us who come to you in faith!" Distant women's voices wafted through the thick woods and reached her ears. She sighed softly, listening to each word and to the palpitations of her heart. "In danger, sorrow and affliction, sinful and suffering, we come to you, Mother of the Most High!" From the eastern crest of the island echoed the angelic hymn. Crossing herself with a trembling hand, and with a churning feeling of contrition, she walked briskly toward the sound.

One hundred and fourteen carved stone steps led to a plateau where the pristine, whitewashed chapel of St. Mary stood like a sea gull gazing at the sea below. St. Mary's Convent was nestled halfway up the slope of the hill on the east of the island.

As the sinking sun lengthened the shadow cast by the convent, Eleni collapsed on the ground, arms through the rails of a steel gate. She lost consciousness, caring not if she ever woke again.

Vespers had ended, and the nuns, two by two, were coming out of the chapel, when suddenly one of them spotted Eleni's body and ran to see what had happened. As she unbarred the gate, two other nuns approached. They struggled to lift her. Her limp body was black with dirt and dried blood from her cuts and scratches.

In a hushed infirmary on the first floor of the convent, Sister Anthusa, a nurse, washed away the blood, examined the bruises, and covered Eleni with a white cotton blanket. She moistened a cloth with vinegar and put it on her forehead.

"Good daughter, who did this to you?"

"The enemy," Eleni whispered, her tear-filled eyes blurring her vision.

"The enemy? Why?"

"I don't know." Eleni wept. Coming out of her daze, she saw a crucifix on the wall. Sister Anthusa followed Eleni's movements with concern. "You're safe here," she said.

"I know." Eleni sighed, and with a slight smile, she faded away. She had confronted evil, and she was no longer an innocent. Her enormous dark-brown eyes blinked, exuding pain, the whole nightmare in the hands of the Nazis still playing itself out in her half sleep.

* * * * *

The town well that provided drinking and cooking water lay west of Moria, a five-minute walk east of the Roman aqueduct. Twice a week, Eleni came early in the morning and filled two ceramic pitchers.

This time, she walked faster than usual, thinking on the way how she was going to make stuffed eggplant for dinner. A jeep stopped behind her. She smelled the fumes and increased her pace.

Twenty steps later, two Germans grabbed her. They took the pitchers out of her hands and mumbled something in broken Greek, enough to give Eleni an electrifying shiver down her spine. She had done nothing wrong. She had said not a word against the occupying force. Something was not right.

For a moment all was blank terror in the giddiness of suspicion. When she managed to look around, she saw a pair of shiny boots, an impeccable uniform, an expressionless face shaded by an officer's cap, and the brass letters "ARKO" pinned to his collar. The other German walked back to get the jeep.

In the hands of Nazis, one learned quickly enough to avoid challenges, dismiss all thoughts of the future, and to cooperate. Eleni's limbs were numb and so was her mind as they helped her to climb into the jeep. Her chestnut-brown hair flowed in the air as the jeep whisked her away. She buttoned the upper button of her blouse and tried to hold her blue skirt over her knees. From the corner of her eyes she could see the commander approaching her body.

Ten minutes later, they arrived at the famous villa of the wealthy olive-oil merchant Costas Cambas. The guards opened the gate, and the jeep moved on to the very end of the road, stopping in front of the marble stairway that led to the main building of the estate.

As they climbed the steps, one by one, Eleni moved away from the commander's breath, her face stiff with trepidation. The commander gave orders to his subordinate who, after opening the door, saluted and left.

Eleni seemed to be in a twilight zone and could not be sure what was happening. In the center of a large room hung a brilliant chandelier representing centuries of elegance. Walnut chairs were equally spaced against the walls. To her left was a chestnut-brown grandfather clock, and at the other end of the room, a fireplace topped by an enormous, austere portrait of Hitler. A banistered ladder led to the loft above, poorly lit by tired bulbs. The only sounds of life were the occasional steps of Commander Strauss and the snapping of fingers.

Much history had unfolded at the Cambas estate, but its only living heir, Nitsa Cambas, had entered the monastic life. The estate had become Commander Strauss's headquarters.

In front of the fireplace was a huge oriental sofa. Heavy drapery allowed very little light to enter. The commander crumpled a newspaper and put it under the wood. It didn't take long; the dry olive-tree wood ignited into flames, exuding a sweet fragrance. When he came back to Eleni, he held two glasses half-filled with cognac. Looking him defiantly in the eyes, Eleni saw him mentally undressing her, a ferocious lion ready to devour his prey. He brought the drink to her lips.

"No!" said Eleni with determination. Her contempt made her nauseous.

"Come," he said. "You don't have to drink. Come and see the fire." He finished his cognac, left the glasses on the table, and assisted Eleni to the fireplace.

"Let's sit here and watch the fire," he said.

"I want to go home," she said. "My aunt will be waiting for me."

"*Jawohl*," he replied and pointed to the sofa.

Eleni decided to cooperate. Maybe, as time passed, he would let her go, she thought, as the commander sat at the other end of the sofa. His eyes reflected the flames, and he spoke words that rhymed in German.

Occasionally, he would get up and poke the fire, and each time he returned to the sofa, he sat closer to her. She felt trapped. As a helpless insect caught in a web sees the cunning spider in every detail—the sharp angularity of the awkward legs, the white cross on its body, and the brutal mouth—so, too, did Eleni, with appalling clarity, see him above her, ready to bear down and drain the sap of her life. She began to smell his breath and the scent of his perspiration. He took off his jacket, and grunting with sudden desire, edged nearer and nearer.

"Please, let me go," she implored, her eyes swimming in tears.

"Not yet," he said, and wrapped his arms around her youthful body, lust and obsession possessing him. Arms like steel bands, unbreakable, heavier with each passing second, bore down on her, clawing her flesh.

Eleni breathed in short, quick gasps, her revulsion near to making her vomit. In the struggle to free herself, straining muscles and nerves, the blood shot to her head, and she thought the veins in her temples would burst from the pressure.

Arrows darted from his flaming eyes. Determined to have her, Strauss stripped himself to his drawers and tore off her blouse. Eleni felt his fierce fingers on her skin as they moved down her bosom to her crotch. With the other hand, he removed her bra and kissed her naked breasts heavily, pressing his thick lips on her nipples. She screamed, resisting; her knees buckled, and she would have sunk to the floor had he not held her fast. She shivered like a sparrow on a cold winter's day; her throat was dry; and as she choked, her neck turned the color of her swollen veins. Then she fainted.

Sprawled on the leather sofa where the enemy had left her, her strands of hair lay on her naked shoulders, making a wild and tortured design on her bruised skin. She crossed her hands over her breasts and felt pain; her nipples were moist and stiff from his sucking; drops of blood from between her legs were drying on the sofa.

Commander Conrad Strauss, sweating, disheveled, and tired, ascended the stairway leading to the bedrooms upstairs. He passed one of his subordinates, winking at him with a sort of charm, maintaining mastery over his conquest. "Comrade, she's all yours." Closing his bedroom door, he shouted, "Relieve yourself, and get rid of her."

Strauss stretched on a recliner beside his bed and lit a cigar. He shifted position, feeling sore in his genitals, and blew out an abundance of smoke, thinking that making love to a virgin was costly.

"Please . . . please, don't touch me," Eleni shouted to the approaching comrade, as she cowered in the corner of the sofa. She pushed a ceramic vase off the table. The vase broke, and tulips and golden daisies spread all over the floor. The comrade squatted and gathered the flowers and the broken pieces. Eleni saw a gentleness in his eyes. This soldier was not the ferocious ugly enemy that had raped her. Yet, her heart palpitated with fear. She held on to the cross that hung around her neck, determined to die rather than submit to more humiliation. She wanted to get up and run, but her knees felt sore and weak. The soldier took the flowers to the kitchen and came back with a wet washcloth. Eleni saw his smile as bait and pulled back, tearing off the chain from her neck.

"Please, don't come near me." She kissed the cross and gave it to him with imploring eyes. "Don't touch me."

Lifting his brows in silent sympathy, he said, "I won't hurt you. Don't be afraid." He handed her the washcloth and put the cross in his pocket without even a glance at it.

Eleni burst into hysterical sobs and pressed the cloth against her face. It was warm and soothing. She wiped her face, coming out of the lethargy that had possessed her.

"Please, let me go," she pleaded, her lips parted in desperate anxiety, hoping.

He saw the terror and fear, but behind those impenetrable eyes was the captive's yearning for freedom. He heard the commander's voice, "She's yours. Relieve yourself, and get rid of her," and felt humiliated. He was not about to comply with the commander's whims.

"I'll help you to get out of here," said the soldier.

Eleni pressed her hand against her breast and bowed, "Thank you." She saw a hopeful sign in his face. *If he really means what he says,* she thought, *I shall be eternally grateful.*

The soldier walked a few steps ahead and Eleni followed.

At the gate of the estate, the soldier spoke to the guard, who saluted and opened the gate as the soldier motioned Eleni to leave. Silently, they walked together a distance from the estate. The soldier took a roll of brand new marks from his pocket and handed it to her. "Take this; buy yourself a new dress."

Eleni looked to see if anyone was watching. The gate was no longer within view; the horror she felt in that accursed estate was far behind her; she was free. In her eyes, the soldier was a guardian angel, but her heart was troubled with rage, momentarily blurring her vision. *Where will I go? What will I say?* she wondered. She bowed her thanks to the soldier, threw the marks on the ground, and ran off without looking back. Puzzled, the soldier stooped and retrieved the money.

* * * * *

When she came out of her daze, Cambas's mythical palace faded out like a dream. Crossing herself repeatedly while looking at the crucifix on the wall, she realized that she had had a terrible nightmare. When she touched her body, she felt sore all over. Sister Anthusa reached out and held Eleni's hand, and as she caressed her forehead she said in a soft, compassionate voice, "Our sinless and innocent Lord Jesus suffered humiliation and death on the cross but came back into a new life."

Eleni's eyes remained still, and she breathed lightly.

"In some sense, you suffered like him," Sister Anthusa continued. "A part of your life has been lost, but the meaning of life is just beginning for you."

Eleni closed her eyes peacefully. She felt only shame. *How will I face this cruel fate?* she wondered.

CHAPTER 6

The Price of Bread

Dawn came to Moria's little houses and huts like a deliverer. It seemed as if the new sun rose as a friend to Takis, to soothe his pain. He stood in front of a small mirror that he had hung on a vine, and for the first time in his life, he shaved off the few whiskers that foreshadowed his manhood. Washing off the soap and blinking his eyes, he looked at himself. He hardly recognized the face that stared accusingly back, hardly recognized the desperate brown eyes. He felt silly as he spoke to his reflection: "First you lost your bike, then you lost Eleni, and God knows what next."

The sun's rays shimmered through the thick foliage overhead, and the azaleas glistened with dew. From the warmth of the sun, however, Takis took little comfort. Eleni's ordeal and presumed rape, the constant hunger and sickness of his people—all this overwhelmed him, filled him with rage and despair, mixed with a consuming desire for revenge. Now, after a sleep haunted by nightmares, he was possessed by a single-minded determination for action. The time for fun, for fooling like children with Nazi domination, was over. All reason dissolved into tumult and rebellion. Throughout the village of Moria, especially among the women, the reality of Eleni's abduction was as painful as the thrust of a knife. Takis loved Eleni with a deep, caring, secret love. He knew that the memory of her kidnapping would not fade easily. But if friendship had any meaning, his three friends had to act, and act now.

Along the shore of the Aegean at the foot of Moria lay the smallest village in the island, a handful of huts called Panayioutha, "the Little Virgin Mary." It was also known as the Fishing Wharf or the Boat-makers Town. So it was with a heavy heart, but strong mind, that Takis set out through the fields and olive groves of Moria on his way to the Boat-makers Town.

As for Eleni's disappearance, he vacillated between hope and uncertainty. And to Takis, this was the final insult; he resigned himself to the idea that he would not survive much longer in Moria. As the Aegean came into view in the distance, he pictured himself making his way across to Turkey to the joy of freedom. But the thought of leaving his friends behind shamed him. How could he be so selfish?

Friendship, a gift from God to the human race, was the source of the energy that empowered Takis to continue in his resistance to the Nazis. Few are the men who know how to live and die with dignity, yet the four friends had sworn to this cause, to live free or to die. To alleviate the pain they suffered when the Germans killed or imprisoned one of their compatriots for insubordination, the four would go to the hot springs of Therma, dive into the mineral water, swim out several yards and clasp hands in a perfect, unbreakable circle. Grasping each other tightly by the hand, they would make plans to escape or to sabotage the occupying forces.

Takis had a plan in mind, but before sharing it with his friends, he needed to talk to the boat-maker.

Mitrakas was a huge man, about fifty-eight-years old. He was sitting in a little room in his hut, drinking sage tea and smoking a big cigarette which smelled of burning rope. Takis waved the smoke away from his face.

"How can you smoke that thing?" he said, coughing.

"Who are you, boy? And what do you want?"

"Barba (Uncle) Mitso," said Takis, in the fashion of the young addressing their elders, "my name is Takis Kalellis, and I'm from Moria. I know your reputation as a master boat-maker."

"That's history, my son," Mitrakas said and drew on his cigarette. "Sit here." He pointed to a wooden stool next to him. Holding his cigarette in front of Takis's face, he smiled. "This is an educated cigarette, you know."

Takis took a look and grinned. "I can see that; it has writing on it." The cigarette was made from discarded butts which Mitrakas gathered every morning from the streets of his little town. He made his own supply of cigarettes by rolling the tobacco in scraps of newspaper.

"You're a smart young man. Now, tell me the truth; why did you come all the way from Moria to see me?" Mitrakas was dressed in a velvet waistcoat—the only inheritance from his father—which was an odd match for his wide-blown breeches. His weather-beaten face, wrinkled by sea and sun, was adorned by a gray, drooping, Stalin-like mustache, and his fiery eyes were ever alert. His enormous knobby hands, strong and skillful, had worked on many a boat. But his ferocious appearance was wholly inconsistent with his innocent soul. Before the invasion, the children had gathered around him in his backyard, watching him as he carved wood for his boats. He would search his pockets for change, which he gave them for candy. He loved the children, and his favorite expression when they made mischief was, "You are *katsirmades!* Accidents of nature."

When the Germans took control of the boat-making business, Mitrakas refused to work, claiming his arthritic condition made it impossible.

"I know you can't work, but I want you to make a sacrament for me," said Takis.

"Don't speak in riddles, boy. What do you want?"

"Three friends and I want to cross the Aegean and seek asylum in Turkey." Takis held his breath and avoided the fierce eyes by gazing out of the window of the little hut facing the blue Aegean.

"Didn't you hear what happened to the last seven refugees?" roared Mitrakas.

"Yes, it was very sad. But all four of us have made up our minds."

"Do you want to become heroes? It's the destiny of our country to produce heroes." He drew on his educated cigarette. "Believe me, if you are caught like the other seven on their voyage to Turkey, the Germans will kill you without a thought."

A garrison of SS men marched by. At a command, they halted. With stony faces (and in hesitant Greek), they demanded of those seated outside the coffee shop directions to Pamphilla, another seaside village three kilometers away.

Through his window, Mitrakas gave them a look of distaste. "It's these green monsters that concern me. They have us surrounded with mines, barbed wire, and machine guns. We're prisoners."

When the SS men resumed their march, Takis said, "I know you are a master boat-builder. I want you to build us a small boat—one that would fit four people."

"And that's a sacrament?"

"Yes. A sacrament saves souls. The boat will save us from slavery."

"Well put, Mr. Takis. And when the Germans or their accomplices discover your plans, what then?"

"It's a chance we have to take, Barba Mitso."

"I don't want to get involved." The cawing of a crow above his hut distracted him; even that was a bad omen. Mitrakas rubbed his chin and cheek with the palm of his hand and said, "I lost my only son in the war between the Greeks and the Fascist Italians in Albania. Three months ago, I lost my wife; she became ill, food was scarce, and there was no much ine. The Germans confiscated my boat, and now I can't even go fishing. My tools are all I have left in this world." His eyes had lost their glow as he told his story. He drew on his cigarette, and a feeling of loneliness enveloped him, touching Takis, too.

His simple tools, laid out on a tall wooden bench, were part of him, an extension of his own limbs. It was inconceivable that he would not use them. Even just looking at them, the boat-maker could see the many products of his craftsmanship.

"Apple trees make apples, and olive trees make olives, Barba Mitso, and the master boat-builder must make boats." Takis's persuasiveness stirred old feelings in the master. A man who is deprived of those he loves and of his possessions can become a hollow man, dying slowly of deprivation, but Mitrakas was an old sea dog who would not allow invaders to possess his spirit for long.

"I'll make you a boat," he grumbled finally, "but you must promise to tell no one."

"I have to tell my friends. We have to pay you."

"Money, I don't need, but can you bring me some food?"

"My friends and I will bring you a supply of food—and cigarettes, too, so you can throw away those educated ones. When can you start?"

"Don't rush me. Come back tomorrow and bring me something to eat. Then we'll discuss the details."

"What about the wood?"

"I said, 'Come tomorrow,' didn't I?"

Takis ran like a deer through the olive groves and arrived in twenty minutes at Aunt Pelagia's hut. She had gone down to the creek to do her laundry. The door was unlocked so Takis knew she was not far away. He entered, and as he waited, he felt his enthusiasm over the proposed boat trip dwindling. *How poor and empty this little house is,* he thought. *It's like all the other little houses—wooden table and chairs, embroidery on the walls, and it smells of zucchini.*

On the wall beside a three-rung stepladder that led to a dark loft hung a full-size portrait of Eleni, dark, graceful, and cheerful. She had an intelligent face with sensitive, refined features. She was one of the few girls in Moria who was able to dress with a certain elegance, for she was a good seamstress. Her shoulders, hands, and feet were beautifully proportioned. She was alert, ingenious, vivacious, and a bit of a flirt. Takis found in her the same force, the same dignity, as in her brother, his friend Bouras.

Timid and bewildered, he sank down under the picture. "Where are you, my sweet, sweet love, Eleni?" From the window, he saw the silvery olive trees and the peaceful meadow unfolding down to the river. He remembered his fourteenth birthday, and the fragrant air of May came back to him. Eleni, Bouras, and he were chasing butterflies in the golden bushes; Eleni's delicate finger held one of the struggling creatures and then let it go, laughing. Takis climbed a tree, and Bouras pulled him down; and the two of them then showed off as they tussled with each other. The memory came brutally fast, vanishing almost at the same moment.

Pelagia, her shawl over her face, ascended the hill slowly, groaning as she carried the heavy basket of laundry.

"Aunt Pelagia, where is your nephew? I've been looking for him."

"Ill fate has befallen us, dear son. Your friend is devastated with shame. I don't know where he is."

"We all feel for Eleni. Is there any news?"

"Not a word. I light candles every day." She crossed herself. "God help us." Her face was furrowed with lines of pain.

"I'd better go and look for him."

"He told me this morning that he might go to Alexis's place."

Takis took the deserted alleys to Alexis's tavern and met his three friends in the back room.

"Bouras, where the hell have you been? We've been searching all over for you," Takis said, hugging him and lifting him off his feet.

"Were you worried about me?" asked Bouras.

"Oh, no. We thought you had abandoned us." The others grinned.

* * * * *

It was Thursday, the last day of October, and a long breadline waited outside Albanis's bakery. There remained only ten minutes before 3:00 P.M., when the rations would run out and the bakery would close, leaving many hungry people without a morsel of bread.

Alexis went in and out of the back room, bringing black olives, fried sardines, and a large slice of German bread cut into quarters. Spitting out an olive pit, he pointed at the four friends. "Listen, you big pricks, you nearly got me killed today." He sounded angry, but Takis saw mischief in his eyes. The parrot in the cage hanging from the ceiling was unusually quiet.

"Who gave you the finger today, Alexis?" Bouras asked.

"Even his birdie seems indisposed," Tsakiris commented.

"Alexis's birdie is never indisposed when all these good-looking Germans are around," Pantsaris said.

Alexis pulled a chair close to the table, put an olive in his mouth, savored its saltiness, and pursed his lips tightly. "It's my bird all right, but not this one," he said, pointing to his pants. His expression was serious.

The friends felt suddenly timid and suspicious, waiting for the trap to spring.

"If this room is your nest, then don't shit in it," Alexis growled.

"Alexis, what's the matter with you? You've never spoken to us like that before," Takis said with concern.

"I've never been so angry . . . I should say terrified! I thought for sure the Germans would shoot me today."

"Why?" Bouras asked, hoping that Alexis had dared something heroic on behalf of his sister, Eleni.

"Because you have been fooling around with my parrot, teaching him to say, 'Hell with Hitler! Hitler go to hell!' And somebody went and told the Germans—maybe that leech Cara Beis. He drops in here—not often, thank God—and sniffs around for news to carry back to the Germans."

"What did the Germans say?" asked Takis.

"Earlier this morning, two SS soldiers came and looked around the place. When they saw the parrot in here, they smiled. Then they headed for the stairs, and I nearly shit in my pants. I took a quick shot of cognac—and you know me with cognac, I nearly became numb. They came down spitting out words I couldn't understand, and I was sure they'd found out what you and I know is hidden upstairs. I was waiting for them to handcuff me and take me off to the Gestapo, and I could see myself ending up like Lefteris—boom! But they were laughing together good-naturedly, and then the stupid bird began to squawk out in German: 'Hell with Hitler! Hitler go to hell!' and he whistled and cocked his head from side to side. I wanted to wring his neck. The soldiers smiled weakly, but judging by the way they stalked out, they were angry."

"And you thought they were going to kill you?" Takis said.

"A couple of German words out of a parrot's beak and you were afraid they'd kill you? I didn't think you were such a scaredy-cat," taunted Pantsaris. He was the clever linguist who had taught the parrot.

"Would you big pricks allow me to finish?" Alexis thundered. "You would be frightened if four Germans entered your home."

"You mean?"

"Yes, when the two left in anger, I had a premonition that they might come back, so I took the cage and ran with it to Papavasile's. He has an identical bird, and when I told the priest the story, he agreed that it would be wise to exchange parrots."

"And that's the priest's parrot?" asked Bouras. He was fascinated at the ingenuity of Alexis and amused by the tale which, even if only for a moment, put the pain of his sister's plight out of his mind.

"Four Germans returned and insisted that the parrot should repeat his performance. The parrot whistled and eventually screeched out, *Kyrie eleison! Kyrie eleison!*—Lord have mercy! Lord have mercy!' I bit my tongue to keep myself from laughing. Then the soldier—the one who had first discovered my German-speaking bird—put his face to the cage, whistled gently to the parrot, and in a coaxing voice, whispered, 'Hell with Hitler! Hitler go to hell!' The bird was terrified and fluttered from perch to perch. The soldier, with an apologetic look, turned to his three comrades and shrugged his shoulders. The comrades laughed at him, and as they turned to leave, he made a final attempt. 'Hell with Hitler!' he said softly to the parrot, and to the amazement of everyone, the bird squawked, 'Amen. Alleluiah!' Gnashing his teeth, the soldier turned on his heel and stomped out."

"You'd better get rid of that bird," said Takis, and his friends agreed.

"But that's the priest's bird. He still has mine."

"Don't get the poor priest into trouble," said Bouras, as the four friends prepared to leave. Flushed with the bloom of youth, their handsome faces smiled at the trick played on the Germans. But Alexis was irked by the way the Germans were now invading his life.

As they emerged from the tavern, Takis and his friends arranged to meet later in Panayioutha, where Takis wanted them to meet Mitrakas and discuss their project.

The breadline had dispersed, but there was a great commotion outside the bakery. People were chattering and looking at a bleary-eyed dog, so thin it was little more than a skeleton covered with faded brownish hair. It had jumped up on Stratya, the errant woman, snatching half of her bread ration and knocking her to the ground. Those who thought the dog had bitten her were exclaiming "Poor Stratya!" while others, pitying the starving animal, were exclaiming, "Poor dog!"

Takis searched the kitchen at home to find food for Mitrakas. Asimakis and Katerina were at work picking olives in the groves. It would be two hours before their return, so Takis took his time. As he passed the family sanctuary, a corner in Katerina's sewing room, something covered with a white napkin caught his eye. As he looked at the icon of St. George and the Dragon, he touched the napkin and felt the bread beneath it. Had a miracle occurred? Had St. George, after killing the dragon, brought them bread? Or had his mother put it there in case St. George should step out of the icon looking for nourishment? Maybe Katerina intended to bless this small slice of bread in the hope that it would become large enough to feed the whole family. With a final look at St. George, and a pounding heart, Takis descended the steps of his house, holding his breath. Under his arm was the precious slice of bread with which he was to entice the boat-maker.

When Takis introduced his friends, Mitrakas put his finger to his lips, signaling them to be silent. He led them into the next room, removed a piece of carpet, and opened a trap door that was hinged to the floor. "Watch your step," he said as he made his way down the stairs to a full-sized basement. It was stark, with a cement floor, and smelled of wood and tar. At the far end, Mitrakas lifted a lantern from the wall and lit it. Two model boats, one bigger than the other, were displayed on a shelf.

"They're beautiful," said Takis.

"Too bad they're so small," added Bouras.

"Come closer. Touch them. Feel them. These are the models, and I use their design to make boats of any size," Mitrakas said, grinning with glee over his own accomplishments.

"Mr. Takis Kalellis from Moria, since your visit here a couple of days ago, I've had sleepless nights."

"Why?" asked Takis, anxious lest he had upset the old warrior.

"All of you, sit down." He pointed to the wooden bench near the models, taking his place opposite them on a three-legged stool. The eyes of the old sea dog scanned the young faces of the friends, who gazed back, wondering what he had in mind.

He pointed at Takis. "Ever since this friend of yours came to me with his dream, I have felt both blessed and cursed. One of the greatest blessings is the love of one's homeland."

"Why do you feel cursed?" Takis asked.

"I want to help you escape this barbaric oppression, so I feel joy in being able to help you, but, at the same time, I am not free to do that which could bring me joy. Treacheries nestle in every corner. Friends betray friends for a slice of bread. I'm afraid."

Takis, in the excitement of meeting the boat-maker again, had forgotten to give Mitrakas the slice of bread. He now pulled it from his inside pocket and said, "Barba Mitso, take this bread as a symbol of our promise to you that you need not worry about this team. We have sworn before God that together we will either live through this ordeal or die."

"I'm not afraid of you, my sons." He kissed the little package and put it in his pocket. "Your project needs a good craftsman. I have a dream that pictures but dimly in my mind what glory your act may possibly bring forth to our land."

The young friends, mesmerized by Mitrakas's rapt features—the look of Jason speaking convincingly to his argonauts—could not be sure what glory they sought.

"Barba Mitso, we want no glory. It's freedom we're looking for," Takis said in a confident tone. His friends nodded their heads in agreement.

"Yes, freedom is our goal," they chimed in.

Mitrakas got up and pointed the way upstairs. "It's getting stuffy down here. Let's get some fresh air and I'll tell you what I'll do to help you escape the vultures' claws."

They all sat in the room overlooking the Aegean where Takis had his first meeting with Mitrakas. They examined the tools laid out on the work bench. Mitrakas made no more mention of payment and apparently was satisfied with the agreement to barter his work for food. He spoke of the hundreds of dowels he would need and explained how they would have to carve them, with exact precision, out of wild olive tree shoots.

On their way back to Moria, they roamed through the olive groves, each one cutting a handful of suitable shoots. They talked about Mitrakas, marveling at his skill and ingenuity in being able to construct a large boat from a little model. They recalled his remark: "I make one rough model and see where it is in error. I make a second with the errors corrected. And then a third, which should be perfect."

About half an hour from home, a fine drizzle began to fall. Dark clouds gathered, and the drizzle turned into a downpour. They didn't dare take time to seek shelter, for they had to beat the curfew, so they were drenched to the bone when they reached Moria. Takis paused on his doorstep to compose an explanation of where he had spent the evening. His father was having his customary before-dinner snooze. In Katerina's eyes, Takis saw anger, which showed in her voice when she spoke to him about his soaking clothes. Wet clothes dry overnight; he knew something else was bothering his stepmother.

"What did you do with the bread?"

"Ate it," replied Takis looking askance.

"Look me in the eye and tell me the truth." Katerina's face was flushed. Takis lowered his gaze, feeling guilty about stealing the bread. He knew his mother was looking into his heart, and he did not want to hear her criticism.

"It was just one slice—enough for one person—so I ate it."

"Your voice says one thing, but your eyes say another."

"I gave it to an old man who was hungry," said Takis with a feeling of relief.

"Why didn't you ask me first?"

"I didn't think you would mind."

"That was a special piece of bread for a special purpose."

Her words hit him like a slap on the face. His anger rose, and guilt reddened his face. What could be more special than giving a slice of bread to a hungry man? He was puzzled that Katerina, always benevolent, often taking food from her own family to feed others, would be so enraged at him. He felt indignant that he should have to justify his action or apologize.

"Papavasile will not be able to celebrate the liturgy tomorrow. I promised him that slice of bread for Holy Communion."

Now his conscience bothered him. Because of his selfishness and his determination to obtain a boat, St. Basil's congregation would be denied Communion. *This surely must be a sin,* he thought.

That night he lay in bed, too troubled to sleep. If he could only make Katerina understand his intentions. Eleni's loving face flashed in his mind, and he felt relief. But the fragrance of the sheets brought to mind yet another nagging dilemma. Would he be able to really love Eleni if her body had been defiled by the enemy?

Flashes of lightning dazzled his room, and from the light was formed a maiden dressed in white. The light flickered over her features—chestnut-brown hair, lively black eyes—and she opened her arms with love and modesty, revealing her beauty. His room became a church gleaming with brightness. She gazed at him and he returned her gaze, thinking that he had seen her before in the distant past, an icon in colors of the rainbow. She was a sweet memory, almost forgotten, and now she came toward him, strong in her love. His tearful eyes blurred the vision, and for what seemed a long time, he was blind to the light.

The sun shone through the window, waking him. It was Sunday morning. With a quivering heart, he thought about Eleni and sorrow again filled his soul. The Germans had ransacked Moria, confiscated his bike, killed his father's friend, and dishonored his life's love, Eleni. A strange dream had brought her back. He was in a frenzy. He clenched his fists around an imaginary bayonet and plunged it into the enemy's gut. "If I could only join the army of liberators!"

The church bell rang a second time, calling the enslaved Moriani to the Sunday liturgy. Takis decided not to go to church. He cast himself upon his knees and wept. "Eleni, my love, where are you now?" From his window, he could see gray clouds gathering in the sky, blocking out the sun. The breeze coming across the mountain filled his lungs with the fragrance of autumn, sweet and ineffable. *Love and death are not more potent than friendship,* he thought, and with a soul still sighing, he set out briskly for Aunt Pelagia's house, hoping to see Bouras. Crossing the silent backyards and snakelike alleys, Takis looked up occasionally at the graying sky. *Surely God the Almighty is angry with me for stealing Katerina's Communion bread. I've sunk to the level of a thief!* he thought. The north wind punished his youthful body with cold, and he felt pain in his joints. "Are you punishing me, Lord? I have never stolen before; never committed a crime. You must be shocked, Mighty One, as you look down from on high upon so many evils."

CHAPTER 7

Why Is the Day
of Freedom Delayed?

The next day, Takis walked the full length of the Cara Tepe camp. Out of the corner of his eye he could see armored trucks, camouflaged cannons, and SS soldiers. It took almost half an hour, and he felt his heart aching. *What would become of the island with these monsters present?*

As he approached the city, a flight of crows made deathly noises over the carcass of a mule lying in a ditch. They had picked the bones clean. An elderly man, hollow-eyed, unshaven, and dressed in rags, chopped at the head of the mule with his axe, and with each blow, the crows fled. The skull finally cracked open, and the man scooped out the brains.

"What are you going to do with those?" Takis asked.

"Fry them, boy, and eat them."

What could be worse than that? thought Takis as he went on his way leaving the starving old man behind.

Although hunger gnawed at his stomach, Takis shuddered at the thought of having to stand in line in the hope of getting some food.

"See if you can get some of that boar meat smuggled in from Turkey," his father had suggested.

"I will," Takis had replied, determined to make his contribution to the Christmas fare.

When he reached St. Nicholas Chapel, a kilometer from Mytilene, he met Bouras and Tsakiris, each holding an end of a thick stick on which hung a small tank of olive oil.

"Where are you taking the oil?"

"We're going to sell it and buy a pair of pants for each of us."

"I've a better idea," Takis said, momentarily forgetting his purpose for going to the city. "Let's sell the oil and then go to a restaurant in Mytilene."

"Great idea!" Bouras said.

"Then our asses will be naked at Christmas," Tsakiris said.

"We can always get around to buying our pants later," Bouras said.

"Right," said Takis. "We've loads of oil at home, and I can double the amount you have in your tank."

It didn't take too much coaxing to persuade Tsakiris to go along with their idea, and his pleasure grew at the thought of a celebration as they entered the marketplace of Mytilene. Within an hour they found themselves at a back table of a small narrow restaurant. Aristides, the owner, tasted the oil and liked it.

"You can eat and drink anything you like," he said to the three of them.

"Anything we want?" They looked at each other, delighted with the bargain. They breathed in the aroma of the displayed foods: stuffed zucchini, fried eggplant, and stewed beans. Even during the famine, Aristides maintained his reputation; he did not serve any meat, for he did not trust the blackmarketeers who had a supply of donkey, dog, and horse meat, but he managed to concoct delicious vegetable dishes.

The wine was sweet and the stuffed zucchini spicy. Suddenly Bouras looked sad. "Hey, friends, someone is missing from our company. His glass is empty."

Takis saw guilt in Bouras's eyes and a smirk on Tsakiris's face. "Where's Pantsaris?" he asked.

"By now, Pantsaris must have completed his poem," Tsakiris said.

"What are you talking about?" Bouras asked.

"I saw Pantsaris this morning—sorry, I forgot to tell you—and he was holding a couple of notebooks and a handful of pencils. He said he was going to climb the mount of St. Elias and was not coming back until he had finished his poem."

"Did he say what kind of poem?"

"A love poem!" Bouras laughed.

"Pantsaris sounded serious. He said it would be a poem about freedom. He even told me the title: 'One More Spring.'"

"Now we are saved! A poem about freedom will free us from the Nazis! Pantsaris is a dreamer," Bouras said.

"Shut up, Bouras." Takis felt annoyed. "Maybe we need a theme to unite us."

Then with eyes dilated, he said, "I've got to go . . . I hate standing in line for a piece of meat, but my father expects to eat boar at Christmas."

"Let's drink another glass of wine, a small one, and then we can all go," suggested Tsakiris.

"I'll never hear the end of this," Takis said and prepared to leave.

"Okay, now that we've blown the oil let's get back to Moria!"

"Not yet, Bouras; let's go with Takis," Tsakiris said.

Two hours later, the line at the butcher's shop was fairly short. And by 2:30 P.M., the inevitable happened: "There's no more meat," shouted the butcher. "The Nazi vultures," he added under his breath.

There was no more to be said. The line dispersed, and the customers, with saddened faces, returned home.

"What shall I tell my father?"

"Takis, it's not your fault that they ran out of meat," Bouras said. "Just tell him the truth . . . you stood in line."

"I filled my belly with the oil that . . ."

"I'll give you more oil tomorrow, and you can go and buy pants for yourselves." Takis was more concerned about what to tell his father.

They trudged on in silence. Takis was guilt ridden. He had failed his father by not getting in line on time to get the meat.

Halfway to Moria, they met Melpomene. Once raped by Nazi soldiers, she had become Melpo the whore. A half-dozen Nazi soldiers now lived in her house on the outskirts of Mytilene. She had eventually succumbed to their continued advances and joined the oldest profession in human history. The islanders looked upon her, an accomplice, with disgust. But Melpo made a living and even supported a three-year-old boy by using her body.

Between good food and wine, Bouras's passions were ignited, and he approached Melpo with a charming face. What kind of promises he made no one will ever know, but he persuaded her to join him and his friends. They walked two kilometers and came across a deserted chapel in a hollow. While Takis and Tsakiris waited, Bouras took Melpo inside, and with a rooster's intensity, proved to himself that he was a man. Tsakiris lasted a little longer. He kept Melpo in the chapel and was insisting on making love a second time when Bouras knocked on the door. "Are you performing some sort of ritual in there?" he called. Tsakiris, perspiration trickling down his forehead, came out with a stiff upper lip, acting as if he were annoyed that someone had dared to interrupt him. Takis did not wish to have a turn. Boggled by the events of the day and the anticipated confrontation with his father, he said, "Let's get back to Moria before we're caught in action." Takis had one more reason to avoid whoring. He had never been with a woman, and the idea of attempting anything in the chapel appalled him.

"What's the matter, Takis? Are you a virgin?"

"That's a pretty nasty remark, friends!"

"Well, what are you waiting for?" asked Bouras. "I'm almost ready for a second turn."

"Stop bragging," Tsakiris said, and then turning to Takis with a smile, he added, "Don't keep Melpo waiting. She asked for you."

"After this, we'll all be going to holy hell," Takis said, feeling the pressure to conform. In his urge to prove his masculinity, he even managed to get an erection. He felt disturbed with himself for succumbing to his friends' wishes. When he came out of the chapel, he pretended that he had enjoyed the interlude, but his turbulent, guilt-ridden thoughts lingered. *How could we do such a thing in a holy place?*

On the way home, Takis stumbled a few times. His friends made jokes about Melpo and her charms. "She must have devoured all your strength, Takis," they said, laughing. Takis's mind remained in a haze. Melpo's image kept following him, and her words echoed in his ears: "Come on, man; get your strength in me." She had spread her firm thighs apart. "Don't be afraid. It won't bite you. I'll wrap my legs round you . . . , my softness will consume your hardness. Don't be afraid." Takis hesitated. Pity was the only feeling he had for Melpo. He did not know how to get out of the situation. She moaned with passion. "What's the matter? Don't you have the strength to take me?" she asked. Takis shook his head No, and as he prepared to leave, he said, "I'm shy, but please don't tell my friends."

By the time they saw Moria in the distance, the sun was swallowed by a cloud in the west. The ravaged village lay under the cloud, as silent and stiff as a cemetery. Something painful shaded the faces of the villagers who walked along silently in a state of oppression. As the boys approached St. Basil's Church, the air felt oppressive: hell had relocated itself in Moria. Women, with sinister and infecting fear, stood in front of their doors, anticipating the worst.

In their helplessness, the three friends wondered what this subterranean threat was. Their confusion grew more intense. Then Stratya, a wrinkle-faced wanderer dressed in black, came toward them. "I wouldn't stay around the streets if I were you," she said.

"Stratya, what's going on?" asked Takis.

"You mean, you don't know?"

"We're just returning from Mytilene," Bouras said.

"You should have stayed there."

"Why?" questioned Tsakiris.

"They killed the priest's son. He was found lying like a dog on the curb by the fountain."

"What?"

"Who killed him? Why?"

Stratya, who served as a midwife in Moria, was the omniscient informer. Eighteen years had passed since she had delivered the priest's son. She had a good idea who had killed him, but she did not answer.

"Why don't you go to the priest's house? That poor soul needs comfort." She walked away, covering her dishevelled hair with her black cloak and mumbling words that no living soul could understand.

Takis and his friends were in shock. They could not understand why the Germans would kill the priest's son, a timid young man who avoided going to parties and was uncomfortable with his peers. He had been destined to become a priest like his father. The boys felt sorry for Papavasile, but they didn't have the heart to go and talk to him. Instead, they sought solace at Alexis's tavern.

The customers and vendors at the marketplace had thinned out. At one corner, a barefoot youth with patched pants and a thin shirt was selling cabbage, leeks, and lettuce. The time ticked by; a couple of hours remained before curfew. Trembling with cold and hunger, the boy shouted expressions in praise of his vegetables, but no one was buying them. Money was scarce. Down the street marched a squadron of SS soldiers, enclosed in an armor of obstinacy and willful ignorance.

Inside the tavern, two men in a corner, oblivious to everything but their game, were playing backgammon. The dice clicked as each took his turn. At the other end of the room was Apostolos, the butcher, drinking wine with his colleague Pavlos, a round-shouldered, white-haired shepherd in his late sixties. Apostolos had brought liver and lamb kidneys, which Alexis had fried for *meze*—delicacy. Takis sniffed the tasty fry, eyeing Alexis. "Anything for us?" he asked.

"We Greeks are bad people," stammered Pavlos.

"I'll drink to that," Apostolos said, clinking his glass. The eyes of both men looked glassy. They had been drinking all afternoon, and Alexis kept reminding them that "the pot turned and found its lid"—meaning that they belonged to each other.

Seeing the three young men, Pavlos and Apostolos resumed their posture, wanting to appear clear headed and wise. "Our life hangs by a hair," Pavlos said, pointing his finger at the three friends. "The wild beasts destroy the tame ones. Be on guard, boys; you heard what happened to the priest's son."

Apostolos, blinking his eyes and shaking his head, lifted his glass. "In wine, one finds wisdom."

"That's what we're going to do," Bouras said and nodded to his friends to enter the back room. Alexis watched with an approving smile. "I have reserved something for you, little pricks . . . excuse me, big pricks. Just go in there quietly."

Alexis set three wine glasses and a dish of delicacies on the table. "Eat these now while they're still sizzling." He paused for a second, tying his apron and twisting his mustache, a habit he had when collecting his thoughts. Bending over the table, he whispered, "Things don't look well at all." He sat at the table, keeping an eye on activities in the tavern.

"The Nazis must be after your ass," Bouras said.

"That's not it." Alexis's face saddened. "I was with Papavasile before he found out about his son's death. He covered my head with his *epitrahilion*, stole, as if he were going to hear my confession, and we both listened to his radio. A broadcast from London reported that a soldier by the name of Costas Koukides was guarding the Greek flag on the Acropolis hill when a squadron of Germans came along with a swastika. They ordered the guard to lower the flag so that they could replace it with theirs. Having no recourse, Costas silently obeyed, and gnashing his teeth in fury, riveted his eyes upon the leader. Then he climbed up a marble column nearby, wrapped himself in the flag, and in a clear, steady voice, sang:

> *I love my country's flag*
> *As I love my life.*
> *I shall not hand it to an enemy,*
> *I prefer to die . . .*

He then threw himself into space and landed in a rocky crevice two hundred meters below.

With his elbows on the table and his hands supporting his head, Takis listened. He did not touch his wine or the fried liver. The news report spurred him on to make up his mind. *This is it. Tonight I'm taking that swastika down from the castle.*

"I have a plan. I'll mix ground glass into this liver and feed it to the German shepherd dogs that guard the Cara Tepe gate."

"Where? Why?" Everyone looked at Takis.

"Don't do anything foolish!" Alexis's voice sounded condescending.

"Alexis, I mean it." Takis's eyes showed determination. "They have gone too far; they have even killed the priest's son. I'm going to tear down their swastika." His face was flushed.

Bouras and Tsakiris were disturbed that Takis had decided to carry out such an act that night, for Mitrakas had not yet finished the boat, and therefore they were not prepared to depart for Turkey, especially at a moment's notice. They looked Alexis in the eye, soliciting some sort of assurance that all would be well. Their glasses were empty.

"You know the penalty for sabotage. Do you want to have two funerals tomorrow?" Alexis pulled up his chair and sat beside Takis. He pushed the glass under his nose and said, "Drink it! Wine makes you feel strong and wise, as Apostolos claims."

"Alexis, I can't drink wine and think that everything is fine. The snakes are sucking the blood out of our very souls."

In his brown eyes, Alexis saw fear and determination. He looked at the other two. Bouras continued munching on the *meze*. Tsakiris could not keep still. Alexis hesitated before telling what he had on his mind.

"I need one of you tonight," he said.

"What for?" Bouras asked, with his mouth full.

"If you guys have balls, you've got to trust me."

They all volunteered.

"I said I need only one person." Alexis really wanted Takis, but sensitive to youthful mischief, he decided to toss a coin. "What's fair is fair," he said. "The winner comes with me tonight. Do you agree?"

"We agree!" they answered.

"Heads or tails?" He spun the coin high in the air and caught it as it fell. "Call it," he cried.

"Tails!" shouted Tsakiris and Bouras together.

"Heads!" said Takis.

Alexis lifted his palm slowly from the table and looked at the coin.

"Takis, I'll see you tonight at eleven behind St. Basil's."

"Alexis, tell us what you're up to," pleaded Bouras.

"Tomorrow, at this hour, join me here and I'll tell you all about it." He made a gesture to them to keep their mouths sealed.

When they met the next day, Pantsaris came in with a copy of his poem. "This will be our national anthem," he said. His posture was erect, and he radiated with pride. There was no response. "Is something the matter?"

"Alexis has something to tell us, and it's serious," Takis said.

"Don't worry. We've time to hear your poem."

"And it had better be good." Tsakiris smiled.

Alexis brought in five glasses filled with ouzo and water. "Let's drink to freedom," he said. They all took a strong sip and turned to Alexis for the latest news.

Alexis described in full detail how the allies were sending weapons through Turkey. The previous night, the second load of machine guns had arrived. Alexis, assisted by Takis, had unloaded the small vessel and hidden the weapons in Mandrach. In time, these weapons were to be distributed to patriots who had banded together in the mountains.

"Okay, heroes, listen to my poem," Pantsaris said.

* * * * *

The reason for the murder of the priest's son remained a mystery. At the funeral, the whole village of Moria lamented the loss of another innocent victim. Engulfed in grief, the priest, his wife, and daughter witnessed the love and dedication of the people who mourned their son. In their sadness they could offer no comfort.

When the body was carried into St. Basil's, Father George, a visiting priest vested in white, was waiting at the altar. He had been

Papavasile's colleague and friend for over thirty years and knew the family well. When the sad news reached him, he came at once to comfort and help his friend.

He hugged and kissed the bereft father, crying with him just before the service. His eulogy was simple and poignant, coming from a heart whose concern went much deeper than mere sentiment.

"It is at times like this that it is not easy to be a Christian. *An eye for an eye* may make sense to a heart filled with grief, but Jesus gave us an unfailing remedy: forgiveness.

"There are no words that can bring solace to a mother and father and sister for the senseless death of young Christos. My own heart aches and I share their grief. As I see the youth resting among flowers in his coffin, I think of God sacrificing his Son for our salvation. And as I look at Christos's mother, I envision the Virgin Mary under the cross. The human pain, a mother's sacrifice, her own offspring crucified. How are we to understand this pain?

"Christos is now with God, and he has left behind a pain that we must share. We live in critical times, threatened by imminent tragedy. We can allow our hearts to live in hatred like those who killed Christos, or we can follow the path of Jesus, who forgave even those who plotted to destroy him. In the death of our son, Christos, Jesus died once more."

Listening to his colleague's eulogy, Papavasile's eyes became dull and lifeless. He longed for God's reason. Inconsolable, he took minimal part in his own son's funeral service. At the end, in a choked voice, he invited the people to pray for peace.

* * * * *

March 1942

Three months passed, and the only ray of hope was the smile on the boat-maker's face. "The boat is ready. As soon as the caulking dries, you can haul her into the sea."

Early on the third Sunday in Lent, although it was springtime, the weather in Moria was piercingly cold. Papavasile, his overcoat pulled tightly around him, entered St. Basil's. In preparation for the liturgy, he lit the candles and ignited the coal in the silver censer. A sweet-smelling fragrance mixed with the cold air and caressed the Byzantine icons. The congregation would arrive in another hour.

The saints, in colorful vestments, peered austerely from their posts. Four fluted pillars rose high, supporting an icon of Christ. The prophets, long-faced, desperate, still wailing for the lost glory of Israel, cowered at Christ's fe t. From the height of heaven, as portrayed in the dome, Christ blessed with his right hand while holding the book of the Gospel in his left. Many centuries had passed since the angels had proclaimed, "Peace on earth." Still, after centuries of painful, spiritual struggle, He blessed: Peace be unto you!

Papavasile's eyes filled with tears. He beheld Christ's wracked, whiplashed body hidden under a beautifully hued robe of blue, red, and purple. He imagined a thorn here and there in his carefully combed hair, and on his forehead he thought he detected dried blood that innumerable layers of paint had failed to cover. Written in his eyes was: "Patience! Learn to carry your cross as I have!"

Papavasile felt weak, tired, and ambivalent. His faith for the one he served with dedication was beginning to falter.

Standing before the holy table and vested in purple robes, Papavasile turned toward his congregation and bowed, holding the book of the holy Gospels. He noticed Takis and his friends. They were among the few young men left in Moria. Takis began reading the epistle lesson for the day. When he finished, he went to the priest and kissed his hand. "Father, my friends and I must see you." The priest nodded, and then half-heartedly read the Gospel lesson. Pausing, he looked at the congregation. Their faces were emaciated, and their weak legs could scarcely support their bodies.

In a period of two years, Papavasile had buried nearly three hundred people. The war brought a quick end to the misery of many. He mourned the death of every parishioner, but the most fearful and pitiful death was by hunger. He had seen people eat dead donkeys, dogs, and mules. The heads and feet were cut off the dogs and the remainder sold as lamb in the city markets. He rushed at all hours to pour a drop of Holy Communion between the dry lips of those dying of hunger.

"Why is the day of freedom delayed?" War, that dreadful enemy of the world, had not only taken away many of his people, but also his son. Though angry and bitter, should he ever meet the murderer of his son, he was not sure how he would react. Could he take vengeance? He was a man of the cloth. Momentarily, his heart was filled with admiration for the brave mountaineers. They were fighters, and their struggle for freedom was sacred.

With uplifted hands, he began the supplication:

"In peace, let us pray to the Lord." His lean, striking face was distinguished by a sensitive aquiline nose, accented with large brown eyes. His gray mustache, though badly in need of trimming, could not cover his full lips and added an air of maturity to his appearance.

The cantors responded with robust voices: "*Kyrie eleison.*"

Papavasile faced the altar so that his worried countenance was not seen by the congregation. Staring into the eyes of the crucified Christ, he continued:

"For the peace of the whole world and the stability of the holy churches of God, let us pray to the Lord."

"*Kyrie eleison.*"

"For the civil authorities, leaders, and liberators of our enslaved country, and for our delivery from every foe and adversary, let us entreat the Lord."

In an attempt to ease his tension, Papavasile recalled the humorous chants he had improvised, parodying the life of a seminarian. How he had sung and satirized his teachers and led his fellow classmates in traditional Greek dances after the ever-watchful bishop had gone to sleep. The attempt was to no avail. His slender fingers clenched the crucified figure on the cover of the Gospel book. As his faithful congregation made the sign of the cross, he sought to grasp an inner strength.

The church emptied, leaving columns of incense smoke rising to the vaulted dome. Takis and his friends approached the priest.

"Father, although we haven't done much to comfort you in your sorrow over your son's death, today we have come to ask your blessing," Takis said.

Papavasile sensed that the four had something serious to tell him. With a warm embrace, he led them inside. When they told him of their decision to leave the island, he smiled, but his eyes brimmed with tears. Behind their eager eyes, he saw the flame of youth, the yearning to escape from slavery. His heart was proud. "I wish my son could have shared in your spirit," he said with a sigh.

Silently, Papavasile led the four youths through the darkened church to the altar. He lit a candle and offered a prayer.

"May God's angel guard you and keep you safe. Bring back freedom."

One by one they thanked the priest as he escorted them to the exit. "Be very careful, my sons," he said, making the sign of the cross over their heads.

"Father, please keep in touch with our families," said Takis.

"I will," said the priest.

"Will you ever visit my sister?" Bouras asked.

"Sorry, my son. I meant to tell you," the priest said apologetically. "I was at the convent last night. Your sister looked peaceful and is in good hands. There is a lot of love at St. Mary's."

Bouras nodded skeptically. If he could only change his mind at this point and forget the escape! The reality of leaving his sister and aunt behind hit him painfully. Did he have a choice?

CHAPTER 8

Elpis, the Voyage of Hope

The meeting place was at Mandrach, a sheepfold in a neglected quarry by the sea, four kilometers from Moria. Mitrakas, the artisan, and Takis and his friends, the four apprentices, had worked for five months in Mitrakas's basement building the boat in small sections. These, covered with rugs lest an evil eye should spy them, they carried to Mandrach. Nobody would visit this place anyway, except to dump a dead donkey or horse. The stench was unbearable, although, for the most part, the sea breeze blew the smell away. Takis and his friends took turns providing something for Mitrakas each day—a piece of dry bread, some figs, a handful of raisins. The old man was getting tired, and his hands and feet began to swell from malnutrition. Takis knew that when people swelled like that more than once, death was near. With trepidation, he spoke to his friends about the situation. "We'd better keep Mitrakas fed, for if he dies, the boat and our passage to freedom will die with him."

"Bite your tongue," said Bouras.

After five months, the boat and oars were finally ready.

"She's beautiful!" Takis exclaimed, throwing his arms around Mitrakas in celebration.

"A masterful job! We must name her. Let's call her *Argo!* "

"Like in 'Jason and the Argonauts?' Cut it out, Bouras," said Tsakiris.

"Call her *Elpis*—hope," suggested Mitrakas.

"The master is right," Pantsaris said. "Let's call her *Elpis*."

"When is the blessed hour?" Mitrakas asked, as he caressed his creation, his aging face glowing with pride.

"Barba Mitsos, midnight on March 24 is the blessed hour. We want to arrive at Aivalick in Turkey on the 25th."

The artisan and his apprentices embraced each other, making a circle. They all knew what March 25 meant. It was Greek Independence Day, a day celebrating the end of four hundred years of slavery under the Turks.

Mitrakas blessed them with tears in his eyes. "May it be your liberation day as well, and may God guide you with favorable winds."

They thanked Mitrakas and camouflaged the boat with olive-tree branches.

"We have two more nights on the island. Let's not do anything stupid to prevent us from leaving," Takis cautioned. "Friday night we take off."

"I'll be there too," said Mitrakas. In his voice was a tone of determination that his apprentices could not help but take to heart.

"We'll meet here by eleven," Bouras said, and they all agreed that they would need at least an hour to prepare before getting the boat wet.

"We might need last instructions from the master," Takis said, looking hopefully at the proud boat-maker.

Takis already knew what he would be doing for the next two nights, and Bouras reminded them that the following afternoon they were to meet at Alexis's tavern for a farewell drink. Together they left Mandrach and headed for Moria.

"Friday night at eleven," they reminded each other, and set off on their various pursuits.

Two hours before curfew, Takis arrived at the Convent of St. Mary. The nuns had given refuge to Eleni after her rape at the hands of the Germans. Slowly she had recovered her strength. Takis wanted to see her for a few minutes before returning home. As the sun was setting, he met her at their accustomed place, under a lemon tree next to the belfry. Her sponsor, Sister Anthusa, welcomed any visitor for Eleni, but she was especially fond of Takis, for Eleni had confessed to her that he was her brother's best friend and that he loved her like his own sister. Looking into his young love's eyes, Takis found that he could hardly speak. Thoughts crowded his mind, and rage swept through him at the cruelty of the Nazis who had contaminated Eleni's beautiful body and taken her virginity—a prerequisite of marriage in Greek tradition. Now, cloaked in black, she stirred his feelings, and his conscience was filled with guilt that he was leaving her behind.

Eleni told him how much better she was feeling and how lovingly the nuns had cared for her in the past five months. Takis had been so involved with his own plans that he had not realized five months had passed since Eleni had sought shelter in the convent, and even now, his mind was preoccupied with his flight.

In her serenity, Eleni sensed Takis's nervousness. She now saw him, just as the nuns did, as a handsome young man. She would always cherish Takis as a friend but never more than that. Besides, she was a year older than he, and in Moria it was traditional for the husband to be at least ten years older than his wife. She looked into his brown eyes and held back her thoughts: *Time and prayer heal all wounds.* She smiled.

In her nun's garb, Eleni looked older than her seventeen years, a full woman growing more attractive with time. Takis wanted to embrace her, but he hesitated, for he felt small, inadequate, not quite a man. Then he reached out and took her hand into his, and together they walked in the shade of the trees.

"Takis, you're pale, and I hear trouble in your voice. What's the matter?" Eleni asked with deep concern.

Takis looked around cautiously, not wanting anyone, even the nuns, to hear what he was about to say. When he told her of his coming flight to Turkey, Eleni began to cry.

"My brother is leaving also? What about Aunt Pelagia? And what about . . . ?"

"Don't worry, you're in good hands," Takis said, preparing himself to return home. "Stay here where you'll be safe. When Greece is free again, I'll come back to you."

On the way back to Moria, Takis felt miserably guilty. He had still said nothing to his father or Katerina about his plans. Occasionally he had talked about the young men who had left the island to find asylum in Turkey, but his father had dismissed the topic. Then one day after the priest's son, Christos, had been murdered, Asimakis had a change of heart. Takis overheard him saying to his stepmother, "Katerina, I don't blame the young people for trying to escape this curse that has befallen us."

After Jimmy and Kiki had gone to bed, Takis announced his plan, concealing his concern about their reaction.

"It's a dangerous plan, my son. Maybe next spring or next summer these villains will be on the retreat." Asimakis looked at Katerina. "And then . . . and then, America, here we come! Freedom. Opportunity. Food—American hamburgers, ham and eggs-over-easy and buttered toast!" He smacked his lips, savoring the image. But he did not miss the determination in his son's face.

Takis felt an inner strength. He believed that Eleni was on her knees praying for him at that moment. He took both Katerina and his father by the hand. "Mama, Father, I love you both very much," he said, almost choking in his desire to make them understand. "Baba,"—he used the name he called his father in serious moments—"what I must do, I must do. The whole plan is carefully worked out."

"But those vultures have eyes all over the island," Asimakis reasoned. "They'll kill you on sight."

"Please trust me," Takis pleaded. "Papavasile has given me his blessing."

"I don't want you to go."

"I could get killed here—just as easily as the priest's son."

"Don't say such things," Katerina cried.

"I can't endure the slow death here in Moria. Would you rather I joined the guerrillas and played with death daily?"

Asimakis pondered his son's words for several minutes. "You know," he said, forcing himself to smile, "I was sixteen when I told my parents I was going to America. Your grandfather raised his cane, whacked me on the head, and thundered, 'And what about our fields and our goats?' 'I'm going to the land of opportunity. I'll be able to send you money and clothes,' I said. But he would not budge." Asimakis sighed. He knew he could not dissuade Takis, and he saw himself in his son.

"Son, I'm totally against your decision, but I cannot stop you from going away." He put his arms around Takis and kissed him. "My father couldn't stop me, not even with his cane."

Katerina buried her face in her apron and sobbed. "Promise me you'll be very careful," she said through her tears.

"It's time to get some sleep," said Asimakis, knowing full well that it was to be a sleepless night.

In Tsakiris's home, the news of his departure got quite a different reception. His father looked at him in awe. "You're sailing to Turkey! You're going back to your roots, my son," he said with pride. "That's my land and the land of your mother and my two brothers."

Tsakiris knew that his father and mother were refugees, Anatolian Greeks who had fled to Lesbos after the destruction of Asia Minor in 1922. But he had never heard his father being nostalgic over Aivalick, the town in Turkey where the boys intended to seek refuge.

"Maybe it's your destiny to open the way for us," his father said. "Go, my son. Go."

Since Pantsaris's father died when he was young, he had only his mother to confront. He looked devastated as he walked along Aqueduct Alley on his way to Alexis's tavern.

"You look like death," remarked Tsakiris, who caught up with him along the way.

"I wish I were dead," replied Pantsaris, who then went on to describe his mother's reaction. "'You only have one mother,'" he said, mimicking her. "'How can you do this to me?' And then she fainted! I was scared. I thought she'd died. I had to slap her on the face twice to revive her. I feel so guilty about leaving."

"What about you?" Pantsaris asked.

"I think my father is eager to get rid of me. Feeding five mouths isn't easy, you know."

"What about Takis? Did he tell his folks?"

"I don't know. Maybe we'll find him in the tavern."

They arrived at Alexis's door at the same time as Takis. Inside they found Bouras sitting alone drinking ouzo.

"You've started without us?" said Takis. "What a friend you are!"

"Where the devil have you been?" Bouras roared.

"What's got into you?" Tsakiris asked in annoyance. "You're drunk already!"

"Sit down, guys," he replied. "I'm drinking out of joy." He wondered if he should tell them his secret. Pantsaris chucked him under the chin and looked into his eyes.

"You're hiding something. I can always tell when you're hiding something."

"Well, did you brave men tell your loving mamas and papas about our coming voyage?"

"Shut up!" Takis put his hand over Bouras's mouth. "Walls have ears, you know."

"We told our parents," Tsakiris said. "What about you? Did you tell your aunt?"

"I'll talk to my aunt tonight," Bouras replied, smirking. He wanted to tell them that he was no longer afraid of women, that on this very day, another woman, not a whore, had brought him into full manhood. But he hesitated. Earlier that afternoon, as Bouras walked to Merope's with a basket of pomegranates and quince, his heart pounded with desirous thoughts. *If Niko is not there and his mother is alone, I'm going to bed with her, I swear,* he said to himself.

To his amazement, he found her—the most beautiful widow in Moria—alone. He looked at her nervously and yet full of desire, and she returned the gaze.

"*Hairete*—greetings! I've br . . . brought you some fruit."

"Pomegranates and quince. How nice! Thank you," she said, picking up a quince and smelling it. She eyed Bouras playfully. "I'm sure they are delicious."

Bouras was tongue-tied. She saw him blushing, so to make him feel more comfortable, she invited him to stay and chat. As she sat on the sofa, a shaft of sunlight caressed her silky hair, and her blue eyes sparkled against her pale skin. She had just taken a bath and, wrapped in a red terry-cloth robe, she smelled of eucalyptus soap.

Bouras sat in a thick straw chair, his thighs tight and his feet crossed under him. She could not help noticing that his eyes were fixed on her knees—above her rolled down stocking tops—protruding from under her robe. The sunlight was also shining on his hair and face, illuminating his expression. She thought to herself, *What beautiful brown eyes. I would love to kiss them. I could make him happy. Yes, yes, Bouras, I want you. It doesn't matter to me that you are younger. Making love is so exclusive, beautiful, and sacred—a gift from God that I miss terribly. It's been eleven months since a man touched me. I want a man, an enduring man to hold me, to touch me, to penetrate me.* But she was afraid to articulate her feelings lest he take fright. With a gleam in her eye, she leaned toward Bouras and said, "If you're thinking of Niko, he has gone to his grandmother's orchard. He won't be back until dark."

The glint in her eyes tantalized him. Her robe parted slightly, and his vision blurred. He sighed. She smiled. She pulled herself closer to him until their knees touched. He felt her naked knees rubbing against his, turning him into a volcano of physical desire. *She must want me, too.*

Ever since that dreadful day of her husband's funeral, Bouras had flirted with the fantasy of making love to Merope. He had heard so many tales of widows and their passions that he was obsessed with the idea of their lovemaking. But he had never dared to make any advances to Merope. He had confided his passion to Alexis, who composed a poem for him:

> A widow's bedroom
> Has the odor of quince,
> I smelled it one night,
> And my troubled mind
> Cannot be tamed since.

The possibility of plunging into Merope's bed excited him. His heart beat with intensity; he sighed, and with a hesitant hand, he reached out to touch her. She took it and pressed it against her breast, helping him to massage her. The mere touch of her swollen breasts, fragrant, warm, and tender, ignited his passion, and Bouras, with a prolonged sigh, pulled away.

"Oh, you're a man full of fire," Merope said with a reassuring smile. She took him into her arms. She understood what had happened and felt a craving, a kind of insatiable void.

"Come," she said, "we've some work to do." She had him by the hand and laid him on a soft couch in a dimly lit den. She excused herself for a few minutes and returned with a steaming washcloth. It smelled of eucalyptus. "Don't move. Let me do this," she said. She removed his pants and cleansed him thoroughly. She patted him dry and powdered his genitals. Like a hostage, Bouras surrendered to Merope's fondling, and as he watched the gleam in her eye, his hand caressed her thigh. She opened and closed her thighs, squeezing his hand and giving him more room.

"A full man," she whispered. "Look at you. Ferociously big!" She could not believe her eyes. "Bouras, you are going to make a woman very happy," she said. She was ready and determined that she was going to have him first. She snuggled next to him. "Please come into me," she said, spreading her legs to receive him.

Gently he lay on top of her, lifting his hips, and guiding himself with one hand, the other affectionately touching her face, eyebrows, lips, and ears. She twitched and jumped for a few agonizing seconds until she had taken him in totally. As he poked rhythmically, a long "Ah" escaped her lips. "Keep hitting me just as you do. Please don't stop."

He worked himself in and out, faster and faster, the breath beginning to hiss between his teeth. She scratched his back slowly to still him. "It is better if you go slowly," she said. Her soreness was succeeded by a pleasurable orgasm. "Come now! O Son of God, I can't wait any longer," she moaned. After a few deep breaths, he let it go.

He lay on top of her, breathing heavily. "Today you have made me a real man," he said, kissing her tenderly. Tears of joy slipped from the corners of Merope's eyes into her hair. She lay on her back wishing that Bouras could be hers forever and hoping that he would at least come back to her again.

Pantsaris looked at Bouras's glassy eyes and tilted head. He nodded to the others to take heed. "If we are to leave tonight, Bouras, you must go to your aunt's and get some sleep."

"And remember," Takis said.

"Eleven o'clock at the meeting place," Tsakiris added.

Alexis came in with a basket. "For the trip," he said. He looked from one to the other, and his eyes revealed mixed emotions.

"We'd better say our good-byes now," he said.

"It's only four o'clock," replied Pantsaris.

"Yes, but we shouldn't wait until the last moment; the tavern might be busy by then."

Alexis brought four steaming cups and placed them on the table.

"Drink this to sustain you," he said. "It's broth."

"What did you make it from?" asked Takis. "It's very tasty."

"Yes, it's really savory," added Bouras. The words were no sooner out of his mouth than he began to choke, for he caught sight of the empty bird cage. Where was the parrot? "I don't believe it!"

"It won't hurt you," Alexis said. "Today, we eat the parrot; tomorrow, I'll cook the cage."

They all laughed.

"Poor Plato," they said in unison.

Alexis embraced each one and wished them "*Kalo taxidi*—safe journey." He wiped his eyes. "When you come back we'll celebrate for a whole week," he said, turning away from them.

"*Paidia*—be careful," Takis said to his friends. "Make sure you take different paths. . . . I'll meet you there. Bouras, go home and get some rest." He was about to leave when the thought of his father crossed his mind. He approached Alexis. "You would be doing me a great favor, Alexis, if you would keep an eye on my father while I'm gone," he said softly. "Comfort him when you can." With a long last look at the tavern, Takis left.

Absorbed in thought, Takis hung around the statue of liberty. He wondered if they would get out to sea safely later that evening; if they would make it across the Aegean; if they would ever get back to Lesbos again.

Dressed in his beige turtleneck and brown slacks, he awaited the opportunity to creep into the dry sewer among the pine trees. This was the first step in his final task—the removal of the swastika, a job he had promised himself to accomplish so long ago. Wrapped around his waist was a burlap sack in which to hide the flag. The sewer smelled of decaying rubbish, and as he crawled on his stomach, he could hear the rustle of other creeping creatures. He held each breath for as long as he could to avoid the stench. He could see a dim light from the glow of the lingering sunset marking the other end of the pipe, and as he neared the opening, his body trembled. His courage almost failed him as he stood up in the open air. His knees were like rubber and sweat trickled down his chest. The sight of the swastika enraged him, and the thought of what he had to do paralyzed him with terror. *I must be crazy*, he thought. *No sense! Who do I think I am? Hercules? Theseus?* He visualized himself telling his friends of his great triumph. *I may not live to tell them. My heart is pounding as if it were about to burst.*

Again he got down on all fours and crawled toward the flagpole. He was a stone's throw away from it when a German shepherd dashed up to him. He froze, thinking he would be torn apart. He held his breath and felt rooted to the ground while the dog sniffed him all over. Takis could feel the drool dripping on to his neck and ears and the wet tongue licking his feet. Having satisfied his curiosity, the dog trotted back to his master leaving Takis, his limbs trembling so that they could scarcely hold up his body. For ten minutes he did not dare lift his face.

He remained like one of the stones strewn around the tower of the castle. When he was sure there was no movement, he decided it was now or never. His hatred for the symbol spurred him into thought. *I must tear it down. I'll burn it. No, I'll tear it to shreds. No, I'll take it and show off my conquest.*

The evening breeze subsided, and the flag hung from its post like a man in a noose.

One more step, one more breath, and Takis was undoing the knots with trembling fingers. He could feel his heart thudding. The fear of being caught and of being hanged on the flagpole made his stomach churn. His mouth was dry and sour, and his clothes were soaked with perspiration. He undid the last knot, and the flag fluttered into a heap on the ground. Now he moved more quickly, rolling it into a small bundle, pushing it into the burlap sack, tying the sack around his waist, and scrambling back into the sewer. He made it!

Emerging from the other end of the pipe, he went up the mountain—an hour's climb—down the other side through tracks no longer traveled. He continued to Mandrach, the meeting place.

While Takis fulfilled his personal revenge and Bouras slept, recovering from his afternoon ecstasy, Tsakiris and Pantsaris returned to Alexis's tavern with a bag of potato peels which Tsakiris had found in the garbage outside the German canteen. They had washed them in the Camares river, thinking they would make a substantial meal on their trip across the Aegean. They fried them in the tavern and found them to be so crisp and delicious that even Alexis was impressed and suggested that Tsakiris set up a potato-peel enterprise after the war. They all laughed, and Pantsaris, thinking that they would enjoy another item on the menu to accompany the potato peels, disappeared for fifteen minutes, returning with a small bundle under his arm. He had stolen a hen from his grandmother's coop.

"Don't ask any questions, Alexis. Just kill and boil it. We need food for the trip."

Alexis, who always had a pot of hot water on his stove, boiled the chicken. He then cut it into chunks, steeped them in wine for ten minutes, dipped them in egg-batter, and fried them. He got a wicker basket used for collecting olives and filled it, putting the fried chicken in one side and the fried potato peels in the other. Between the packages, he hid a bottle of wine and a note: "Drink this when you arrive and think of me. Until we meet again. Alexis." He topped the basket with hay, gave it to Tsakiris, and the two boys left.

They headed for Mandrach, each taking a different route. An hour and a half before curfew they rejoined each other a stone's throw from the sheepfold. Apprehensively, they surveyed the area. Takis and Bouras were hastening through the olive groves, their eyes and ears on the alert. And then the moment came. The four joined minds, bodies, and souls, overcame their fears, and with courage, moved on in search of freedom.

The Aegean had one-foot swells, and the sky was overcast that night of March 24, 1942. Takis and his friends pushed their fourteen-foot boat against the rising waves. Wiping the sea spray from their eyes, the young islanders stared intently at the dark horizon. Shoes and socks already in the boat, pants rolled up to their knees, they searched the sea for rocks, water-logged freight containers, timbers, all deadly menaces to their newly built craft. A few feet from the shore they climbed in and began to use the oars. Before the war, rowing had been their Sunday afternoon pastime, and their bodies quickly returned to the old rhythm. What was once a game had become their passage to freedom.

The solitude of the sea made them keenly sensitive to every sight and sound. Slowly, they began to lose sight of Mitrakas; the old boat maker had stood by the shore and waved them farewell: "*Yia ke hara sas leventes, ferete piso lefteria*—health and joy to you, brave sons; bring back freedom." His words still echoed in their ears. Behind them, the sea breeze smoothed out their course. Far ahead, some sixty kilometers away, lay Turkey, visible only as a dark silhouette of the mountains of Asia Minor, studded with sporadic flickering lights.

Once at sea, they worked with nervous energy, moving their oars in time to hold a straight course. Each occasionally looked overboard, checking the seas rolling beneath low thick clouds. Struggling in the dark against the waves, they lost themselves in the vastness of the infinite. Suddenly, somewhere under the curling swells, Takis thought he saw something black running parallel to their boat. Bouras looked over the other side and saw something similar. Alarmed, Tsakiris and Pantsaris also leaned over, and all four agreed that the whooshing noise of the dark shapes sounded like passing torpedoes. "Whatever it is, it's not a submarine," they tried to reassure each other. The boys laughed with relief when a school of dolphins splashed by. The friends began to row again, each keeping a regular pace, their eyes staring into the darkness. They fell suddenly silent as premonitions of danger raced through their thoughts. Bouras, still uneasy, volunteered an omen he had heard once from his Aunt Pelagia: "A dolphin is the symbol of joyful living."

"Right! Playing with death is joyful living," said Pantsaris, who was already beginning to feel fatigued.

"What kind of nonsense is that?" Tsakiris asked. "Would you rather write poetry in bondage?"

"Some people are braver than others," Pantsaris said, as a large wave crashed against the bow jolting the boat sideways.

"*Paidia ypomoni*—patience," said Takis as he stood up to stretch his legs. He tried to maintain his balance, but the sea kept rocking the boat like a toy. It was another disturbing sign that there was danger yet to be met and conquered. He sat down quickly. Slowly the boat regained momentum as the friends rowed with serious intensity. Lesbos was no longer in sight, and Takis began to feel an eerie emptiness. *Will we ever see Lesbos again?* he wondered. His premonition about the dolphins was danger, not joyful living. A shiver coursed through his entire body, but the others did not notice.

Suddenly, a huge vessel parted the waves before them, a floating hulk thrashing thunderously to the surface, sending tons of water at their boat. In a panic, the friends gripped the oars tightly and tried to row away. The swastika on the side of the vessel flashed in front of their eyes. It was a German submarine. Only ill fate could have led them to the exact spot where a German submarine would come up for air on its nightly patrol of the Aegean.

Dropping his oar, Takis huddled beside his friends. "Just as we promised," he whispered. "We live together or we die together." Takis knew his capacity for holding his breath under water, but he was not about to desert his friends.

"I'm scared," stuttered Pantsaris, trembling.

"What can they do to us?" Tsakiris said in bravado, though his heart had dropped to the pit of his stomach.

"In case we're caught, we . . ." But Bouras was unable to finish the sentence for terror immobilized his mind.

Hiding his fears behind chattering teeth, Takis muttered, "Before they hook us up like fish, let's jump overboard and try to swim back."

"We wouldn't stand a chance," Pantsaris objected.

"Their torpedoes would blow us to smithereens," added Bouras.

"Let's pull ourselves together," said Tsakiris. "If they catch us, let's play dumb."

"That should be easy for you."

"Shut up, Bouras. Tsakiris's idea is clever," Takis cut in, his head clearing. "We'll tell the Germans that we took a ride and our boat drifted away. It became dark, and we got lost."

"And they'll believe us?" Pantsaris asked.

A sudden crash and the hatch opened! Two sailors holding machine guns stepped out of the narrow opening. "Don't move!" they shouted through the darkness. They pushed an inflatable life raft off the deck and then jumped into it. As the churning sea brought the Germans near the boat, the four friends struggled with all their strength to pull away. From the tower of the submarine, lights flashed right and left. A volley of shots thundered against the rising waves, hitting the stern of the boat. Water broke through the shattered hull and quickly filled the bottom.

As the searchlight passed over them, Takis lowered himself into the water, telling the others to follow. At that moment, he realized he was still in possession of the swastika which, in the confusion, he had forgotten to throw away. The boys joined Takis, the freezing water urging them on in their flight to survive.

Takis stretched his arm and pointed west. "*Adelphia!*—brothers! Back to Lesbos," he cried and dove deeply. The others followed. As much as they tried, they made little headway. They knew their friend could swim at best twenty-five yards under water with one breath. For a few horrifying seconds, he was nowhere to be seen, and they thought they had lost him. Then they heard him calling them to swim faster. It was too late—the searchlight had found them.

The inflated raft edged next to the three, and the two marines pulled them aboard, one by one. Sick with defeat, they watched as Takis swam farther. He took another plunge and disappeared among the waves, the searchlights bobbing around him. Within minutes the raft, riding a white-crested wave, approached Takis. He dove under it, making his way to the floating wreck of their boat.

Once again the marines fired at the boat, reducing it to rubble. Takis was swimming parallel to the wreckage, trying to hide behind it, when he heard the shouts of his friends: "Takis, you'll get killed. Come with us. Remember our oath!" One of the marines threw a life jacket, and Takis, realizing the inevitable, grabbed it. He looked at the two marines, stern and ferocious instruments of the Third Reich. "Nothing escapes them—thoughts nor plans nor movements," Takis mumbled to himself. "I should have listened to my father." As he settled himself near his friends, his terror increased, for he realized he was sitting on the swastika.

The two marines plied their oars right and left, trying to stabilize the craft and bring it alongside the submarine. *This is the end,* thought Takis. *We'll be joining the other seven students captured in their boat and executed without trial. That's exactly what will happen. We'll be lined up in front of a firing squad tomorrow.* He had lost control of his nerves, and his whole body was shuddering. With tearful eyes, he looked at his friends and said, "It's all my fault."

"Takis, your brain must be freezing," whispered Pantsaris.

Deadly silence prevailed as the four friends, after nearly an hour in the water, were taken aboard the submarine.

"Poor Mitrakas, your labor was in vain," said Takis, as they watched the last scraps of their boat break up and float away.

"A shattered dream," Pantsaris added.

"God help us!" Bouras said, grabbing his friends. They were drenched and cold, and their teeth were chattering. Huge vultures with wild claws, the Nazi marines dragged them inside the submarine. With a tremendous thud, the door slammed, closing out the sea. The captain of the submarine ordered them to be taken below and given dry clothing and food.

The four friends huddled together in a narrow room around a small table. They turned their gaze to several freshly opened tins of meat. They were hungry, and the sour taste of horse meat didn't seem to bother them. One marine towered in front of them, and another behind held his machine gun at their backs.

"*Paidia*, there is no earth more beautiful," Takis said.

"Where there is freedom," Pantsaris added.

"I think we need to change our names," Bouras insisted.

"We'll call you Bouras Earth." Pantsaris smiled.

"I like that name, for I feel rugged and harsh like the Greek soil."

"I want to be called Water, for I can live on it and under it," Takis said.

"I want to be called Fire."

"You are Fire, Tsakiris," the others said together.

"You've burned many girls' hearts in Moria."

"Thanks, Pantsaris, you're truly a poet," replied Tsakiris. "We'll name you Air because, like a breeze, your words always caress our souls."

"Guess who is the poet?" Pantsaris smiled. A marine interrupted, and from the harsh tone, the friends understood the message: they were forbidden to speak.

Young boys spend leisure time fishing.

BELOW LEFT: Katerina and her son Takis climb 114 steps to St. Mary's Shrine to light candles and pray for peace.
BELOW RIGHT: Takis's dream is to become the best goalkeeper in Greece.

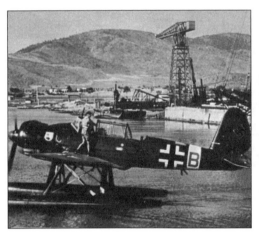

LEFT: With the arrival of the Nazi plane, the spirit of the island changes.
RIGHT: Like rain, the paratroopers descend on the Greek land.

BELOW LEFT: The Nazis march through Yugoslavia on their way to invade Greece.
BELOW RIGHT: A German soldier guards the first prisoners.

Painting of a Cretan wielding a shepherd's staff confronts a paratrooper.

BELOW: The Nazis order those to be executed to dig their own graves in the painting below. Stylianos uses his shovel for a different purpose.

A newspaper headline: Athens in the hands of the Germans.

rddeutsche Ausgabe

Aug. / 54. Jahrg. / Einzelpreis 20 Pf.

Norddeutsche Ausgabe

Berlin, Montag, 28. April 1941

VÖLKISCHER BEOBACHTER

0.60

Kampfblatt der nationalsozialistischen Bewegung Großdeutschlands

Athen in deutscher Hand

allschirmtruppen besetzten Korinth — Leibstandarte „Adolf Hitler" nahm Patras

'Αθήνα στά χέρια τών Γερμανών. Μονάδες άλεξιπτωτιστών κατέλαβαν τήν Κόρινθο. Τό Σώμα Στρατοῦ
Adolf Hitler, πῆρε τήν Πάτρα.

German soldiers pose in front of the Acropolis.

A German solder guards a silent city.

News of the Nazi invasion sends a shock wave through the children.

BELOW LEFT: Patroklos refers to the poem: Better one hour free than forty years in slavery.
BELOW RIGHT: Takis senses a force holding him in check as he watches his bike being confiscated.

The marketplace is deserted.   Houses are confiscated.

BELOW LEFT: Alexis in front of his tavern defiantly awaits the arrival of the enemy.

BELOW RIGHT: At the back of Alexis's tavern, five steps and an iron door lead to a secret room where he hides American weapons.

Father Lefteris joins the liberators.

ABOVE: Ready to fight for freedom.

LEFT: Resistance increases daily.

Captured resistance fighters are hanged in the American Square in Athens.

BELOW LEFT: Merope seeks comfort at her husband's grave. Lefteris was the first victim of the Nazis in Moria.

BELOW RIGHT: Invincible, Bouras is determined. "There will be no Nazis in Lesbos."

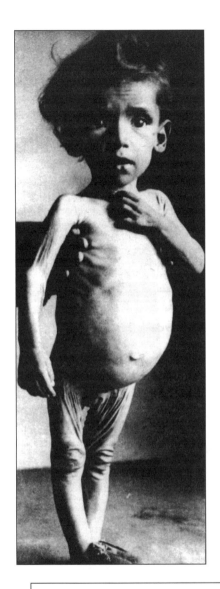

Πεῖνα. Ἡ μεγάλη τραγωδία τῆς Κατοχῆς. Τόν χειμώνα τοῦ 1941-42 καί μόνο, πεθαίνουν ἀπό τήν πεῖνα 260.000 ἄτομα. Παιδάκια στούς δρόμους μέ τουμπανισμένες κοιλιές, νεκροί σέ κάθε γωνιά, καροτσάκια πού μεταφέρουν μέρα-νύχτα τά πτώματα στό νεκροταφεῖο. Μιά μόνο λέξη ἀντηχεῖ: Πεινῶ.

Hunger was the great tragedy of Nazi occupation. During the winter of 1941-42, 260,000 people die of starvation. Children with swollen bellies wander in the streets, death is found in every corner, wagons carry the bodies to the cemetery night and day. Only one cry echoes in the air: I'm hungry!

Emaciated, the hungry forage for food in garbage disposals.

Mother and child grind broomseeds to make flour.

ABOVE LEFT: The Roman aqueduct observes Nazi atrocities against freedom-loving people.

ABOVE RIGHT: After the rape, Eleni finds refuge behind the walls of St. Mary's convent.

ABOVE: The castle endures the emblem of conquest, swastika.

LEFT: Under the Statue of Liberty, Takis discovers an underground tunnel leading to the castle where the swastika threatens the innocent.

Barba (Uncle) Mitsos in his boat for the last time. The Army of Occupation will take it away.

BELOW LEFT: Barba Mitsos: *Why is freedom delayed?*
BELOW RIGHT: Mandrach, the escape point for the four friends.

ABOVE LEFT: In Haidari, the prisoners wait for One More Spring.
ABOVE RIGHT: Anestis offers hope in his interpretation of their dreams.

BELOW LEFT: Perhaps our American allies will liberate us.
BELOW RIGHT: After the Haidari nightmare, Christoforos packs surviving possessions and prepares to come to America.

The Day of Liberation. Moria celebrates Eleni's wedding.

It's time for dancing!

ABOVE LEFT: Patroklos Pantsaris, the poet.
ABOVE RIGHT: Peter M. Kalellis (Takis), the psychotherapist, in the door-way of Alexis's tavern.

BELOW LEFT: Stratis Bouras, proprietor of a paint factory.
BELOW RIGHT: George Tsakiris, the Potato-Chip King.

ABOVE LEFT: Alexis's nephew Vasile takes over the tavern.
ABOVE RIGHT: Once again the Four Friends meet to celebrate life.

BELOW LEFT: Aging and ageless Papavasile reminisces about the dark days.
BELOW RIGHT: Katerina joyfully awaits the arrival of her son Takis.

CHAPTER 9

O Precious Liberty!

At daybreak the submarine docked on the island of Crete. The four friends were handcuffed, put on a jeep, and taken to the outskirts of Heraclion. There, two SS marines locked them in a small dungeonlike cell with no light or windows. "This dark inferno is our prelude to hell," cried Pantsaris. The rest said not a word.

Later in the day, the two marines escorted them to Nazi headquarters, two kilometers away. They were taken to Stefan Patcher, a German officer, sitting behind a huge desk skimming through papers. He looked up, surveying the prisoners over his gold-rimmed glasses, and then, glancing to his left, he spoke to a civilian interpreter. The civilian had heavily oiled black hair, a dark face, and devilish eyes. He bowed to the officer and went closer to the four friends.

"I want you to pay careful attention to what I tell you," he announced in perfect Greek.

The four nodded.

"The Oberst Lieutenant (lieutenant colonel) respects and rewards people who speak the truth," the interpreter said, smiling at his superior. "You snatched away the German flag from the castle of Lesbos. Such an act is considered sabotage against the occupying forces." The interpreter paraded in front of the four, and then with an abrupt twist, he faced each one in turn, asking the same question: "Why did you remove the flag?"

"What flag?" Tsakiris asked, an innocent expression on his face.

The interpreter slapped him violently across the cheek with the back of his hand. The other three tried not to acknowledge Tsakiris's pain. Tsakiris's eyes remained obstinately open, giving his friends courage. The physical pain was not as severe as that caused by his anger.

"What flag?"

"We haven't seen any flag."

Two SS soldiers brought in the burlap sack, tore it open, unfolded the wet flag, and spread it in front of them. Takis's eyes brightened with remembered exultation and dimmed just as suddenly at their dashed hopes. As he watched Patcher undoing the collar of his uniform, he sensed the enemy's wrath. He felt a dry bitterness in his mouth, a tightness in his chest. *I got my friends into this mess because of my revenge,* he thought. *Now all of us may be shot because of my craziness.*

The interpreter consulted with the lieutenant and then addressed the four captives. "You committed sabotage against Germany, and you attempted to escape. Your punishment could be death by hanging." The interpreter looked each one in the eye, and raising his left eyebrow, he asked, "Now which one of you stole the flag?"

Takis realized that if he did not speak, he would risk all their lives. If he boldly acknowledged his guilt, then maybe he could save the others.

"Who is responsible?" the interpreter said sternly.

After a few seconds of silence, Takis replied, "I am."

"I am," said Bouras.

"I am," said Pantsaris.

"I am," said Tsakiris.

"Then all of you must die," shouted the interpreter.

Takis swallowed with effort, feeling the noose of guilt around his throat. He felt ready to cry but controlled his tears. Mustering enough strength he whispered to his friends, "Are you crazy? You didn't do it. I did!"

"You're not making any sense," replied Bouras.

"We did it together, remember?" Pantsaris said.

"I'm not crazy. I'm your friend," Tsakiris replied.

Then, with determination, Takis turned to the interpreter. "I took the flag because I hate the Germans. I hate what they did to our homeland. I hate you, Mr. Interpreter, for being a Nazi accomplice."

The interpreter's face reddened, but he remained quiet, and leaning over the lieutenant's desk, he once again consulted with him in German. He came back to the four, a smirk on his face. Pacing to and fro in evident rage and clearing his throat, he said, "The Oberst Lieutenant is a good man, a very good man—as a matter of fact, an admirer of Greek civilization. He's willing to forgo the death sentence, but you will still be punished severely."

The four glared at the man behind the desk, who wriggled his strong, belligerent nose. They found it hard to believe that it was he who held their lives in his hands.

I'd like to poison you and all your cruel masters, Takis thought, looking vehemently at the enemy.

A side door opened, and a soldier brought in handcuffs. The lieutenant gave further instructions to the interpreter.

"The army of occupation has plans for you," said the interpreter, and he nodded at the soldier with the handcuffs.

"They'll probably send us to Germany and make soap out of our bodies," Bouras mumbled.

"They might train us to be good Nazi soldiers," Tsakiris whispered.

"They could brainwash us, you know, and send us back to Greece to fight against our own people," said Pantsaris.

"Compulsory labor, maybe!" suggested Takis.

"Or death!" emphasized the interpreter.

Once handcuffed, they were escorted to a dark dungeon. "This will be your home for a while," announced the interpreter. Removing the handcuffs, the soldier pushed the four friends through the door, locking it behind them.

The walls of cement, wet with moisture, were more than seven feet high, topped by a barbed-wire ceiling that served as a skylight. The cell door was a sheet of thick steel reinforced with cross bars. A slot at the bottom allowed food to be passed in. The cement floor was bare and smooth except for a hole in one of the corners which smelled of urine. During the night, cockroaches invaded the cell, the insects' ticklish touch keeping the prisoners awake.

Dawn eventually came, bringing with it more despair. Every few minutes, a drop of yellowish water not even sufficient to wash their faces leaked from the faucet over the latrine, and the smell was unbearable. The slot in the door opened, and a plate of food was shoved on to the floor. It was not an appetizing sight: a chunk of strong-smelling cheese, spoiled and filled with worms, and a piece of dry, crunchy corn bread. Not much of a breakfast, but the friends devoured it anyway.

Two weeks passed by, and the four friends still waited.

"At least we are still alive," said Bouras.

"For how long?" Takis asked, displaying his swollen hands. His friends pulled back in horror. They examined their own hands, and they could see that their fingers were slightly swollen, the skin was flaking, and in some areas, scabs were forming. As the days passed, Bouras and Tsakiris developed a problem with their groins, which became increasingly itchy.

"We'll die of some terrible disease in this accursed place," complained Takis.

"That's to be expected," said Bouras. "We haven't had fresh water, food, or a bath for two weeks."

Hobnailed boots cracked against the cement corridor outside their cell. It was time for the last meal of the day, and they could be sure that the soup would be the same as yesterday's, the same as tomorrow's—

a tasteless bean liquid. They held the bottom of the bowl and tipped the soup slowly into their mouths, making sure their infected hands did not contaminate it. With their stomachs calmed and in the darkness of the fetid cell, they lay beside each other on the floor and closed their eyes. Their minds visualized the little town of Moria, and their hearts engaged in separate fantasies.

An enormous erection made Bouras toss from side to side. In his dream, he was making love to Merope when her son Niko knocked at the door. A vivid recollection of his last visit to Merope surfaced in his mind: how affectionately she had taken him into her den and had bestowed upon him the greatest bliss. He sighed and stretched, unable to satisfy his passion.

To Tsakiris, slumber was far from coming. He saw himself frying potatoes and barbecuing octopus on a grill in the tavern. Alexis had set the table and poured ouzo in abundance. There was to be a big celebration in Moria.

Pantsaris was sobbing in his sleep. Takis shook him by the arm, and he woke up in a fright, looking down at his feet. "I had a terrible nightmare!" he cried. "My poem on freedom was published, and everyone in Moria held up a copy and sang:

> One more spring,
> Oh, precious freedom!
> No more death;
> No more treason.

"And then the Germans caught me and poured cement over my feet, and it steadily rose up my body until I couldn't move. I was crying. Papavasile appeared holding Eleni by the hand, and when they saw I was cemented to the ground, they laughed at me and sneered, 'You're a pseudopoet, pseudopoet.' Then they left me to die."

"What a horrible dream!" said Takis. "I would hate to think what it might mean. You'd better just forget it. It's only a dream."

Takis lay down and tried to rest, but his thoughts traveled to the Convent of St. Mary's where he saw Eleni in her nun's habit and her freshly washed hair smelling of the leaves of a walnut tree. He kissed her rosy cheeks and felt her warm tears on his lips. *Stay here at the convent where it's safe. I'll come back to you someday!*

CHAPTER 10

Accursed Slavery
and Dishonor

On the night of the fourth Sunday in Lent, Papavasile lay awake, struggling, agonized and deeply troubled by the events of the last few days. A small radio, camouflaged behind an icon and a votive light, provided news from the underground. His eyes burned feverishly, and tears stained his cheeks. In the corner of his room, his sanctuary, he could see the icon of St. Michael the Archangel, his silver sword glimmering in the light of a candle. He whispered in pain and wonder: "Smite them down with thy powerful sword!" He imagined the silver sword dripping with blood, and his heart, too, seemed to bleed. He trembled, and his voice became weak, and he seemed to see his country, his people, trembling and bleeding. Not just his town or his congregation, but the whole of Greece becoming a concentration camp menaced by Nazi cruelty and death. Old folk died of starvation; young men were slaughtered by the hundreds; young women were raped and dishonored—a whole nation was drowning in a river of its own blood. The priest grabbed his beard and pulled on it as he listened to the news on his illicit radio.

To date, 166,000 Greeks have been coerced into compulsory service. The United States government has issued an official report with regard to German atrocities in Europe. The report reveals that 1,765,000 Jews have died in the gas chambers at Birkenau; this figure includes 900,000 Poles, 150,000 French, and 45,000 Greeks.

"A diabolical campaign of brutality and terror," he said, his eyes fixed on the icon of crucifixion in his study. Next to it hung the icon of St. Michael the Archangel with a silver sword in his right hand.

"What offense, what sin, must our ancestors have committed, O Lord?" he asked aloud like a dirge in the dark room.

"We enlightened other nations with our letters and civilization, but the invaders have drowned our country. We taught them the freedom of spirit and body, and they have chained us in fear, pain, and hunger. . . . I know you are a God of justice." Papavasile's thoughts failed him, and he knelt. Wiping his tears, he said, "I cannot abandon these people that you have entrusted to my care. Nor can I ask them to have patience any longer and endure the cruelty inflicted upon them by the Nazi masters. We have been enslaved for more than two years. I want to wrestle with the enemy as Jacob wrestled with your angel, until the light of justice appears."

A sudden knock at the door startled him. He sat erect and tried to pull himself together. His glance settled on the icon of St. Michael the Archangel-Warrior, still illuminated by the flickering flame of the votive light. Papavasile lifted an oil lantern and opened the door. The light fell on the face of a youth dressed in an unbuttoned shirt and patched khaki trousers.

"Who are you and what do you want at this late hour?" asked Papavasile. "Are you a patriot? An accomplice? A friend or foe?" His voice revealed his anger.

"My name is Panayiotis. Father, please bring Communion with you and come at once. We have an hour's journey." He took a few deep breaths and continued gasping. Losing his balance he fell on the brick steps of the entrance.

Papavasile put down the lantern and examined the youth, discovering the warm blood on his hands. "You are wounded."

"Yes, the enemy bullets have chewed up my body."

The priest, kneeling beside the wounded youth and caressing his hair, saw Panayiotis's face contorted with pain.

"We must go to my friend Dimitri," he sighed.

"Come. Let me bind your wounds before you lose any more blood. I have clean, white cloth inside."

The priest helped the youth into the house. Meticulously, he bandaged the wounded areas as he listened to the story.

"My friend Dimitri and I are freedom fighters. For five hours this evening we fought against fifteen Germans until Dimitri was wounded. I lifted him in my arms and carried him to a crevice where I hid him, and then I made my way to you." He looked at the priest with passionate eyes. "I don't want him to die without confession and Communion."

"You should stay here and rest," the priest said. "Tell me where your friend is, and I'll go and find him."

"No, Father, I must go with you to show you the way. But we must hurry if you are to touch his lips with the sacred holies."

"Then I will ask Stellios, my cantor, to come with us." The priest folded his *epitrahilion,* wrapped the Communion cup in a red cloth, put a small cross in his inner pocket, and looked around to see if he had forgotten anything—a prayerbook he did not need, for he knew the prayers by heart. They hurried off.

A few dim stars flickered among the clouds, brightening what was left of the night. Holding the small chalice under his hat, he ascended the steep mountain. His long gray hair flowed in the cool night breeze. In front of him was Stellios, holding a camouflaged lantern and assisting Panayiotis in his weakened condition. The priest gathered up his black robe and quickened his pace.

"Father, prepare Communion for me, too," Panayiotis said with a tremor in his voice. "Death is approaching."

Stellios helped Panayiotis to the ground and placed his stole under the fallen hero's head. Papavasile turned and knelt beside him.

"I have committed no major crime in my life, but I have killed several tyrants who threatened our freedom," Panayiotis began his confession. He sighed in anguish. Something secret and terrible still tortured his turbulent mind. His breathing became shallow.

"Go on, my boy. God is compassionate."

"My friend Dimitri and I swore to avenge my sister's rape. Because of the Nazis, my sister Melpo is now a whore in Mytilene." He burst into tears. "The enemy contaminated her and brought dishonor to our home."

Papavasile put his arms around him. He wept. Tears rolled down his emaciated cheeks. He groaned and thought, *The same old painful stories I have heard so often. When will the Lord show us his mercy and save us from this accursed slavery and dishonor?*

"My friend and I armed ourselves with rifles and ammunition and swore revenge a thousand times." Light and strength shone from his eyes as he looked into the priest's eyes, stirring Papavasile's heart with the love of a father.

Papavasile answered with comfort. "If those are your only sins, the Lord will forgive you."

"I have no other sin. Please hurry; death is sucking my last breath. Then, find Dimitri and give him the holy of holies so that he, too, can die like a Christian."

"Where have you hidden him?" asked the priest.

Panayiotis breathed deeply to collect his strength and spoke slowly. "On top of this crevice not too far from here are two cypress trees, one beside the other." With each word his voice became weaker. "Take the narrow path to your right; about a hundred meters away you'll find a cave among wild holly-berry trees. Dimitri lies there."

Papavasile unfolded a red silk cloth, poured a few drops of wine into the small chalice, and whispered a prayer.

Panayiotis lifted his head, with his last strength, and with fear, faith, and love, his trembling lips received Holy Communion. A magnificent rapture spread over his countenance. Then in his delirium he spoke. "Mother . . . have you seen . . . the glory of Greece. . . . Dimitri, light the lantern. It is dark. Melpo, wear your wedding gown. Dimitri and I are coming. There will be a glorious . . . wed . . . wed . . . ."

One after the other, the stars flickered, and the morning unfolded to welcome the glorious dawn. The birds hidden among the myrtle branches chirped in pairs, a blithe song for the forthcoming spring and a dulcet dirge for the loss of youth.

Lifting Panayiotis in his arms, the priest made his way to the cave as he had been instructed. Stellios followed, bearing the Communion.

"There he is, covered with myrtle branches!" Stellios placed the Communion cup on a stone and uncovered Dimitri.

"Father," he cried, "he is dead! His chest is as cold as marble."

"It seems that both brave friends died at the same time."

The priest placed Panayiotis next to his friend and sat near them, touching their faces and weeping. He felt that same pain when he lost his only son. Now these two valiant youths were also his sons. In sorrowful haze, the cantor looked with compassion from one to the other, from the living to the dead.

"We'll bury them here where the soil is pure, and when freedom comes we'll plant two small cypress trees upon their glorious graves, a shrine to remember," said the priest.

Papavasile removed the khaki clothes from Dimitri and used his black robe as a shroud for the body. They began to dig a grave with a silver scimitar that had hung from Dimitri's waist.

Carefully, priest and cantor placed the two bodies together and covered them with wild flowers and freshly-dug soil. The priest said a prayer. To Stellios's amazement, Papavasile then dressed himself in Dimitri's khaki uniform. "Forgive me, Dimitri, my son," he said. "I must continue the fight for you." With trembling hands he tied his belt. The war that had taken place in his heart for the past two years had finally been resolved. He looked at his cantor with a sympathetic smile and said, "It is the fate of our race. Even priests must fight. Until a moment ago, I was a pastor of many souls in our small town. From now on I shall fight the tyrant. I shall be the avenger."

Stellios could not believe his ears! A priest, a man of God, would go out and kill?

Papavasile shouldered Dimitri's rifle and spoke in a tone of sadness and prayer to the freshly covered grave. "My sons, I shall take your place among the mountaineers. In due time, I shall visit your grave to bring you glad tidings—the vanquishing of the enemy—that your souls may rejoice." He turned to Stellios, laid one hand on his shoulder and extended the other. "Our nation has many priests to preach the holy Gospel, but the fighters are few, and we must fight for our freedom."

"Forgive me, Father, I must say a word or two."

"Speak, my son."

"It is unfair . . . to allow elders to fight while we, the young, stay at home like women. I am only nineteen, but I can aim well. Let me be the one to join the famous liberators."

Stellios's brown eyes glowed with enthusiasm.

"You, Father, have already sacrificed one son upon the altar of freedom." His sincere words touched the Father's heart.

"This I did not expect from you," he said. "No man is too old to defend his country." He handed the Holy Communion to him. "Take this back to the church and guard it with your life."

"If that is an order, I shall obey because I not only respect you as a priest but also as a father."

The priest embraced Stellios and kissed him on the forehead.

"Give me your blessing, Father," said Stellios, his voice breaking.

"We shall see each other again on the day of freedom," said Papavasile as he blessed his cantor.

Both men knelt before the grave, and the priest offered a prayer:

"My Lord, you are a witness to the heinous tortures and degradation of our nation. I am not painlessly betraying you, for priesthood is deeply rooted in my heart. But Mother Greece is crying for help, and I cannot deny her my support. Forgive me, my Master, and give me courage and strength. I am joining the mountaineers, the brave liberators, to fight against the barbaric forces; and when my country is free, I shall again serve you with dedication. Please forgive my decision, O Understanding Savior."

CHAPTER 11

Compassion for the Enemy

The world within the Convent of St. Mary was serene and orderly, but Eleni could find no peace, for she was constantly worried about her Aunt Pelagia. Finally, a year after her rape, Eleni left the convent and went to live with her aging aunt. About a kilometer west of Moria among the green olive orchards was a solitary hut where the two women spent their days cleaning, mending, and existing on the bare necessities.

When the Moriani discovered that Eleni had returned, they treated her as an outcast, for she had had dealings with the Nazis. To avoid the malicious ridicule, Pelagia and Eleni confined themselves to their small plot of land, cultivating a vegetable patch and caring for their hut, often wishing for Bouras's return. To have a man around would have been a great help.

December brought bitter cold weather, and the women warmed themselves by the fireplace. A flickering lamp by her side cast its yellow rays on Pelagia's face. Gradually, Eleni felt an inner peace. One night she was looking out of the window, watching the approach of a snowstorm. The whistling wind swirled from the mountains and began heaping the snow into the valley. Flakes stuck to the windowpanes, blotting out the world. Eleni placed an oil lantern by the window and prepared for bed. Suddenly, she thought she heard a voice outside. She listened intently. She could faintly hear a cry for help.

Could it be my brother coming home from foreign lands? she wondered.

She wrapped herself in a woolen coat and covered her head with a thick scarf. Cautiously she opened the door and stepped out. Her feet sank into the snow and made a crunching sound. "Who's there?" she called. "Where are you?" The only answer was the whistling of the wind and the groaning of the trees. Then she spotted footprints. In spite of her apprehension, she began to follow them. They led her to a body lying in the snow. She knelt down and cradled the head of a man in her lap, wiping the snow from his face. He was fair haired with a light complexion, and his clothes were torn and wet. He looked at her, and in his blue eyes was a silent plea: *Lassen Sie mich nicht sterben*— don't let me die.

"I'll help you, but I can't lift you by myself— you must help me."

He closed his tired eyelids in affirmation and made an effort to stand, but he was so weak that Eleni carried most of his weight.

When they entered the hut, Pelagia woke up in a fright.

"What is it, child?"

"A wounded man! A stranger."

"A stranger?" Pelagia asked as she tried to pull herself together.

"A wounded stranger who needs help. Come, give me a hand."

"But he's an enemy! Look at his uniform!"

"Well? Should we let him freeze to death in the snow?"

Confused, Pelagia said, "He's trying to tell us something."

"Yes, he's saying he needs help. Don't just stand there. Give me a hand."

They laid him down on a thick sheepskin rug. After removing his torn, blood-stained uniform and wet shoes, Eleni covered him with a woolen blanket. She dried his hair and rubbed his numb hands and feet, and then cleansed his wounds, gently covering them with ointment Pelagia had made from bitter roots and olive oil. His eyelids quivered, and he gave a deep sigh of gratitude. He was safe. Eleni raised his head so that he could sip a cup of homemade wine. He opened his eyes and gave his rescuers a sorrowful smile.

Aunt Pelagia feared Eleni's act of kindness. "Have you not heard the story of the peasant and the snake? The peasant found a frozen snake, and feeling sorry for it, he put it under his shirt to warm it. The snake revived and gave the peasant a fatal bite. The peasant's dying words were: 'Never trust an evil creature.'"

Eleni placed an earthen vessel filled with well water in the fireplace to make sage. "Stories are stories. What could this stranger do to us?" she said.

As she knelt over her brew, she had a notion that the soldier's eyes were fixed on her. In spite of her aunt's warning she made up her mind to help him.

The following morning an image flashed in Eleni's mind. "I know this man!" she thought. Her heart palpitated with such intensity that she rushed to her aunt.

"Aunt Pelagia, he's the man who helped me escape from the German headquarters!"

"Child, are you sure?"

"Absolutely! God must have sent him our way."

"Jesus Christ conquers and disperses all evil," Pelagia said as she crossed herself three times.

Eleni took a soft towel and dipped it into a kettle of warm water. Kneeling at the young man's side she gently wiped his face. She wanted to say something, but her lips trembled, and she had a lump in her throat. The stranger looked at her, as an enslaved soldier looks at the liberator who rescues him from the grip of the enemy. His face became animated, for it was at that moment that he, Fritz Bittrich, recognized the girl whom Conrad Strauss had raped, the girl whom Strauss had offered him as a trophy. He remembered the agony in her face when he let her go free. Struggling, he reached into his pocket and took out a small leather wallet. From it he pulled a golden cross and chain and gave it to Eleni. Recognizing the cross as her own, she cupped it in her hands and kissed it.

"*Danke. Ich werde Sie nie vergessen*—Thank you. I will never forget you," he said.

Three days passed. The sky was gray and heavy and the trees were laden with snow. Eleni did not sleep much over the next few nights. She laid her head on her pillow thinking of that horrible night. Images kept coming back—Strauss, her sullied body, and the soldier who had set her free.

Aunt Pelagia left at dawn, as she always did on Thursdays, for her job as a cleaning woman at the Gianellis. Eleni was alone with the wounded soldier. She tiptoed around the hut, attending to daily chores. As she wiped the window, she admired the white-mantled olive grove that bordered their plot. Icicles hanging from the roof of the hut dripped gently like teardrops. By squinting her eyes, she could see the green, yellow, and pink of a rainbow glistening through the icicles. Snowflakes stuck to the window forming an exquisite tapestry.

Eleni stepped quietly to the kitchen and prepared a cup of hot sage and brought it to the soldier's bedside. He opened his eyes. She then fetched a cup for herself and sat near him, looking into his face. Slowly, they sipped the sweet-smelling sage. The fragrance was heady. She wished she could read his thoughts. She liked him. *Was it compassion, gratitude, or other feelings?* Not a word was uttered, yet the vibrations of love steadily entwined their souls. A fantasy that this was a man whose kisses she could cherish, whose affection she could trust, developed rapidly in Eleni's mind.

Fritz sipped the last of his sage, and taking his cup, Eleni placed it beside hers on the floor. Now she had no fear. She caressed his forehead and clasped her hands over his. She wanted him.

Silently, his strong arms stretched gently forward, and he stroked her long, dark-brown hair. She bent over him, and their lips met, gentle and then relentless, until they moaned with desire. She unbuttoned her blouse and skirt and dropped them to the floor. Lifting his covers, she joined him. The sheepskin rug was soft and warm, like a nest. Never before had Eleni felt or acted like this.

The two youthful bodies adjusted perfectly to each other. They looked into each other's eyes without exchanging a word. Their movements were tender, springing from an unconscious awareness. Each gesture followed naturally to the next, without any reservation.

She allowed him to take possession of her. He moved and maneuvered her tenderly, careful not to hurt her, leading her with sureness. Her heart yearned for such a man, tender and strong. Never before had her flesh pulsated with such heat and fury. She clasped him with her thighs and pressed her breasts against his chest. Her head struggled upward, holding on to his tongue with her lips. Vibrating and moaning, she exhaled a gasping cry.

Then, their bodies in sweet exhaustion came silently apart. He drew the covers over her as she lay against his chest, and they fell asleep.

Two weeks later, Fritz Bittrich, now completely healed, stood in his crisp, well-ironed uniform before Strauss and reported: "The Greek guerrillas have captured a quarter of a company of our men on the outskirts of Moria. They have taken them to Agiassos mountain, leaving the wounded behind and thinking I was dead. I had a narrow escape. Fortunately, a native woman rescued me."

Throughout his tour of duty on the island Fritz Bittrich was ever mindful of his extraordinary rescue from death, and when he found himself in a position to repay his debt, he eventually did so with gratitude. Because of his technical training he was consulted about a plan to blow up an electric installation in Moria. It was an emergency plan the Nazis intended to put into effect should they have to retreat. Once they were safely at sea, the whole area was to be detonated. The idea of such destruction of land and life greatly disturbed Fritz. *But what can I do*, he thought. *I am only one person*—and I am part of the system.

CHAPTER 12

A Prelude to Nazi Justice

May 19, 1942

In the evening, six German officers sat at a tavern by the sea. They ate and drank and joyously laughed in celebration as they talked the language of power. It was another day of conquest for their superrace, and a day to be recorded in history, marking the deportation of forty-six thousand Greek Jews from Salonika to Auschwitz, where the number of human exterminations was to increase to millions.

The arrival of the summer months brought sizzling weather to the island of Crete. The sun seemed to be in collusion with the enemy, the searing heat producing unbearable conditions on the island. Takis felt his prison uniform clinging to his skin; if he had the strength, he could have wrung the perspiration out of it. The smell of stale sweat and unwashed humanity pervaded the barracks, and the prisoners were lethargic and irritable.

Oberst Lieutenant Stefan Patcher spoke to the Greek interpreter about the four German soldiers who died of malaria and suggested that the four young rebels from Lesbos be employed in disinfecting the rivers.

Takis and his friends were assigned to their new job and provided with tank suits, chemicals, pumps, and instructions. Although always under escort, they felt they were fortunate, because while working they followed each river to the sea where the interpreter gave them permission to swim. The sea water also had a curative effect on their health, healing their sores and allowing their skin to renew itself.

They killed thousands of mosquitoes, and the interpreter appreciated their diligent work, rewarding them with a small piece of bread at the end of the day.

Near the end of October, the rains came, causing the rivers to flood and marking the end of their disinfecting job. The friends were worried lest they be transferred to another prison or to an outdoor project in the cold weather. Then came the news that the Germans were going to utilize all the prisoners in the construction of two huge buildings on the outskirts of Heraclion, one as an infirmary for their troops and the other as a recreation center.

An inventory of the six hundred prisoners was taken; construction workers and builders were selected first. Takis told the interpreter that he and his friends were good at carpentry. Having watched Mitrakas, the boat-maker, he felt that hammering in nails and cutting wood would be easy for them.

More than three dozen men were drafted for the project, including the four friends. They hammered thousands of nails, driving in each one with poison and curses. One evening, Takis confessed to his friends that he no longer hated the lieutenant who had taken away his bike, because he had driven three hundred and thirty-three nails into every part of his body. "Nailing that lizard-face made me feel good," he said. "I hate no more."

By December 1942, two rectangular buildings were standing. The four friends assisted an older man, a master carpenter, to lay a floor in the recreation building. They worked slowly, dragging the job out until spring.

Months of hard labor toughened muscles and sharpened skills. The warmer days of March reminded the friends of their carefree days when the youth of Lesbos looked forward to the first week of April, the week when they all took the traditional first swim of the season.

With the precision to which all prisoners were accustomed, Stefan Patcher and his subordinates held roll call on the first Friday morning in April. The interpreter saluted smartly and, having reported that the best builders had been selected for work in Athens, he read the list of the chosen names. The four sighed with relief that their names were not included. Half a dozen SS men guarded the newly formed line and prepared to escort it to the harbor.

Patcher then asked the interpreter to call the four friends forward.

Two SS men marched up to Patcher, saluted him, and turned to handcuff the four friends.

"Why handcuffs?" asked Takis in uncontrolled panic.

Tsakiris burst out in protest, "We have been good workers for a full year. Why such senseless treatment?"

Patcher responded in a curt tone through the interpreter, "Because there is a file on you in Athens. We have been informed—from a source that we cannot reveal—that four men, assisted by three women, concealed and transported weapons in a coffin. The four young men are presumed to be in league with a tavern owner in Moria. The German headquarters in Athens requests your presence for further interrogation on this serious matter. You will be leaving this evening."

CHAPTER 13

Haidari, Hell Revisited

Athens, April 1943

*Apagoreverte i kykloforia politon metaxi
6:00 kai 6:00 proinis*

Circulation of civilians from 6:00 P.M.
to 6:00 A.M. is absolutely forbidden

No twinkling stars could be seen over the Acropolis. Athens, the majestic city of Pallas Athena, was veiled in a gray mist. Young and old rushed home to beat the curfew, and behind barred doors they awaited the coming of "one more spring" and counted the days since the invasion, now in its third year.

It was on this night that Takis and his friends were placed aboard a fishing boat and carried by the whirlwind of the Aegean to a landing spot where they were picked up by two German soldiers. The helmeted Nazis, their machine guns ready, prodded the handcuffed friends forward through the silent squares. Behind their impassive appearance, Takis saw disciplined, ruthless men, strict and polite in peace and fierce in war. Propagators of the Third Reich, they were strong from an inner programming received in youth and committed to a love of their country, which claimed superiority over all other nations. The friends were fearful of their destination. "Haidari," Takis whispered, his heart restraining terror.

Haidari, enclosed in a crenelated wall, rose some 350 yards above the level of Piraeus, the major harbor of Greece. Perched on a steep slope, Haidari was wooded from bottom to top. At the summit was a level area of seventeen acres, a third of which was occupied by buildings and the remainder covered with olive and pine trees. During the First World War, Haidari had served as a barracks and later, as a federal prison. When rumors of a second world war spread, the Greek government converted the estate into a training center. On April 26, 1941, Haidari became a Nazi concentration camp.

"Halt!" A blatant command interrupted the rhythmic gait.

They stopped. Barbed wire garnished an enormous steel gate that groaned open before them.

"*Heraus . . . heraus*," persisted a guttural voice. Once through the gate, the armed guards on duty pointed the way. The camp was protected on all sides by coiled barbed wire, and neither Takis nor his friends were able to see the boundaries, but they felt the evil presence which would separate them from the free world.

The group was ordered to stop, and the four friends, afraid of their imminent separation, attempted to shake hands. A cold weapon blocked them, and pointed to a boxlike room without windows. A short man in short khaki pants and T-shirt followed them, holding an ox-hide whip. Once left alone with them, he flogged them mercilessly. Takis had a chance to whisper: "Brothers, sighs and groans, yes; tears, no!" Then, as the whip hissed through the air and lashed him across his head, he fell down unconscious. Soon after, the other three sprawled on the filthy cement floor, half-conscious and groaning.

Hours later, as they regained consciousness, still feeling the pain of the whip, they could hardly stand up. Now part of the interrogation plan included isolation. The four had to be separated. Four helmeted soldiers came and forced each young man to follow a different direction. "*Yiassas Paidia* . . . health to you, friends, until we meet again," Takis whispered.

"*Heraus!*" shouted the armed guard delegated to lead Takis. When he turned to wave good-bye, his friends had disappeared.

Takis shuddered as the guard pointed toward a dirty stairway littered with cigarette butts and dust. He sensed the gun pointed at his back urging him to descend. Slowly, the dark staircase swallowed him—Dante's descent into hell. Noises from outside could no longer be heard, and the sunlight turned into darkness.

Hell Night began. The other prisoners, dressed in prison garb, no underwear, fatigue caps, and wooded flip-flops, were herded into a large alcove. Through the locked windows came the muffled sounds of the dry Athenian night—distant bells of grazing sheep and the monotonous croaking of frogs. Within a few minutes, the odor in the alcove was repelling and unbearable.

Initially, Takis could distinguish nothing. He moved only by instinct. He slowly became conscious of movements and strange, muffled sounds—a distant cry for water, an incoherent babbling of words, gasps, and pantings. *At least I'm not alone*, he thought.

His eyes gradually became adjusted to the darkness, and he saw the face of his prison guard next to him—pale with eyes flashing fear and suspicion. Takis cowered instinctively, his knees turning to rubber.

Suddenly two iron hands seized him from behind and threw him like a ball into a cell. The guard locked the door behind him. *God, what's next? I'm buried alive*, he thought. Trembling, he closed his eyes and prayed that he was only having a bad dream.

He reached out to touch the walls around him. He calculated the dimensions: about sixteen feet high by seven feet square—a rectangular box, a standing coffin. On the floor was an uneven stone facing the locked door, it was the only furniture in the cell. He felt the stone from all angles, and by evening he had grown to love it. It became a chair, and during the night a pillow.

A rusty iron door containing a window without glass separated him from the grim corridor. A dim light shone through, revealing messages on the walls. Takis struggled to see them.

> At the time of trial, calmness is your only weapon. . . .
>
> Death will frighten you less after you go
> through first-degree tortures. . . .
>
> If you lose courage, you lose everything.
>
> Hope is your only salvation. . . .

He shivered. "What's first-degree torture? What could that be?"

Takis's heart raced with fear. *Where are my friends?* he wondered. He continued searching. About a foot from the ground was written: "If you survive the tortures of Haidari, you will be a hero."

Takis read on.

> I have lived here three days and four nights, tied hand
> and foot. Avoid thinking as much as you can. Pray for
> death. It's easier to face.
> > Protectively,
> > Ponemenos—the Wounded One

"No! I don't want to die," whispered Takis.

* * * * *

Next morning, Takis woke up shivering. He wished he could put his head under a faucet and let warm water pour over him.

Then a drop of water fell on his forehead. "Maybe it's from the damp ceiling," he thought, as he wiped it off. Another drop fell, and then another. He looked up. The roof of the cell had been removed! He was sure it had been there the day before. Ugly laughter impinged on his thoughts. Looking down on him from above was a ghoulish face with a twisted smile. Takis stared back in bewilderment. Water, increasing in temperature, continued to drop on him. It streamed into his eyes, down his nose, into his mouth, and down his chest. His whole body was burning. The final dousing was accompanied by more sadistic laughter. A voice commanded him to look upward again. The ghoulish face spat upon him. In pain, Takis lowered his head. Again he was commanded to look up. More spitting and insults. *God, how long is this going to last?* His neck ached terribly, and he was having difficulty raising his head. Then with a deafening pound, the ceiling panel closed. The game was over.

* * * * *

Takis learned that there were approximately seventy cells. Between each group of twelve cells were the latrines, and bordering the back was a strip of experimental garden tended by a few privileged prisoners who had survived the initial horrors of Haidari. Beyond the garden were a dozen gallows, a reminder to the prisoners of their possible destiny should they attempt an escape or an anti-German activity.

Some fifty meters in front of the cells lay an enormous roll-call square where the prisoners gathered each morning and awaited orders to join the work-squad line or the execution line.

There were also rules to be followed: do not ask questions; reply "*Jawohl*" when spoken to; and do not complain about the food—accept it gratefully and scrape the bowl clean. Prisoners were also forbidden near areas where heavy artillery was stationed.

At three o'clock every afternoon, clanging sounds in the corridor announced the serving of the one and only daily meal. It was Takis's fifth day in the camp. He was hungry, but he could not even part his blistered lips. Resting his head on the stone, he let his mind wander, trying to ignore his gurgling stomach. As he dozed off, a man appeared; a friend and comrade. Before long, Takis and the man found themselves on the island of Lesbos, wandering among rocks and ravines that led to the sea. The evening aura mixed with his joy, and Takis felt lucky to have escaped. In the twilight, he identified his comrade. It was Alexis, the man who shared ouzo with him in the back room of his tavern.

"I know who you are! How did you get here? Where are you taking me?"

"Away from the hell of Haidari."

"But what about my friends?"

"We'll come back for them."

"Why did you choose me? They, too, are young and innocent . . . I dragged them into this. . . ."

"You did what every man must do—fight for freedom."

Takis felt proud. He climbed up on a rock and stretched his arms toward the sky. "Alexis, I'll fight!" he said.

Facing the sea, Alexis handed him a flute and said, "Brother, pipe our nation's sorrows." Then he began to sing.

> Greece can never die,
> She is afraid of no one.
> Give her a few hours to revive,
> And a glorious nation
> She'll become.

The murmuring waves foamed upon the sand and wet Takis's feet. They had come to hear his playing. Then a boat came into view, and Takis could see a helmet and two fast-moving oars. "That's not a German boat. Nor is it Greek. It must be American! At last they have come!" shouted Takis. "Our allies have arrived, just as my father always dreamed they would. Oh, Father, I wish you were here to see your American friends. They haven't let you down. They have come to avenge Lefteris's death."

Under the helmet of the oarsman, Takis observed a ruddy face. Sewn on the upper part of his sleeves was the emblem of the American flag.

"Welcome! Freedom from the sea!" screamed Takis.

Alexis and Takis moved with the speed of a shuttle, carrying weapons from the boat to the shore. The stranger from the sea helped stack the weapons silently on the shore. Takis and his reclaimed friend unloaded several dozen rifles, machine guns, and three cases of ammunition. They covered them with khaki sailcloth. The American marine then returned to his boat and rowed swiftly away. "Why couldn't he stay longer?" Takis wanted to kiss his hands in gratitude and tell him, "Friend, I'm an American, too, thanks to my father."

They lost sight of the boat behind the waves.

Takis raised his voice. "Come back! What am I to do with the weapons? Come back and tell me what to do!"

His pleas were in vain. "Blessed Allies," he murmured, looking at Alexis's despondent face. "They start a war and always let the little nations finish the fight for them."

"Maybe it's time to fight for the freedom of our own nation," said Alexis. "Greece is tired of shedding blood and being betrayed."

Takis sat alone by a rock and began to play his flute:

> Good fortune . . .
> Send us more valiant men on a swift ship
> To scatter and burn the barbarian fleet. . . .

A flashlight devoured everything—the ocean, the deep blue sky, the stars, and Alexis. He scratched his head with both hands, his vision still blurred. He reached for the stone under his head. It was a dream, but so real. He put his arms around the stone and vowed that no one would ever know that he and his friends had helped Alexis distribute loads of weapons to the freedom fighters.

Takis heard keys turning as another cell was opened.

The man in the neighboring cell groaned as from a beating. The warden's words, "*Heraus . . . ,*" were followed by more beatings. Takis stood on his tiptoes to see through the small opening in his door. A brazen face with two steady eyes stared back at him. He held fast to the window, compelled to look straight into those cruel, insidious eyes. After a moment, the eyes withdrew.

An unseen hand switched on all the lights, blinding the eyes of those who had been sitting in darkness. A young woman walked by Takis's cell. Pitch-black hair hung uncombed over her dirty face and swollen eyes. Her dress, without color or form, revealed breasts hanging and suffering from abuse.

The guard unlocked the door of a cell and waited for her to enter. She struggled to throw her hair back so that she might see, but her arms hung paralyzed. She approached the wall and tried to part her hair against a hook. The guard, clenching his gnarled fingers around her head, shoved her against the hook. A painful cry escaped her lips. "*Skylia tharthi imera sas*—dirty dogs, your day will come."

* * * * *

The initial interrogation was intimidating, but the most severe torture did not officially start until the sixth day. Takis had no time to himself once the quartet was taunted and hustled through the doors that led to their individual cells—no time to think; no time to rest; no time to familiarize themselves with the cramped, austere cells into which they were thrown.

A door slammed, and a shrill voice pierced the prisoners' ears, echoing through the narrow hallway. Pairs of curious eyes peeped through the little openings of their cell doors. A jangling of keys, and a guard forced Takis's door open.

"Come out, Greek hero! The Third Reich is going to initiate you and your friends today," said the guard.

Takis felt his skin creep with fear.

In the corridor he joined his friends.

"What's happened to your face?" Pantsaris shivered at the sight.

"Sh. . . . Pray nothing worse happens to us."

"It's all blistered!"

"I'm okay," said Takis.

The four reached out and embraced each other for a few precious seconds before the guard pushed them forward. Takis turned to look at him, a tall, jaunty Nazi soldier whose eyes reflected fury shaded by the green helmet. His face was pale and stern.

On the stairway to which they were directed, Bouras stumbled and fell. He touched his chin and blood dripped into his hand. At the sight of the wound, Takis tore a strip from his shirt and offered it to Bouras, who agonized. "The crocodile behind us tripped me."

A brusque "Halt!" nailed them to the spot. The four looked at each other, and although no words were spoken, each knew what the other was thinking: *Together we live; together we die.*

Freshly dissolved lime splattered on the walls cleared their nostrils as they marched through a poorly lit hallway. Behind the rows of locked doors were patriots from all parts of Greece, all subjected to the machination of Nazi cruelty. The four dared not ask where they were being taken.

The corridor ended at a huge double door with bronze handles. *I hope this is an exit to the free world,* thought Pantsaris.

One of the guards rang the bell, and while waiting for the door to be opened, Pantsaris unfolded a wrinkled paper which he kept under his shirt and whispered the lines:

> *Life is not a single lane,*
> *To walk ahead on steady feet;*
> *Life holds out multiple routes;*
> *We choose our fate—our street.*
> *Prison and concentration camps*
> *Are darkness, fear, and woes.*
> *What is the fate of those inside?*
> *Their destiny, only God knows.*

"That's promising," Bouras said.

"I agree," added Takis as the guard snatched the paper, seeking translation.

The door opened and the four friends were ushered into a large room. Heavy odor of barrack soap and boot polish filled the air. Four windows allowed ample light to fall upon a portrait of Hitler occupying half of the wall behind a large oak desk. Dark paneling, shellacked parquet floor, and a chandelier suggested a new sort of mortuary.

As Takis entered, he immediately recognized the green eyes that had thrown him into the cell. The light-reddish hair was perfectly trimmed, and without the helmet, the face looked unpretentious as he spoke to

Niketaras, the Greek interpreter in his freshly starched green uniform. His grooming was impeccable. He stood at attention in front of Takis as he awaited orders from his superior. A repellent smell of soap and sulphur exuded from his person.

Maybe this man will ask us a few questions and let us go. We didn't hurt anybody, Takis thought.

Niketaras spoke words that cracked like a whip:

"Hauptmann Heins Gruber wishes to demonstrate to you four young rebels the power and severity of the Third Reich. If you are smart, you will confess any anti-German activities of your countrymen. Otherwise, the chamber next door will make you immortal heroes." Hauptmann Heins Gruber got up from his desk and came closer to the four.

Their hearts raced as they stood in front of Gruber, who scrutinized them from head to toe. Feeling annoyed that he could not ask the questions directly, he spoke to the interpreter again.

"The Hauptmann wants to know why you are so swarthy."

Takis explained that the islanders spent their summers by the seashore.

"Awaiting your allies?" Niketaras barked with a sneer. Gruber nodded to the interpreter to continue.

"Takis Kalellis, Patroklos Pantsaris, Stratis Bouras, and Yioryo Tsakiris: You distributed American weapons, you removed the German flag from the castle of Lesbos, and you attempted to escape to Turkey." Niketaras, his eyes soliciting approval, looked at Gruber. Takis sensed that more accusations were to come.

"We need a new poem," said Bouras to Pantsaris.

"We need a miracle," replied Tsakiris, pursing his lips.

"What are they saying?" asked the Hauptmann.

"They want a miracle," replied Niketaras, rolling his eyes.

"What are we waiting for?" Gruber extended his hand, pointing the way.

Niketaras opened the door and led the four friends down a corridor to a large room where a radio was playing music unfamiliar to them. The room resembled a meat refrigerator; it was bitterly cold. The furniture consisted of three benches set against stark walls.

Bruno Koch, a fat, baldheaded man, rose to his feet. Light reflected from his head, and his small piggish eyes seemed to be sinking in his bloated face. He saluted, and then inspected the four friends, ordering them to sit down. Gruber saluted him and ordered the interpreter to guard the four rebels. As Takis was sitting on the bench, his eyes fell on Niketaras's hand. What a grotesque sight! He had two thumbs on his right hand. "It's a bad omen," whispered Takis. "That man is accursed. He bears the mark of Cain."

The four followed Bruno Koch's motions. Lazily, he pulled a rope that was suspended from a pulley in the ceiling and attached it to a wall. Near one of the benches stood a small table bearing an array of instruments: a plaited cowhide whip, a carved club, and a rod of barbed wire. All of the instruments bore traces of dried blood.

Koch ordered Takis to step forward. He tied his wrists behind his back and then nodded at Niketaras to start the proceedings. Niketaras turned the radio to a different station, broadcasting music so loud it was deafening. A woman sang a vibrant Mozart aria, and Koch began to pull the rope. Pantsaris fainted at the sight, and Bouras and Tsakiris witnessed the horror of Haidari as Takis was lifted to the ceiling.

"No!" shouted Takis.

Bruno Koch was possessed with power over the unfortunate victims, whose life and death were in his hands. He understood that if he did not perform his duties well, a more suitable candidate would be found for his post.

Those who survived his cruelty later learned from other survivors that the torturers employed in Haidari were, in fact, ordinary criminals selected from the German prisons.

Bruno threw a bucket of water in Takis's face. The water entered his gasping mouth, causing him to cough. Two hands squeezed his ribs to bring up the water he had swallowed. The interpreter tried to force a cold instrument into his mouth, but he locked his teeth in obstinacy.

"Open your mouth!" shouted the interpreter. "Open your crazy mouth or you'll choke on your own tongue. Come on! Slowly. Open up."

Takis felt a knot in his throat. His mouth cracked open and he took a deep breath.

The interpreter, unaffected by his pain, sneered, "Would you like some water?" He threw the remains of the filthy water into Takis's face. His tongue absorbed it like a sponge.

"What did you do with the weapons?" The perspiring faces of Koch and the interpreter hovered around Takis.

"Speak up, miserable bastard, or you will die!" the interpreter advised impatiently. "What did you do with the rest of the weapons?"

"Tell them, Takis!" shouted Bouras from the corner.

"Tell them what?" Koch approached Bouras, swinging his club against his boots. "Maybe you know about the weapons."

"All I know is that he has no knowledge of weapons."

"You're a liar!" Koch tapped Bouras on the forehead. "I'll get to you next."

"Maybe we could find another method to make your friend talk." Koch pulled a wrinkled newspaper from his pocket; *Das Reich*, a four-page daily announced the achievements of the Third Reich. He rolled it to form a tube and set it afire with his cigarette lighter. Koch brought the torch deftly under Takis's chin. The flames licked Takis's face.

"Stop it!" screamed Tsakiris, and began to vomit.

The smell of burning paper and hair filled the room. In spite of fear and pain, Takis remained silent.

"For your own good, speak!" shouted the interpreter. "As a Greek, I advise you. Speak, and they will probably let you go free."

Takis, wrestling to avoid the flames, the stench of burning flesh, remained obstinate. As the torch burned out, the damp air cooled his singed cheeks. Relief.

They lowered him from the rope.

Koch and the interpreter felt their defeat. "We'll take you back to your cell to recover and think. There will be further questioning tomorrow."

Trembling in the hands of his foes, Takis staggered toward the door.

"*Kourayio filemou*—courage my friend." In his semiconscious state, Takis recognized Bouras's voice. They looked at each other for a brief moment. "I guess I'm next," said Bouras.

Covered with wounds, clothes in tatters, Takis trudged from the torture chamber and leaned on the entrance to his cell, weeping.

The arrogant guard stood by, disinterested, inured to the sight.

CHAPTER 14

A Man Must Endure

Takis could not open his eyes. The eyelids were heavy and painful, and the lashes were stuck together. Behind his eyes, the hive of terror was loose on him, and each cell in his brain had become wasp-winged and deadly; each cell was shaped like an hourglass; and each cell felt the power of flight and the invulnerability of the swarm. His eyes blazed. Helplessly he looked around. All was madness and loathing, but he wanted to survive. Momentarily, his world appeared small, congested—just a tiny drop, a bubble which he needed to burst so that he could emerge into the daylight. But he could not lift a finger . . . his arms felt disjointed, his hands, as though they were missing.

An invisible presence in his body searched all the pain-filled crevices and carefully examined them. Noise seemed to drill into his eardrums, gradually subsiding in his joints and leaving his body like a dead weight.

In his anguish, Takis imagined apes surrounding him, dancing a macabre dance and grinning inanely. They jumped persistently, grasping him by the shoulders and hanging on his body. Then laughter exposed their decayed yellow teeth and spongy gums. Takis tried to shake off the ugly creatures, but the more he tried, the tighter they clung, and his joints could no longer endure the pain. His whole body ached.

"A man must endure," whispered a voice. "If you lose your courage, you lose everything. Fainting might relieve you for a little while . . . death might be desirable . . . but neither is the answer." Takis kept hearing the echo of his own thoughts.

A man whose physique was familiar to him stood near.

"Takis, my son, it's me—your father."

In a daze, Takis blinked. "Father, is that really you?" His guttural voice had no strength.

"Yes, it's me."

"How did you find where I was?"

"It's a long story."

Takis closed his eyes and remained silent for a few moments. He had trouble knowing whether he was asleep or awake. He breathed heavily, seeking solace from his pain in the stupor of slumber.

"You must be in so much pain."

Asimakis felt helpless. The floor seemed to vibrate. Takis was having convulsions. Only a few minutes earlier, he had been burning with fever, and now he was cold and dizzy.

His father touched him gently on the arm and on the chest. Removing his jacket, he rolled it into a ball and placed it under Takis's head.

"Father, go away. Deny me. Tell them you don't know me. Tell them anything, but get out of this hell." He hesitated as other thoughts whirled through his mind: they have brought my father here to torture him—it must be the most terrible punishment to see one's own son bound and tormented.

"Son, I feel terrible for causing you to be in this state. Me and my stupid patriotism. Forgive me."

"I don't know what you mean."

"When war was declared, my American friends advised me against returning to Greece; they said I should bring the whole family to America. But I acted like a hero. I could have made sure we were all safe."

"It's not your fault."

"I didn't think that Hitler would last three months. What did I know?"

The door opened, and in came an SS officer smoking a cigar. He was tall and thin, with a violin face under his braided hat. He watched as Takis suffered and then delivered a long, calm speech in English to Asimakis. When the German officer left, Asimakis translated the speech to his son. "The officer said: 'It's written in the Bible that Abraham was called to sacrifice his son. God wanted to test his faith. You were brought here to witness the sacrifice of your son that we might test your love. You and your son will be set free if you confess the truth about the weapons.'"

"What else did he say?" asked Takis.

"Nothing."

Takis sensed fear in his father's voice.

"Father, how did you get here?" asked Takis in a hoarse whisper.

"Two weeks after Alexis was summoned and sent to Haidari, I received a message from him through a young German soldier. . . ."

"Alexis is here?"

"Yes, he was betrayed by Cara Beis who revealed his involvement in hiding the weapons."

"What about the coffin and the weapons?"

"How do you know about them?"

"The Greek interpreter in Crete," Takis replied weakly. "After the Germans captured us at sea, we ended up in Crete where we worked for almost a year. There we learned that the Germans knew of four men and three women from Moria who had carried coffins filled with weapons, and that the four young men were in the habit of spending time in a tavern in Moria. Someone betrayed us."

"You mean you and your friends?

"Yes, Father."

"I can't believe it! Well, son, after you left, I, too, became involved," confessed Asimakis. "I had often seen Alexis helping to carry the dead. We averaged three to five funerals a day in Moria. Then, one day, the first or second of March, Alexis came to our house asking for help. I followed him to St. Basil's, where a funeral procession was taking place. There were two men and three women, and a covered coffin. One of the women was Stratya. The two men with mourning bands on their left sleeve— Apostolos, the butcher, and Pavlos, his friend, avoided looking at me. When I asked Stratya who was in the coffin, she shrugged her shoulders and replied, 'Ask Alexis.' Apostolos said, 'It's my father,' as he wiped his eyes with a white handkerchief bordered with black ribbon. I didn't see any tears, so I expected something strange was happening.

"I didn't pursue the matter until Alexis said, 'We're going to Afalon.' 'Why not the local cemetery?' I asked. 'It's full up,' said Alexis. He motioned the men to get going, and then he whispered in my ear, 'This is not the time to ask questions.' And I, like a dummy, thought I was helping to carry a dead body to the grave. It was at the moment when we left Moria behind us that Cara Beis, the hooked-nose snake, came along the path toward us. Alexis told Stratya to start moaning, and the other two women in black joined in the sobbing, murmuring a dirge: *Heartless Death, why did you take our father so soon?* When Cara Beis wanted to look at the deceased, with wailing and tears the women pushed him away. 'It's sacrilege to open a coffin ready for burial,' Alexis explained. Then Cara Beis, making the sign of the cross, embraced the coffin, attempting to open it. Alexis quickly gave him a blow on the head, and he fell to the ground—knocked out. The funeral procession resumed.

"That night, Alexis's tavern was thoroughly searched and taken apart. Alexis was summoned, examined, and let go. A young German soldier whom Alexis had befriended advised him to get out of town immediately. Alexis packed a bag and was about to leave when Cara Beis and two SS officers broke into his house at midnight and took him away.

"Alexis's arrest propelled me in the fields. Between premonition and fear, I knew it was a matter of hours before Cara Beis would attempt another of his betrayals. During the day, I hid in caves and crevices at St. Elias's mountain and at night I crept back home for some food and clean clothes. A week later the young German who tipped off Alexis brought your mother a note from him that said, 'Takis is in Haidari!'

"I cannot begin to tell you our joy. We stayed up all night. We talked about you. Oh, how we've missed you.

"'I'm going to bring Takis home!' I told your mother." Asimakis embraced his son tightly. What he could not tell his son was the rest of the conversation with Katerina.

"What if the Nazis kill you?"

"That's a chance I have to take."

"What about Kiki and Jimmy?" she pleaded.

"You know I love all of you, but when I think of Takis . . ."

Tenderly, Katerina touched his lips with her fingertips, "I want you to go and bring him home . . . but I'm terrified. What if I lose you, too?"

"Alexis's friend, the young German soldier, came to our house several times. He liked Kiki and Jimmy and brought them bread. One evening your mother slipped something into his hand, and the following night he returned to show me the coin she had given him. 'Get as many of these as possible, and I'll help you to get into Haidari to see your son,' he said. When I married Katerina, she was given a dowry of one hundred and fifty gold coins. She collected the money and came to me. 'Take all these, give them to the Germans, and bring my Takis back,' she said. I am going to offer all of it to General Steckelhuber in the hope of gaining your freedom."

"What about my friends, Bouras, Tsakiris, Pantsaris?"

"Are they here?"

"So far! And we've been through so much."

"I promise you to do my best."

"Dad, did you hear anything about Alexis?"

"When I came to Haidari, I asked everyone I could about Alexis from Lesbos, but nobody seemed to know anything about him. Then I came across a Greek interpreter. He seemed a good man. I slipped him a gold coin and asked him about Alexis. 'Yesterday he was shipped to the prison of Averof,' he said."

"Compared to this hell, Averof is heaven."

"Perhaps," said Asimakis.

CHAPTER 15

Degrees of Pain and Courage

Asimakis stood outside the main office waiting to see General Steckelhuber. He thought of the gold coins he was going to offer the general in the hope of gaining his son's freedom.

"The general will see you now." Niketaras said, leading him into the office.

"Your son is being sent to the hospital today." Steckelhuber watched the American father through a cloud of smoke, observing his reaction. "Your son will be in good hands," he added, "but you and I have some unfinished business to discuss." Stretched comfortably in an easy chair, he gestured to Asimakis to take a seat.

Asimakis showed no emotion. The Nazi cruelty he had witnessed had numbed his feelings, and he no longer felt pain, joy, or fear. His only concern was for his son's survival, and thus his mind was perfectly clear: at an opportune moment and with extreme sensitivity, he would surrender to the general all his earthly possessions—the gold coins, a paid-up insurance of $20,000, and, if the general wished, his own life. He began to make his proposal.

After hearing Asimakis speak, the general rose angrily to his feet and stubbed out his cigar. "A bribe?" His laugh was like a hyena, his teeth showing.

"Dollars are of no value to us, Mr. American. In a very short time, there will be only one kind of money, the Deutsche mark."

"I want my son's freedom," Asimakis said.

"I have already laid down the conditions: confess the truth."

"What truth?"

"The truth about the weapons and their source. That is the price of freedom for both father and son. Fair?"

"Fair, General Steckelhuber, but I don't know of any weapons, or their origin."

129

"Very well, comrade American." The general's face was white with rage. He pressed a bell, and from the next room came Hauptmann Gruber. After listening to the general's commands, Gruber escorted Asimakis to a jeep. Shortly after, Asimakis was taken to an olive grove near the border of Haidari where the camp isolation cells were located. He was put in a boxlike cell with no windows. The stench of the camp filtered through pipes fitted to tiny holes in the walls.

After three long days, Asimakis heard the squeaking of his door. Momentarily blinded by the light, he could distinguish only the silhouettes of two SS men. When they demanded to know if there was any change of mind, the prisoner recognized the voices of Steckelhuber and Gruber. Interrogations were repeated one day a week for the following three weeks, but Asimakis remained firm. He maintained that his status was that of an American citizen of Greek descent, a family man having no knowledge of weapons.

Gruber was ready to submit the American to additional torture and certain death, but Steckelhuber, believing that a few more weeks in isolation would bring about the desired results, wished to detain him further. Besides, he did not want to be accused of the death of an American and preferred to leave him in his cell. Thus, if he died there, it would be of "natural causes."

"Comrade, the hospital reports that your son is recuperating very well. You may even be able to visit him—provided, of course, that you cooperate." They closed the door behind them, leaving Asimakis with the sordid smell of earth. The smell reminded him of a barren mountain in Moria where the Germans had set up cannons and planted mines.

On August 15, the day of the Dormition of the Virgin Mary, a chaplain came to give Holy Communion to those in isolation. Asimakis was found dead. It was reckoned he had expired the previous day, for although his body was swollen, it exuded no odor.

* * * * *

"Water . . . wa-a-a-ter." A groan of thirst, a parched tongue, and a feverish face. A gentle hand brought a straw to his mouth. Soothing, cool water quenched his inferno. Takis blinked his eyes once, and with a faint smile of gratitude, fell asleep again.

The infirmary was located on the top of a hill in Helioupolis, the city of the sun, a southern suburb of Athens. The antiseptic smell bounced off the whitewashed walls of the long, rectangular ward where rows of cots occupied by the wounded and fractured bodies of the prisoners were lined. While preoccupied with the casual study of the alien terrain where his spirit had broken into irreversibly fragmented parts, he wondered how many men and women had broken under the fearful tortures of the Nazi system. He wondered if the grotesque phantoms of their damaged spirits haunted the alcoves of the barracks in Haidari, recruiting others into their defiled ranks with howls of horror watching them coming apart at the soul.

Thick cotton blankets, freshly ironed sheets, and angels of mercy in white uniforms tended the sick with graceful movements. With a gleam in his eye, Takis admired their rosy skin and blond hair neatly tucked under white caps. They spoke gently, with self-confidence. With his eyelids half-closed he could see the silhouettes moving around quietly; one in particular reminded him of Eleni. "Eleni must look just as beautiful in her black cassock," he thought, suddenly feeling the pain of separation and the possibility of never seeing her again. Sleep came and blocked out the thought.

Twice a day, the patients were allowed fresh air. Many of them guided their own comrades to the veranda, where recuperating prisoners reclined on wooden chairs. Here they felt less alone, able to share their pain and their destinies. Each had a story to tell. All had developed an inner strategy for survival that daily nurtured them as they gazed toward their homeland. From the veranda they could see the Acropolis hill, where ancient glory and civilization prevented the weak from becoming too weak, and the powerful, too powerful. Yet, below the veranda and around the infirmary were tangles of barbed wire, a vivid reminder that this temporary paradise was an extension of hell, Haidari.

They learned from one another that, upon their recovery, they were destined to return to Haidari. And there, again, they would be subjected to the dictates of the Nazis. But they realized that having survived the tortures and interrogation once, there was nothing more to fear, not even death.

Four weeks later, Takis was given his final medical exam. The examination was crude and unemotional, like a demonstration in an anatomy class. The doctor touched his swollen shoulders and pressed his chest with steel fingers, leaving impressions on his pale flesh as if it were wax. Not once did their eyes meet. He spoke to the nurse, who translated in broken Greek: "You are as well as you can get. You are ready to return to Haidari."

His body ached, but Takis was delighted with the news. In spite of the conditions in the camp, he looked forward to seeing his friends and his father. His face gleamed with hope.

* * * * *

September was still moderately warm. All day long, the prisoners worked, digging, pushing wagons, breaking stones, building, erecting walls, and hammering roofs—the labor seemed endless. For Takis, the first week back in Haidari was a time of adjustment. Although under surveillance, Takis persistently searched among the crowd. He finally found his friends and expected to locate his father. Haidari consisted of thirty-six barracks, each containing three hundred prisoners. His friends were in barracks #7, a large brick building which stood out prominently in the middle of the compound. It had not been cleaned for months; old mattresses and broken bunks lay on layers of filth, and slimy water oozed from the cracks in the walls.

The reunion with his three comrades was joyous. They introduced him to some of their new friends, who were delighted when Takis gave them a packet of cigarettes, a commodity so scarce and precious in the camp that many of the prisoners cut each cigarette into three pieces to make it last longer. Takis told them that from July 15 to September 15 in the hospital he had accumulated more than three hundred cigarettes, which he kept to share with his friends. Bouras lit one and motioned to Tsakiris and Pantsaris to do the same. Takis felt a few inches taller, and he looked around to see if anyone was watching— maybe his father would see him. Awkwardly, he held a match to the tip of the cigarette and began to puff. Pantsaris began to cough and sputter while Bouras choked and gasped for air. The friends began to laugh, coughing and gasping at the same time.

When Takis asked around if anyone had seen his father, nobody seemed to know anything about him. In the last week of September when there was still no sign of his father, Takis went to the officers' building and requested to see the general. In his classic cold manner, General Erwin Steckelhuber assured him that Asimakis was safe and sound. Takis, his eyes riveted on the general, felt his stomach turn. He detected evil in the general's face and words. *What does he mean, my father is safe and sound? Is it a ploy to deceive me?* he wondered.

"Where is my father? I wish to see him."

"You cannot. He has returned to your island where he's working for the Third Reich." Steckelhuber lit a cigar and looked at Takis through the curling smoke. "He's a smart man. He's reporting on the weapons being unloaded there, and he's tracing their source."

My father working for you? he thought. *My father an accomplice— impossible!* He shook his head in disbelief. He knew his father was a man of integrity and a dedicated American. He wanted to attack the general and choke him with his bare hands, but his arms were too sore and weak to be effective. He flexed his hands, and as he turned to leave, the general spoke again.

"You can be free also. Right at this moment." The general stood up, pretending benevolence and pointing to the door. "The truth can set you free," he mocked.

"The truth is, General, that I want to see my father."

"Think over what I've said."

Later in the day, Takis met with Pantsaris and Tsakiris near roll-call square. The two friends were upset because Bouras had developed erysipelas, an excruciatingly painful disease which takes the form of a tumor; Bouras had one the size of an egg on his right cheek. They didn't know to whom to go for help until Pantsaris suggested that Niketaras might be persuaded to intercede for them. Takis felt some relief, hoping that in the process of getting attention for Bouras, they could find out information about Asimakis.

Niketaras finally arrived with a doctor, who began tending to Bouras. Pantsaris, eager to help Takis, began to ask the interpreter questions. "What has happened to Mr. Asimakis? Has he been sent to another prison?" Takis and Tsakiris listened intently. Looking at the friends, Niketaras said sarcastically, "Comrades, relax!" The three friends stood facing the interpreter, awaiting an answer. Takis's heart was in his mouth. His premonition was verified when he saw the evil look in Niketaras's eyes.

"When did you see your father last?"

"The day I was taken to the hospital," replied Takis.

"The next time you see him, it will be in the next life."

"Your Nazi friends killed my father? Tell me it's not true!"

"It's not true. They didn't kill him."

"Then where is he?"

Takis grabbed Niketaras by the lapels and shook him. "I want you to take me to him. I want to see my father," he screamed.

Pantsaris and Tsakiris pulled him back, and Pantsaris, pinching his arm, said, "Are you crazy? The interpreter is on our side. He's trying to help us." He winked.

"Don't be stupid. I only help those who cooperate."

"Please, Mr. Niketaras, take me to see my father," Takis pleaded.

"I'm not sure I can do that."

"Please."

In the evening, when they lined up for their ladleful of soup, Niketaras came with a message. "Bouras has been taken to the infirmary, and Takis's father is in isolation."

"When will I be able to see my father?" Takis asked anxiously.

"I'm working on it. Don't rush me," replied the interpreter.

* * * * *

Bouras dragged himself out of bed. Although six weeks had passed since his experience in the torture chamber—for it was now November of 1943—he still had not recovered completely; but the hospital staff thought otherwise and returned him to Haidari. Tsakiris, through patience and cunning, was put to work cleaning potatoes and polishing kitchen utensils, jobs that yielded him a couple of ounces of bread and all the potato peels he could want.

As for Pantsaris, he had written a poem for Niketaras's children, and for that he was owed a favor. Niketaras, although a Nazi accomplice, was illiterate, and so he assigned Pantsaris the task of copying reports, making him swear never to reveal any of the information. Pantsaris was sure that his oath of confidentiality amounted to something, and so he persuaded Niketaras to use his influence to have Takis transferred to barracks #7.

* * * * *

The barracks were locked before evening roll call and reopened at daybreak. Although lock-up time meant bedtime, the prisoners often had difficulty sleeping. The insects cautiously came alive to begin their night work. The prisoners could hear the faint rustle of small wings, the secret transit of spiders, the waxy promenades of huge roaches down the concrete galleries, and sometimes the scuttling of rats in the garbage area. Some of the captives gathered in groups and talked; others, wide awake, lay on their backs, their thoughts traveling through the free world of love, hate, and struggle. Two men moved restlessly. One was John Demos, the provider of cigarettes. He had a short blond beard and the eyes of a hawk. During the daytime he was a nonsmoker, but when darkness fell, he chain-smoked while keeping vigil. By the time Demos was on his third cigarette, the ward was enveloped in a smoky haze. When possible, he concocted a mixture of tobacco and poppy seeds and rolled his own brand. The prisoners inhaled deeply as their nostrils were seduced and their wills weakened. Demos invited the indisposed prisoners to the infinity of the world where the sun was bright, the meadows green, and the water of the rivers crystal clear—an earthly paradise. The three hundred souls tossed and turned, looking plaintively at the tiny glow of their torturer's cigarette.

Demos sat hunched over as he smoked, guarding his precious cigarettes. Occasionally he cleared his throat, spitting noisily on the floor. In the outside world, he had been a peddler of roasted chickpeas at an insignificant corner in Athens by Constitution Square. Now, in his mid-forties, he was a tobacco merchant in a godforsaken place that even the devil feared to approach. As a chickpea vendor, he had never been addressed as Mr. Demos, and no female had ever shown any interest in his pale face. His new situation gave him a sense of importance. His greedy eyes did not recognize that Death was but a step away, ready to shoot dice. Without paying any attention to Death, Demos grasped at his present opportunity and became a significant personality, a well-fed, sought-after personage with experience in exploiting his fellow-men. Takis and his friends watched him with irritation.

The mattress next to Demos was occupied by Tharapis, a shrewd businessman and the proprietor of a cigarette lighter stolen from a German officer. In exchange for a light, he required the first puff. He out-did Demos in his harshness and ugly intentions. He had been a beggar, a profession suited to his laziness. These two vipers hated each other, and the prisoners hated them both.

Further down the room lay Mr. Leonidas, a middle-aged, respectable man. Although he was from Athens, everyone called him Spartiati, for he had the physical appearance of a Spartan. Leonidas, with his blue eyes and caressing voice, appeared to be the product of a school of etiquette, for his movements and demeanor were gentlemanly. His behavior was instinctive. He knew how to talk, how not to talk, and how to ask for a favor. He seldom gave offense. But he suffered like the rest; pain and frustration showed in his eyes.

Well before dawn, Leonidas was wide awake. Acid juices in his stomach caused him painful cramps, and his mouth tasted of bile. As he looked at his sleeping son Fotis, his disconsolate heart struggled with hate and affection. His son had broken a bakery window and stolen three loaves of bread that were part of army rations. The Germans had traced the thief, and both father and son had been sent to Haidari. A survivor of Haidari's tortures, Leonidas's right hand was paralyzed.

By midnight, Leonidas managed to suppress his inner turmoil, and with a bittersweet smile, he stroked his son's hand. Then he got up quietly, put on his army boots, and crept toward Takis. "Are you awake, Takis?"

"Yes. I can't sleep. I keep thinking of my father," said Takis.

"Is your father in danger, too?"

"He volunteered his life to save me."

"I hear that your father is an American."

"Yes, and a proud one!"

"Where is he now?"

"Strict isolation," replied Takis.

"Strict isolation is rough." Leonidas shook his head. "Hunger causes hallucinations. You see food paraded before your eyes every day. You smell the kitchen odor that is piped into your cell . . . and you chew your tongue. Terrible! Terrible! I went through it."

"And you're still alive!" Takis's eyes dilated with excitement.

"One must have hope as well as endurance," Leonidas said.

"Don't they give you any food?" Takis's eyes welled up with tears.

"Sure . . . salty sardines and water once a week."

"If my father whispers a word of what he knows, Lesbos will be put to the torch. But I know he'll not reveal any secrets. He'll probably tell them a story, and then maybe they'll allow him back in the camp."

"You're a naive young man. I won't repeat what you've just told me. But take my advice. Don't share any secrets in this rotten place."

* * * * *

When toiling under the conditions of compulsory labor, little time is available for thinking. The past becomes a vague memory. But at night, talk and sharing are important aids to survival. Barracks #7 became a ciborium of memories—of their homeland of Lesbos, of events centered around Alexis's tavern. Alexis, that glorious creature with his accommodating personality which knew no limits. He would do anything for a friend. Now, Alexis, too, was rotting in a prison.

"All the prisoners in this hell feel the way we do," Takis said.

"They yearn for freedom."

"They have loved ones at home."

"They are homesick."

"How are we going to survive this hell?"

It was past midnight, and although the bodies were weak and tired, the minds were still active. There was always the fear that one man among them might be a traitor. Takis was suspicious of the prisoner Dalabaras, who occupied the mattress opposite Leonidas. He had a ruddy, full-moon face with large, blue eyes, usually bloodshot. They called him Abari, a Turkish word meaning "cesspool." Abari's body was a mass of flabby flesh; it was difficult to believe he came out of a woman's womb. He was like a dirty monstrosity made by butchers. This awkward mass moved dexterously on a pair of crutches. The right trouser leg hung empty and the lower portion of his left leg was missing. Abari had come into the world bearing the curse of hate and jealousy and of delight in wronging his fellowmen. He came to the concentration camp from a blockade, and there appeared to be no concrete evidence against him. One day, Leonidas told Abari that he was capable of becoming a good, upstanding man and that his character would improve if he could only cripple all those around him and make them like himself. Abari never forgave him for the remarks.

Bouras lay on his stomach next to Dalabaras and dozed off. Bouras had a purpose in befriending Abari, even though he found it unpleasant. It meant being with him constantly—dressing with him, undressing, washing, and even sleeping next to him—and at the same time putting up with his harsh words and the contempt of the prisoners

When Leonidas and Fotis noticed the close ties between Bouras and Abari, they wondered about Bouras's loyalty.

"Why is Bouras talking to that leech?" asked Fotis.

"I don't know, but I can find out from Takis." Leonidas got to his feet and approached Takis.

"Why is your friend keeping company with him?" he asked, gesturing toward the sleeping monster.

"He'll tell you himself, Mr. Leonidas." Takis went over to Bouras and shook him by the shoulder. "Wake up! Follow me. Your idea may get you into trouble." Takis knew earlier of Bouras's plan.

Bouras and Takis sat down with Leonidas and Fotis.

"What's the problem?" asked Bouras with annoyance.

"Bouras, tell Mr. Leonidas and his son why you're befriending Dalabaras."

"Befriending? I'd like to poison the bastard!"

"But you're always with him!" exclaimed Leonidas, incredulous at Bouras's response.

"I fish information out of him. He's an accomplice to an accomplice— you know who I mean . . . that snake Niketaras."

"I don't like it," said Leonidas. "Some of our colleagues in this hell are bound to think you are an accomplice too."

"Mr. Leonidas," Takis interrupted, "Bouras and I, and those two young men you see in the corner over there, we are compatriots and friends. We grew up together; we'll die together if we have to. Bouras would never betray anybody. Besides, not everyone has the guts to hang around a traitor like Abari."

Fotis listened with intense curiosity. In Takis's behavior, he saw the self-reliance he wanted to have.

"Well then, let's hear what you got out of Abari," said Fotis.

"For the past few days he hasn't had any worthwhile information to pass on to Niketaras, so this morning he decided to draw on his reserves. He remembered that an Athenian family called Theodorou once extended their hospitality to a Jewish family, proprietors of Tobias Jewelers on Stadiou Street. This information alone wouldn't be sufficient to warrant their arrest, so he was planning to elaborate on his story. He's always hoping to strengthen his association with the administration."

"Such information could wipe out the whole Theodorou family," said Fotis.

"What can we do to prevent the crime?" asked Leonidas. "If we wait until tomorrow, it may be too late."

Suddenly, a window was shattered from the outside. Fragments of glass cut into those who lay in the row beneath the sill. The prisoners fled to their mattresses. The night guards arrived in one violent full-throated roar of havoc, shining their high-powered flashlights on the prisoners. Takis felt the strong light entering his retinas like acid. Like a crazed venomous pack, the guards descended on their victims. First the darkness, then the light, and now screams and cries of the prisoners, violated, broken down to creatures less than human. Takis lost all control, and in that first hour something died within him, and something new and extraordinary surfaced.

"A t t e n t i o n ! All of you, up!" The shrill voice of the treacherous Gruber reverberated throughout the room, and his flashlight searched the ward.

"All of you, on your feet! Animals, serpents, dogs. You dirty pig, who are you? Why aren't you on your feet?" He flashed his light on the bed-clothes of Dalabaras, whom he was unable to distinguish. Bouras explained that it was the crippled man.

"Very well!" he said, striking his boots with his whip. "You sons of the devil, you won't sleep tonight. I'll be back. Do you hear?"

The savage Gruber was in the habit of carrying out his invasions at midnight or daybreak, interrupting their restless sleep with curses, kicks, and blows, blindly delivered as he lurked in the darkness. Mental terrorizing became more powerful than physical. Often he jumped into the ward through the window, and any hint of insubordination resulted in two or three prisoners being whipped nearly to death. He succeeded in terminating conversations and increasing sleeplessness that evening. After his visit, the men withdrew into themselves, lying on their mattresses, alone with their thoughts. Here and there a cigarette would glow, or the bright flame of a lighter would reveal the enslaved extending across the floor.

Silence prevailed for a few more minutes.

"This mechanized monster cannot reduce us to animals. We are not animals! When his ancestors were cannibals, we were giving the world civilization. We must survive to tell the truth!" Leonidas shouted. "As prisoners, we may be deprived of every right, exposed to every insult, condemned to death, but we still possess power. We must walk erect without dragging our feet, not because Nazi discipline dictates, but because we want to remain alive to tell the world."

Thunderous applause greeted Leonidas's speech as he retreated to his mattress. Sitting cross-legged, he searched his pocket and produced his cigarette holder made of olive branch. He kissed it and blew through the stem. "Will you search that pocket," he said, pointing to his right side.

"I can't find any cigarettes," said Takis. "I'm afraid I've given mine all away. I could borrow one from Demos."

Leonidas, who did not want to admit that he had been robbed, said, "No, don't do that. It doesn't matter. I just wanted to talk to you anyway." The poor soul was distressed lest Takis should think he had used such a pretext to get a cigarette, but he needed a cigarette to soothe his heavy heart. "Forgive me," he said. Their conversation was suddenly interrupted. Fotis, the tall, muscular son who had pretended to be asleep leapt off his mattress, flexed his hands, and went over to Demos for a cigarette.

"Leave me alone, kid. Cigarettes are for men— they can afford them and . . ." His sentence was stopped in mid-air as the youth pulled him up by the armpits and threw him to the floor. With devilish speed, he stuffed a handkerchief in his mouth, tied his hands behind his back, and snatched up the seven cartons of cigarettes.

"Comrades," Fotis shouted, "there are seven hundred cigarettes here! That means two each. Stay where you are, and I'll bring you your ration."

The three hundred captives were delighted, and the agony of the night was transformed. Leonidas was dumbfounded.

The cigarette merchant, beaten and defeated, crawled on to his mat. His silence signified agreement, at least for the time being. Angrily, he covered himself with a ragged blanket, trying not to succumb to feelings of alienation and weakness. Conscious of his isolation, and now the loss of his cigarettes, he felt upset. The ugly peddler of chickpeas was without companionship both in and out of Haidari.

Leonidas looked nervous; his son's action bothered him. Takis, who had no sympathy for the peddler, eventually convinced Leonidas that Fotis was justified in what he had done. "Three hundred prisoners are grateful to Demos tonight, even if he doesn't realize it. He has made the men happy."

Leonidas shook his head. His mind traveled back home to his caring wife. What would she have said had she seen her son attacking a hustler over cigarettes? He envisioned her anxiously reading the newspaper. No doubt, every morning she was first in line for the community paper to see if the names Leonidas or Fotis Katakamenos were in the execution column.

"Tell me, Takis, who suffers more, the crucified or the mother of the crucified? Whose is the greater pain, the slave's or the slave's family? Who pays the greater penalty, the soldier who fights for freedom or his loved ones who remain at home?"

Takis raised his thick eyebrows. "Touchy, loaded questions, Mr.

Leonidas. I really don't know. I would need time to think about them."
He excused himself and prepared to return to his mattress where his
friends lay, still awake. *Pain is pain,* he thought, *and each person suf-*
fers his own, and only that person knows the degree of his pain. He had
taken but a few steps when he turned around and rejoined Leonidas.
And in that split second, the answer to Leonidas's question surfaced in
his mind.

"The mother of the crucified suffers more. In watching my torture,
my father probably suffered more pain than I did. I'm sure he's still in
pain."

"It's a terrible sight. And the total helplessness that the onlooker
feels is devastating."

In the dimness of the night, Takis saw despair in Leonidas's face.

"Yes, to see your own flesh and blood tortured to the point of death—
that cruelty defies description!"

Calmly and without hurry, Leonidas continued, "As a reprisal for the
death of the German soldiers, the prisoners of Haidari are handed over
to the executioner every day." His penetrating eyes looked at Takis. "We
know that within a few days or months our turn will come, that death
is not far off. But those who love us die every minute of every day. And
as if that were not enough for them to endure, they are consumed with
guilt, thinking they are not trying hard enough to save us."

CHAPTER 16

The Price of Freedom

"Oh, the Greek-American hero is here again! What is it now?"

Takis had awaited word from Niketaras about his father's situation, and after seven days passed—which felt as long as seven weeks—he was overcome with worry. After reveille, he asked to see the general.

"I know my father is in isolation, but I really want to see him," Takis said, fettered by chains of anguish.

"I thought you had come to tell me about the smuggled weapons!"

"There is nothing to tell," Takis replied, his hostility boiling. He felt the powerful presence of the conqueror's arrogance bursting out of his neatly pressed uniform.

The law of the SS was *Mercy is an old luxury!* However, Steckelhuber, dissatisfied with such a definition, modified it. His rule became *Mercy is a crime. It is a form of cowardice.* Being a fervent adherent to Nazi policy and having had experience in Russian camps, he was sent to govern Haidari early in the summer of 1942. His promotion was speedy; his stripes were bought with gallons of blood, and having climbed up pyramids of human bodies, he ascended to the present position of general. He gave the impression that he cared little for either his stripes or the glory of his office. Such an impression was false. It was his desire to create a society reflecting his image. There were no limits to his cruelty. He knew no shame or sympathy, for sympathy meant mercy. The sight of the mutilated bodies in Haidari and the painful groans of dying fathers and sons brought him delight.

With his shiny leather whip, Steckelhuber pulled open a file drawer and retrieved a folder which he placed on the table. After flipping through a few pages, he closed the folder. Towering over Takis with simulated sadness on his stony face he said, "I'm terribly sorry. Apparently your father suffered a heart attack. He died on August 15. I'm sorry."

"Liar! Liar!" he screamed. "You killed my father!" Venom of vengeance pumped in his veins.

"I had nothing to do with his death."

"You tortured him, and that's the worst kind of death." Takis could not even cry. His chest heaved. He felt rage and a desire to kill the general, his ferocious eyes searching the room for a weapon. On the mantelpiece stood a limestone urn. If only he could lift the urn, he would throw it at the general and crush his head.

"You appear anxious to die."

"I'm anxious to see my country free!"

"You are a foolish young man. I'm offering you a chance to live, and you reject it."

"My hometown was surrounded by fifty thousand olive trees—a labor of centuries—and you uprooted them to make an airstrip. You confiscated all our possessions. You took away my bike. And now you have killed my father. Why?"

"That's the nature of war, Greek hero."

"To eradicate the human race?"

"To refine it," Steckelhuber said, raising a pompous eyebrow.

"Nazi justice!"

"Count your blessings. You are still alive—at least for a while."

"Death would be preferable to the hell you are subjecting us to."

"Aren't you afraid of death?"

Takis was too heartbroken to reply. Sadness at the loss of his father overwhelmed him, but his eyes remained dry, and at that moment life seemed futile and death a welcome relief.

"What's your answer?"

"I wouldn't be afraid to die if death served a purpose."

"*Heraus!*" shouted the Commander, and he kicked Takis out of his office.

* * * * *

Haidari was a strange world. Omens and superstition were a defiant stream with which no one could easily contend. The incarcerated automatically adhered to certain traditions. They hurried to wash themselves so that they might be first in line for the dream-tellers. Leonidas could not comprehend how these heroes, strong men who had fought for freedom, could believe in such things.

Anestis had the reputation of being one of the best dream-tellers, a talent he had developed since his imprisonment. He was a master shepherd from Thessaly, who, in his mid-sixties, still stood tall in his large frame; and although age had tempered his pace, he was as strong as an ox. A rim of white hair encircled the base of his bald head, the high coloring of his cheeks was a reminder of mountain air, and his thick eyebrows shaded eyes darting messages that could wound an enemy.

The Germans had confiscated his flock of some three hundred sheep, and they had brought him along to tend them. But the animals lasted only a short time. Some were sold in the black market by Nazi accomplices; the lambs were served to the SS; and the leanest were thrown into the boiling pots for the prisoners' mess.

Anestis, who had been in Haidari for over eight months now, was regarded as a source of wisdom. He gave the impression he was a simple man, the sort one finds in remote villages. But he could speak his mind, be authentic without worrying about the consequences. Defiantly, he stood up to the Nazi pursuers, and each time he had the chance, he would point a menacing finger: *Would that God grant me twenty more years that I may tell the world about life in Haidari.* He sat for hours on a broken chair, bent over his staff. His treasured flock having been drastically reduced in numbers, he had little left but the memories of his younger days, days that had given little enjoyment. He recalled the strong impulses he had suppressed, the pleasures he had sacrificed for the sake of his sheep. "You can enjoy yourself tomorrow. You are still young . . . you have plenty of time for fun," he had told himself. And now as he leaned over his staff, he thought of the lost opportunities, and scratching the earth with his staff, he pondered on life and how it had deceived him.

Leonidas did not believe dreams had any relevance to everyday life, but on Sunday morning he woke up feeling very disturbed over a dream which seemed so real that he wondered if perhaps it had a meaning. Several years before, he had nurtured a fig tree in his backyard, and it had grown from a small shoot to a large tree yielding an abundance of sweet figs. In his dream, a thunderbolt struck the tree, shattering it to pieces.

"A fig tree is a source of sweetness. It yields figs on a continuum, six to eight weeks every year," explained Anestis. "But the thunderbolt is an act of God." He looked into Leonidas's eyes with compassion. "The tree represents a life split asunder; it seems to me that you are to suffer a grave loss."

Leonidas hung on every word, waiting to hear more. He saw sadness in the dream-teller's face and wondered if tragedy was to befall his own household. But then he dismissed the thought, reminding himself that there was nothing prophetic in dreams. He gave Anestis a cigarette and lit it for him.

"Thank you," said Anestis, taking a deep puff. "Don't worry. Since we are tormented and deprived of all sources of joy, we are haunted by dreams." He took another puff. "Sunday morning dreams are fulfilled by noon; if you don't hear anything by then, nothing bad can happen."

One evening before lock-up time, Takis came across Anestis sitting on his broken chair. In a flash his mind transferred to Mitrakas, the elderly boat-maker in Lesbos, and he recalled how he and his friends had loved his company as he constructed that memorable boat. Takis sat down beside Anestis, the setting sun resting on their faces.

"Who are you?" asked the bearded shepherd. "Where are you from, and why are you here?"

Takis wanted to tell him the story of his father, for he knew that the old man would understand. However, that was not to be. A guard approached, his club pointing to the barracks.

Damn him! thought Takis. His fond memories—of Moria, Eleni, Alexis's tavern, his home, and Katerina making his favorite *sfougato* (souffle) and *potatokeftedes* (potato fritters)—could not be shared today.

Anestis followed Takis up the pathway to the building, and when Takis looked around, the old shepherd waved *Yiassou* and was swallowed up in one of the cells at the end of the row.

Anestis had been spared interrogation, for his record was clean, and he was needed to tend the twelve remaining sheep. His work consisted of cleaning and protecting the little flock from the barbed wire. He used the hook of his oak staff to pry a sheep loose from a thicket or pull a wandering one out of a hole. The prisoners looked upon him as a godsend, a patient and intelligent man who could understand human pain and respond with a word of comfort. His sensitivity in interpreting dreams was astounding.

One morning, one of the sheep was missing. Anestis left the flock near barracks #9 and, with staff in hand, went around the buildings, seeking the wanderer. His search ended when he found it in front of the headquarters. Gruber, spotting him from the window, rushed out and attacked both the old shepherd and the sheep with a braided leather whip, knocking them to the ground. Anestis, getting to his feet with the aid of his staff, glared menacingly at the enemy.

"*Heraus!*" shouted Gruber as he continued the beating. The bleating sheep came close to her master, who reached out and fondled her. He knew he could put an end to Gruber, for he had the death-giving blow of a lion, but the consequences for the prisoners would be too great. There was little else to be done but stand firmly facing the German and attempt to kill him with a look.

"You'll get a repeat of this if you dare to come near my headquarters again, you dog. Do you hear?" He raised the whip.

"Good!" replied Anestis raising his staff.

"Bastard! You are a rooster!"

Whoever taught Gruber to speak Greek had evidently told him that "rooster" was an ugly epithet.

Anestis burst out laughing. "Yes, I'm a rooster!"

"Does that amuse you?" Gruber suspected a slip in his language. "Hey! Look at me!" he commanded.

Still laughing, Anestis looked him in the eye.

Gruber grabbed him by the thin waistcoat. "Tell me, you cunning devil, what does 'rooster' mean? Your answer will be rewarded with a cigarette."

Tsakiris, who had a smattering of German, came to the rescue and assured Gruber that he would also find the intended insult funny.

"Isn't 'rooster' a Greek word?"

"It is, but it is not an insulting word," explained Tsakiris. "In fact, to call an old man a rooster is a compliment. It means he's strong and healthy and likes to chase after women—like Don Juan!"

"Ah! I understand . . . good . . . rooster." He opened his cigarette case and gave Anestis the promised reward.

The last Saturday in September was agreeably warm. Two hundred of the Haidari prisoners had been executed during the week, a reprisal for the death of two SS soldiers who had been killed in Halandri. The prisoners felt dejected and solitary. The shepherd, now surrounded by a little band that included Takis and his friends spoke words of comfort. Not only a shepherd of animals, but of humans as well, Anestis listened to their dreams and guided them. At night time, like Pythia, he accepted customers as he sat cross-legged on his mattress. In his life as a shepherd, he had swooped like a blackbird over towering cliffs, fallen into ravines, slept as lightly as a hare, climbed to the eagle's eyrie, and quarrelled with wolves. On the mountains of Thessaly, he had kindled fires, seen the soaring star, and in the night breeze had inhaled deeply of the heavens. He had never hurt an ant or angered a man. He had carried newborn lambs in his arms. But now, God willed that he graze humans. His customers came one by one. He held their hands in his calloused palms and looked earnestly into their eyes. He listened attentively and thoughtfully, and then assumed an indescribable expression of understanding, kindness, and wise tolerance. His harsh shepherd's voice became deep, dulcet, and charmingly animated.

Like the prophets of old, he had a habit of raising his head, as if coming back from another world, and fixing his sunken eyes on his client. He had great powers of persuasion and offered advice in terse words: "Do not be afraid of your dreams."

Pantsaris, the poet, with the fair hair and blue eyes of the early Greeks, looked handsome in his gray pants and yellow shirt—a gift from Niketaras—and black sandals with wooden soles. He described his dream to Anestis: "I was on horseback, dressed up in the finest costume I have ever seen—a costume only permitted to kings. It was made of the Greek flag with a belt of the Stars and Stripes. My shoes were red and shiny, and atop my hat, which was embellished with silver stars, was perched a brown eagle."

"What a dream!" exclaimed Anestis. "A revelation, my boy! You dream like a poet! Was anyone else dressed in such a uniform? Think!"

"Yes, there were some others dressed just like me."

"Did you have any weapons?"

"No, nothing like that."

"Were you riding or walking?"

"I was riding the horse through a village, and then I came to a country road that led me to a strange city."

"Hum . . . ! Your dream is not . . . have you got another cigarette?"

Having received the advance payment in his hands—three whole cigarettes, given generously—he continued. "Well, your dream does not mean release. You won't go home . . . not yet. The red shoes indicate that something is going to happen very soon, and the shoes also mean sorrow—not a great sorrow, since you were riding a horse rather than walking. You left one village and went to another, a strange city. Either today or tomorrow, you will leave Haidari—more likely, today. The red of your shoes and the riding of the horse mean swiftness. Perhaps you will be taken to the prison of Averof—I can't be sure. There is no sign of death. The flag is honor. Maybe you will stand trial and be found not guilty. The belt of the American flag stands for protection. The eagle—that is the best part of your dream, for a bird means life, represents loftiness of spirit."

"It is also the American symbol of the armed forces," added Takis.

"That's it! This is not just a dream, it's a revelation . . . for all of us. The American forces will deliver us."

Pantsaris embraced his friends, and they embraced the other prisoners standing around listening, and the song and dance began:

> Fish cannot live on land
> Nor flowers survive in sand;
> And we, the sons of Greece,
> Can no longer live
> Unless we be free.

* * * * *

Pieces torn from an underground newspaper found their way into Haidari. Eight prisoners on labor detail in Skaramanga each smuggled in a section, and a special workshop of faithful readers put the puzzle together. In the evening, the paper was furtively read, and arrangements made to share it with the various barracks.

The men in barracks #7 waited anxiously on Saturday night for their scheduled reading. Occasionally the glow from cigarettes showed the emaciated silhouettes and shaved heads, their ears alert, and necks turned nervously. No artist could paint the true agony apparent in the faces of the prisoners as they awaited news from the outside world. The stillness of the room was strangely disturbing.

The messenger with the news arrived and read to the eager listeners. His voice was hushed like the whispering sound made by a mare drinking water. A shadow separated itself from the phantoms in the background. It silently moved forward, stopping at a group of prisoners.

"Have any Germans been killed today?" asked the shadow.

Nobody minded the interruption. It was Giorgalas from barracks #9, the six-foot-eleven quarry man who had once made the earth tremble with his pick. At the side of his huge, half-naked body his left hand hung limp; he, too, had his share of torment. He volunteered to represent his barracks and carry back the news.

"Any news?"

"In Athens," the messenger read, "Archbishop Damaskinos personally instructed his priests to hide Jews throughout Greece. In cases where it was not possible to conceal a Jew or his family, he advised them under strict confidence to issue pseudocertificates of Christian Baptism.

"In Salonika, Bishop Gregorios hid several hundred Jews and thereby saved their lives. He himself placed the Torah scrolls under the altar of his own church."

"What's that have to do with us in this rotten hell? Can those men of God do something for us?"

Several faces looked at Giorgalas and told him to keep quiet and listen. The messenger pursed his lips and continued in a softer tone:

"Papaioannou, a respected pharmacist, was sentenced to death today for hiding the Nachamoudis—a Jewish family in Athens. The execution will take place at Auschwitz.

"Angelos Evert, chief of police in Athens/Piraeus, has, thus far, issued twenty-two thousand forged identity cards to help Jews escape from Greece. It is one of the ironies of history that Chief Evert's grandfather emigrated to Greece from Germany. Thanks to his German surname, the chief of police was not kept under the close surveillance experienced by other Greek officials."

"Have any Germans been killed today?" Giorgalas persisted.

"Yes—a German officer in Kallithea."

It was the answer they dreaded to hear. In the ensuing silence, the newsreader folded the paper, hid it in his pants, and returned to his quarters.

Leonidas unbuttoned his olive-green shirt and sighed. Protocols and Nazi policies whirled through his mind. Today the crime; tomorrow the list of those who would pay for it. *It could be me, my son, or anyone here*, he thought, knowing that prisoners were always the potential victims.

While he agonized over such thoughts, Leonidas watched the cigarette vendor trudge toward Fotis, his enemy.

"I need a cigarette." He sighed.

"Take them all, Demos. I am not angry. I wanted to fulfill a wish for our brothers. They may die tomorrow."

"But you destroyed me."

"Only your cigarettes. . . ."

"I held on to them because they were the only thing I had left in the world. My family . . ."

"What about your family?" said Leonidas.

The crippled Dalabaras pulled himself into the circle.

"In 1941, my mother died of T.B. There was no medicine. Are you sure you want to hear more?" asked John Demos.

"Sure, sure, go ahead."

"My father died of starvation a few months later. It was a horrible death. His whole body swelled up and broke out in boils. With his last breath he called out for a bite of bread. He died with his mouth open, still waiting for a morsel. Six months later, my sister Stratoula died of hunger, slowly and painfully. She melted like a candle."

Leonidas, lying on his mattress, lit a cigarette and passed it to Demos, lighting another for himself. They smoked in a silence of understanding and tolerance. Fotis's heart pounded with foreboding. His name or his father's could be on the execution list. Takis and his friends crept near to share the warmth and silence of the circle. They were comforted by listening to stories and being part of the scene that calmed their frayed nerves. Leonidas, his eyes moist, caressed his son's shoulders with one hand and then the head of John Demos. A sacred ritual had begun. Demos puffed on his cigarette, making rings with the smoke and wishing they were free.

"It is impossible for a man to be born evil," said Leonidas. "It is all a matter of upbringing and environment."

Many of the prisoners fell asleep, others sat discussing the major issue of survival. But their conversation was suddenly overridden by a serene voice.

"O God, this mournful night, when the wind shouts like a sinful soul rejected by the grave, think of those stretched out in their tattered cots. Let them rest to gather strength to endure tomorrow's pain."

The prisoners could barely distinguish the silhouette of the man on his knees at the far end of the room. Arms uplifted in prayer, Christoforos, a Greek from Cyprus, his bearded Christ-like face upturned, was talking to God, as was his habit. Sometimes he claimed that he was God. Now he prayed with fervor and passion.

"No happiness can compensate for the woes these prisoners have suffered. Send no happiness now. But while your angels rejoice send Death to step into this dismal grave, gently and softly so as not to waken those asleep. Let him lean over them like a sister—not like a mother, for mothers embrace tightly. Let him kiss them on their blistered and wrinkled lips and take their breath away."

In the somber atmosphere, the men retired for the night. Takis felt exhausted. He pulled his thin blanket over his chest. The curtains of courage fell. His heart was full of fear and pain. He wanted to scream to clear his spirit, but fatigue stifled his voice.

The hours before dawn were decreasing, renewing the stress in the camp. Takis had survived and lived to see another spring. With dawn a step away, he took a prolonged look, embracing Lesbos and Athens, and thought over future plans, deeds, and dreams—should he live to be free. The moments before dawn flew like countless feathers from his fingertips, and he felt compelled to keep his hand open so that they could leave one by one. He could not possibly count them as they dispersed in the air, nor could he reckon how many still remained in his palm. Terror at the speed of time whirled him into space, while two tender white hands of a woman stretched out to him, and tearful eyes begged him with yearning to come closer. She was tall and beautiful, wrapped in a lace tunic, giving the semblance of a Greek statue, a goddess that came to life. A basil flower he had planted at the southeast corner of his home, a marble slab in a country road where he once sat, the riverside where he and Eleni had played . . . many dreams . . . plans unfinished. "One more spring," Takis said, terrified that it might be a farewell to life. He needed to stay a little longer. He was unprepared to bid farewell to life. Another moment was granted. He heard a woman's voice: *It's not time yet!* She reached out and held him back, talking to him and arguing. *Who told you the hour is here? Only I know when your time has come.*

"Who are you to appear at such an hour?" he wailed.

I am Hope! I accompany man from his birth to his death.

"No! You are a deceiver who makes promises that encourage people to lean on you."

Half awake and half asleep, not totally aware of the origin of his thoughts, Takis was befuddled. He mourned for his father, who had died in the isolation cell, and for Lefteris and the priest's son. Takis's father always spoke with pride about America. Time and again he had taken Takis to the seashore and, pointing across the Aegean to the horizon, had said, "Son, do not despair. As surely as you now see me and I see you, our American allies will come from that part of the sea. It won't be long." Takis imagined he could hear his father's voice. Yes, it was quite clear. Through a gray mist came his father, Lefteris, and Papavasile's son, sad and unhappy at the enslavement of their country. "It will not last much longer," Takis explained. "One more spring . . . perhaps one more summer."

When he opened his eyes, it was already daybreak. *I must have dozed off for a few minutes,* he thought. The apparitions of the dead had disappeared. He found himself leaning against a wall. His head was heavy, his mind confused and disoriented, and his body numb.

The prisoners got up, took their raggedy towels, and headed for the washroom. Bouras's undershirt hung unevenly, as if it had been beaten on a limestone rock or chewed by hungry mice.

The morning sun reddened the eastern horizon. In ten minutes, the whistle for mess would sound.

The camp of Haidari was hauntingly quiet on that Sunday morning. In his room, Gruber laughed self-consciously as he recalled the incident of the shepherd and the rooster. He strutted out into the yard and paraded around, slapping his boots with his whip. Today he looked like a frustrated bull enraged before the fight. It was difficult to see which of his whips he had with him—the rubber one he used during the compulsory labor details, or the one of cowhide, which signified executions. He waited for the line to form for morning mess. It had to be straight and orderly, otherwise he felt it his duty to whip it into shape. Gruber was granted the luxury of witnessing the results of his terrible power, his rapacious encounter with innocent people; he was far removed from the grief and destruction that his visitation inevitably brought to the targeted population. It mattered little to him what the whip lashed—backs, faces, knees—and as he whipped, he shouted, "Do you see my whip? It is the lucky whip! Sing loudly, rascals! Sing! I'll be hanging you up in an hour. You have a good voice . . . oh, what a voice! Sing, you devils!" He held the cowhide whip. Those who saw it shivered. Death was in the air.

Breakfast was served at six o'clock. Marmalade was on the menu. Takis and his friends exchanged a few words about the German officer who had been killed in Kallithea, a suburb of Athens. It was inevitable that a list for execution would be produced, even though it was Sunday. They still had forty-five minutes at their disposal. Forty-five minutes could mean a whole lifetime, according to the measures in Haidari. There was time to make decisions and prepare themselves by drowning every weakness and mobilizing their strength. They had no power to influence events in either the camp or the outside world. They were no match for the machine guns pointed at them. They had no means of alleviating distress except through prayer. But words would not come, so Pantsaris composed a prayer for all to share:

"Lord, we witness the horrors of the invaders. We know children are dying of hunger, innocent men are executed. . . . We need to survive. We must live on to tell the story of the enslaved. Grant us another day."

The sun rose over the eastern mountains, the falling leaves breathed sighs, and the myrtles shed tears. The olive orchards seemed to be in mourning, and Parthenon, dressed in his golden apparel, wept and wailed under the saffron gauze of dawn. Ten minutes remained for those whose lives were to be terminated. Amid the dust and the cursing, Takis and his friends huddled beside each other, now and then spitting on the ground, angry at their crooked destiny. Every gleam of joy had instantly vanished. There were no recollections of happy times. The prisoners, three thousand of them, became restless. They pushed each other without care, every man concerned for his own survival. The enervation, the insults, and the harsh words reached a climax. Most of the prisoners had not had their morning smoke to calm down the luckless day's distress.

Six soldiers, then six more, and then a countless number marched past the prisoners in an immaculate single file, moving with such precision that they seemed otherworldly, superhuman, surrounding their subjects. Under their arms and pressed against their sides were their automatic guns. Takis felt their soul-chilling presence, an articulate tribute to the mechanized forces of Hitler. They were elite, slim, and malignant.

The ear-splitting whistle was followed by the loudest voice, the braying of Gruber. While the prisoners awaited their fate, a commotion arose among the crowd. Giorgalas, the hard-working giant with hog-bristle hair from barracks #9, was splitting cigarettes. His son along with fifty other men had been hanged a year ago to the day as a reprisal for killing a German soldier. In his memory, Giorgalas distributed half a cigarette to each prisoner; he remembered how his son had asked for a cigarette before his execution, and there were none to be had.

"May God rest your son!" said each prisoner, grateful for the little gift. Anestis lit his cigarette, and as he inhaled he said, "I wonder who'll be splitting cigarettes this time next year." It was a dreadful thought. The prisoners turned toward the city. Athens was still asleep. The sun gently lifted the infinite blue veil woven by the moonbeams during the night, and the soft breeze from the Gulf of Saronikos scattered the morning mist. The prisoners of Haidari watched the rays of the sun, and in them, each one saw his child lying in the cradle, his mother, his father, his young wife. But the faces watching the sun were despondent, crushed by the claws of their rude nightmare, the probability of the death of another two hundred prisoners before the sun set. A flock of birds, like souls of the slain on their way to heaven, flew over the camp, and the candidates for execution, with pleading eyes, urged them to say farewell to their dear ones at home. "At least they will live free."

The first sun rays ignited boundless feelings in the imprisoned hearts. Takis and his friends still looked afar. Acropolis, like an empress of the past, solemnly slipped out of her royal purple robe and gradually vested herself in a gold-woven gown. Pairs of swallows, chasing each other around the barracks, prepared for their journey south to their winter quarters, and the morning breeze lovingly caressed the rose laurels. Minutes ticked away, anxiety subsided, and the prisoners inhaled deeply of the voluptuous fragrance that brought them relief. They watched the most glorious bride in the world, Enchantress Athens, yielding to the sun like a hetaira. Their souls succumbed to ecstasy. They were ready for anything. Fulfilled. A melodic piping of a distant shepherd echoed in the camp. Anestis caught the tune, put his pipe to his mouth, and played it softly. The four friends picked up the sentiment and started to sing. One by one, the prisoners joined them in the familiar song of Rigas Pheraios, a patriot of the past: *Better one hour of freedom than forty years of slavery and prison.*

CHAPTER 17

Waiting for the Allies

The Germans perfected their drilling to such precision that a thousand soldiers, at a certain angle, appeared as one. Their boots thundered as they marched in goose-step fashion. The prisoners knew there was something different planned for their morning, for the band was playing as the mechanized men moved forward. Every beat of the drum was a step, and every step brought them closer to roll-call square where, under strict surveillance, the lines for compulsory labor were formed, and on special days, the execution line.

The music stopped, and Gruber, escorted by Niketaras, emerged from headquarters.

"He's decorated himself to impress us," Takis said, tossing his head in Gruber's direction.

Gruber, small in stature, could easily pass for Napoleon: a grand sight with brass badges shining on his collar and gold braid around his cap. He proudly displayed the stripes and chevrons on his sleeves and the medals dangling from his chest. He paraded in front of the prisoners, counting heads.

Bouras could not control his tongue. "Gruber looks like an agitated wild turkey the way he pauses and struts."

"How about Niketaras?" Tsakiris remarked. "A new suit! Shiny shoes! Whose blood paid for those?"

Bouras surveyed Niketaras from head to toe. The traitor held a list in his right hand, and a cigarette between the thumb and index finger of his left.

Tsakiris, who could not stomach the traitor and sought ways to poison him, said, "Snake face! The product of an unsuccessful abortion! His day of retribution will come."

"And we'll be there to see it!" added Bouras.

The noise of a grinding motor, a deafening sound, made hundreds of heads turn. An olive-green truck was heading toward the gate near barracks #15.

They're coming! The words echoed and reverberated in their heads. Each man had his own interpretation: *Coming to get us! Coming to free us!*

"Is there a trailer connected to the truck?" asked Leonidas.

"I can't see any," replied his son Fotis.

"Then there's going to be killing today," mumbled Leonidas.

"No, maybe they need more workers at a different camp," said Pantsaris. Three times he made the sign of the cross, and then he began to dig at a stone near his foot. He poked it and kicked it until he had worked it free, so that a small indentation remained in the ground. He spat into the hole and then covered it over with soil. Anxiously, he took an old piece of shirt out of his back pocket and tried occupying himself, tying the cloth into knots. Unable to ease himself, he stuffed the cloth back into his pocket. He looked around to see if anyone was watching. Only his friends had seen. Hesitantly, he looked at Takis and then showed him his little notebook. "Bury me in my grave with my poems on my chest."

Takis took his hand. "I'm scared, too," he said.

The truck entered roll-call square, stopping in front of the general's quarters. Two SS officers stepped out, each holding a black leather briefcase under his arm. They entered the building.

"Oh, those briefcases are bulging!" said Leonidas.

"They probably contain long lists of names," replied Fotis.

There was a general hubbub among the prisoners. Takis moved closer to Leonidas.

"Today, they'll execute trees, benches, doors, flies, fleas, everything . . . prisoners won't be enough! And when Hitler erases the human race, he'll wage war against the celestial powers!"

The prisoners laughed quietly, releasing some of the tension.

The two SS officers returned to their truck, their briefcases now empty, and drove away. Deathly silence prevailed for a few seconds . . . the atmosphere was still.

"Humans! O humans! Bloodthirsty brutes and sanguinary snakes," thundered the echo across roll-call square. It was the voice of Christoforos defying the moment. With the face of an ancient prophet and his burlap mantle flowing out behind him, he crossed the line of prisoners and, invincible, he passed in front of the giants of the Third Reich.

"Why so much hate?" Now his voice mellowed and his expression became benevolent. "Humans! O humans! Bloodthirsty humans, why so much hate? Why so much self-destruction? We are all humans. We are all components of the universe whose creator I am." Repeating his lines, he continued on his way.

Some of the prisoners laughed, and others sensed that in the insane world of Haidari, Christoforos, the crazy theologian, was the only sane man. Takis and his friends applauded, and others joined in, but when Gruber barked "Attention!" the clapping ceased.

Anestis put his arm around Pantsaris. "Do you see, my good poet? What did I tell you? Crystal clear! What a dream! I told you yesterday that there was no need to fear death. Listen to the old shepherd."

Takis, less anxious since the departure of the messengers of death, put his hand on Pantsaris's shoulder. "Do you feel better?"

Anestis broke in. "Fear is human . . . but it is the law of the camp, the tradition of the prisoners of Haidari, to die with dignity. If you cannot face death standing up and singing, if you cannot accept your fate without hysterics and faintings, you forfeit your life, and you cannot be a Greek."

Bouras, Tsakiris, and Pantsaris looked at each other with incredulity. "Facing death standing up and singing! What is the old shepherd talking about?"

The door of the headquarters opened, and two huge, well-fed wolf-hounds trotted out. General Erwin Steckelhuber, Hauptmann Heins Gruber, and Niketaras followed behind. The groups of prisoners tuned down their voices in anticipation of orders. Takis stood by his friends. Could this be their day of execution after all?

"Your hats! Take off your caps! What are you waiting for?" Gruber snarled.

"Awaiting our allies!" Leonidas remarked.

Some of the men laughed.

To impress his superior, Gruber shattered the laughter.

"A T T E N T I O N !"

The general, a tall, skinny man, was wearing leather gloves on his huge hands. His face, with its stiff, crude features resembled those of an ape and did not seem suited to his crisp blue uniform and black boots. His neck was short so that his head appeared to be sitting on his shoulders. Beside him stood the shapeless Lieutenant Gruber, a donkey in a lion's skin, who acquired a sense of importance by virtue of the great personage whom he escorted. On this occasion, he felt particularly powerful, for he was to read out two special lists.

The presence of General Steckelhuber stopped all whispering. The camp was transformed into a living cemetery. When the general had finished inspecting the guards, he spoke to Gruber who bowed and saluted.

"*P R O S O H E !*—A T T E N T I O N !" shouted Niketaras, who then turned to Gruber with a bow.

In Haidari, Niketaras the interpreter was known by two names: in the torture chambers he was called Niketaras, and in the camp, the prisoners called him "*Stavroti*—crucifier."

Niketaras lit a cigarette and silently looked over the list, now and again raising his head to look at the prisoners.

"The turncoat is watching," Takis said.

"Let's call him dog-fish," Bouras said.

"That's a good name," agreed Takis.

Gruber took a leather-bound notebook out of his pocket and, breathing heavily, checked off certain names with a red pencil. Hearts pounded and knees buckled as he glared at the prisoners. He closed the notebook, and putting it back in his pocket, waved his hand from left to right: "At ease."

A large truck, with six German soldiers sitting in the back, drove past them in the square. A wave of whispers flowed across the rows of prisoners.

"It's a detachment!"

"It's an escort squad!"

"Maybe some of us will be transferred to another camp!"

"It's the execution squad!"

"It might be a shipment to Germany!"

"Or to our eternal life," said Leonidas.

"A T T E N T I O N ! S I L E N C E !" screamed Gruber.

During the commotion, John Demos squatted down and crawled from one group to another collecting cigarette butts from the ground. He could salvage tobacco for rolling new cigarettes, and then later offer them for sale. Takis looked at him with contempt. How could he carry out this petty act at such a serious time?

"Shame!" whispered Takis.

"Condemn me now, but the survivors will thank me later." His ever-inventive mind was at ease, for Demos had not considered that he might be listed among those to be terminated. He believed he would live forever, and he paid no attention to threats of death.

Facing the silent men, Steckelhuber began to read the list. He called two names, paused, and pointed to the right where the prisoners should stand. He called out two more names . . . and then two more . . . and the prisoners held their breath. He uttered a few words through the interpreter: "Get your chattels—things! Quickly!" There was a generous look on the general's face, causing a sigh of relief in the hearts of those who were called. Takis knew they would not see those six prisoners again, for in a few moments they would be running joyously to their homes, their mothers, wives, and children. They could go anywhere. They were F R E E !

Steckelhuber cleared his throat as he glared at the faces gazing at him. He folded the list, placed it in the inside pocket of his coat, and pulling another list from his left pocket, he handed it to Gruber.

"Questioning," murmured Leonidas.

"Questioning?" Takis asked, looking at the frightened faces.

Gruber read another list of names and told the men to line up in front of the general. These were the prisoners who were to be questioned. Bruno Koch and Niketaras, the inquisitors, would again play their games. Takis's knees trembled, and his spine tingled with fear as he remembered the grim instruments and the blood-stained torture chamber. *The hell of Haidari is merging with the cruel winter of 1943,* he thought. The recollection, like a shower of icy water, froze his body, and thoughts of revenge and sadistic treatment of the torturers, momentarily took possession of him. His throat tightened, and his breathing became shallow.

"Are you all right?" Pantsaris asked.

"Ready to vomit!"

Gruber produced another list for Niketaras to read. It consisted of a hundred and twenty names of prisoners who were being sent to work in Piraeus. Niketaras shot out the names like a machine gun.

As each name was called, the prisoner responded, "Present," and sighed with relief that he was spared, at least for another day.

Takis was disappointed that he and his friends were not on the list, and while wondering what was in store for them, his thoughts were suddenly interrupted by a strange sight. The prisoners were standing aside to make a path for a man who, with the aid of a cane, was trudging toward Leonidas. It was Nicholas Mitakos, a handsome man, a popular doctor from Volos, a city north of Athens. He had been charged with insubordination and sent to Haidari. Although he was only forty-five, he looked sixty—maybe because of the tortures he had suffered. He had no intention of informing on the three Jewish sisters that his wife befriended and whose escape she made possible. When his wife refused to divulge the names, SS soldiers shaved her head and tore off her clothing, leaving her naked in the public square tied to an electric pole to die slowly. Then they handcuffed her husband and took him to Haidari.

Each time Dr. Mitakos returned from questioning, he was unrecognizable for three or four days. His clothes, a strange collection of rags, hung limply on his thin frame. The thorny whip had no mercy for the man who had dedicated his life to the healing of others.

Takis saw the doctor, and his whole body shivered. He was burned around the face, and his lips had turned to a scabby crust oozing with pus. Soup was about all he could manage to eat. Now he sought solace near Leonidas, and as he neared him, Niketaras called his name: "Nicholas Mitakos."

There was no answer. Niketaras spoke to Gruber, and both men came toward the doctor. The prisoners followed the two instruments of terror with their eyes.

"Why didn't you answer 'Present'?" Niketaras demanded.

The doctor pointed to his lips and tipped his untidy mustache. Niketaras again spoke to Gruber, and turning to the doctor ordered him to stand erect, salute, and say "Present."

The doctor said not a word but spat on the ground.

Mercilessly, Gruber lifted his whip and lowered it—one, two, three times, lashing the doctor's head. Blood coursed down his sunken cheeks and dripped from his chin.

The prisoners watching the scene were petrified.

"Takis, we shouldn't stand here doing nothing!" whispered Pantsaris.

Leonidas turned his fiery eyes on them. "Don't be foolish!"

Suddenly Pantsaris fell to the ground, crawling among the feet of the prisoners. Moving quickly, he grabbed Niketaras by the feet and tumbled him flat on his face. Within seconds, several pairs of feet performed the "grape dance" on top of his body. Takis, Bouras, and Tsakiris had just enough time to swing a few punches at Niketaras's ribs.

"Lieutenant Gruber! What's going on?" Steckelhuber shouted.

"Nothing, Sir. I think the interpreter fell down," replied Gruber.

Gruber lifted Niketaras to his feet, dusting his uniform. The prisoners moved slowly back to their places.

Niketaras had hardly composed himself when Dr. Mitakos approached Gruber and said in a lacerating voice, "Strike if you must, but God demands justice, and so do I."

Shadows crossed over their heads, a flock of crows flew by like the souls of the slain on their way to heaven. Fear of death united the prisoners at this feast where uninvited beasts roamed hungrily.

Gruber and Niketaras returned to their posts to continue their orders for the day. Four blacksmiths, six builders, and three electricians completed the labor crew. The interpreter pointed to the right side of the headquarters where the hundred and twenty laborers were to assemble. Then in silence Steckelhuber handed the last list to Gruber. The prisoners were tense as they watched Gruber's every movement. For a few minutes, the general spoke angrily into the humid, hostile air, inciting the minds of the prisoners with a language they did not understand. Their feet were tired and cold, and they shifted from one foot to the other.

Unemotionally, Niketaras interpreted the general's speech: "You already know that each time a soldier is killed by your compatriots, two hundred of you must forfeit your lives. Last night, another officer was killed in Constitution Square in Athens. Therefore, today, two hundred of you are scheduled to die. Some of you will be hanged at crossroads in Athens."

"Ah, is that so?" Takis inquired, a tinge of sarcasm in his voice.

"Yes, that's so!" responded the interpreter.

Gruber began to announce those who had been selected.

The prisoners waited in silence, each one praying that his name was not listed.

"Dalabaras!" Gruber shouted.

Bouras was stunned. Standing beside the condemned man, he asked him why his associate Niketaras had made no effort to save him.

"Bouras, I'm no longer an accomplice," he replied.

Takis raised his eyebrows at Bouras. The ex-traitor had transcended human weakness. He leaned upon his crutches and swung himself along to the execution line. Disgusted with his plight, his demented eyes full of anger, he turned to the prisoners and said, "Forgive me, fellows. I have sinned, and now I must pay the price. Have courage!"

Gruber and Steckelhuber would never understand that this solitary death, the death of Dalabaras, would bring him glory.

The general yawned as the death list was read.

"Present!" "Present!" "Present!" Each emphatic "Present!" was a story that spoke of Alamana, Thermopylai, Salamis, and the fifth century B.C. when the Greeks fought glorious battles against the invaders, rescuing their homeland with their blood. These brave prisoners represented civilization. The soul, the true soul of Greece was still alive to fight another battle against the barbarians, the battle of life against death, freedom against slavery.

"Fotis Katakamenos."

Leonidas shuddered when he heard his son's name.

"Present!" he shouted, as he grabbed his son's arm. "Don't move, Fotis. Human destiny dictates that in death, parents precede their children. I shall take your place. You have a life ahead of you!"

His selflessness brought a lump to Fotis's throat. He fell into his father's arms and wept. Takis and his friends joined Fotis. Seeing the terror and disbelief in his eyes, they put their arms around him.

Leonidas left his son with the four friends to join the line. A cry pierced the air: "*Filoi, tharthi e sera mas*—friends, our time will come!"

Noticing the commotion, Gruber and Niketaras approached the prisoners. Through the interpreter, Gruber ordered Fotis to join the execution line. Fotis hugged and kissed his father. "*Kali antamosi*—until we meet again."

Gruber and Niketaras grabbed Leonidas by the arms and forced him back to the crowd. "Don't rush your death," Niketaras said.

Takis and his friends felt inconsolable as they stood weeping beside the bereft father.

Giorgalas, with the dislocated arm, looked taller. He had decided that death was more desirable than life in Haidari. He came to bid the friends farewell—he had a premonition he would be in the line-up with Fotis.

"Did they call your name?" Takis asked.

"No," replied Giorgalas, "but my ear is burning."

"Were you warned in a dream?" asked Pantsaris.

"Never have dreams."

Gruber continued reading the list, occasionally glancing at the anxious prisoners. When he stumbled over Greek pronunciation, Niketaras came to the rescue.

"Pa . . . pa . . . ge . . . ge . . . or . . . "

"Listen to that! The butcher is chopping my name. I know my last name sounds like a train, but there's no need to butcher it," said Giorgalas.

Gruber continued to struggle.

"If he doesn't say it correctly, I won't say 'Present!' I'll let him crunch on it until midnight." Giorgalas made his audience laugh.

"Perhaps, it's a transfer," suggested Takis.

Giorgalas was taken aback and looked at Takis with a sour face. "Do you think me unworthy to die for my country?"

"Comrade," Takis added, "whatever it is, we will be thinking of you. We might even join you."

With the assistance of the interpreter, Gruber finally got the name out.

"Papageorkakopoulakis!"

"*Paron!*—present!" Giorgalas walked to the execution line, where he stood defiantly under the gaze of Nazi justice.

Many of the prisoners bowed their heads in admiration. The execution line was now complete.

"How many?" inquired the general.

"Two hundred, Sir."

Gruber folded the list and put it into his pocket. Under his watchful eye, the condemned men, escorted by twelve stern SS soldiers, marched, five by five, toward the trucks.

Gruber asked the interpreter to tell the squad to sing. It was not a suggestion but a command—no one asked them if they wanted to sing. The few minutes they had before death brought a heavy mourning to their hearts, yet the SS insisted upon entering even the privacy of their souls. They wanted to trample, crush, and flay the enslaved hearts, so that no moment, not even the end of their lives, would exist without a criminal presence.

The song began:

> *Mavri ne nikta sta vouna—*
> Black is the night on the mountains . . .
> Endless night is land.

The remaining prisoners stood silent, their heads bowed. They felt a mixture of relief that they had been spared for another day, yet guilty that their comrades had been chosen to die.

The band struck up. General Steckelhuber's work was finished for the day.

Like conquerors, the SS escorted their group.

On the east side of barracks #15 stood the two armored trucks covered with khaki tarpaulin; cages to carry the condemned. Each man called had to remove his outer garments and run to the cage in his underwear. Dalabaras, the last to be called, moved swiftly on his crutches, but when he attempted to push himself on to the vehicle, he fell flat on his face. It was an impossible task for him. The SS pretended to be oblivious to the cripple's dilemma. Gruber, witnessing the scene, scratched his head and frowned. Two prisoners jumped from the cage, rolled Dalabaras on to his back, and gently lifted the body into the truck. They gathered up the crutches. "Give those to Gruber—he might need them. He can put one in his mouth and the other up his ass." Dalabaras burst out laughing.

As the drivers started up the engines, four SS soldiers armed with machine guns jumped into each truck and sat on guard. With a deafening noise and groaning engines, the armored vehicles drove on to the gates, and as they closed behind them, the air of freedom caressed the faces of the condemned. Solemnly, the prisoners sang their national anthem. They left behind Haidari, encircled with barbed wire like a thorny crown. The thorns held torn pieces of human flesh and bloody rags, proving that escape was out of the question. Barbed wire tore the mantle of freedom.

From behind the barricade of wire, Takis and his friends watched the departing trucks until they were out of sight. They took off their caps and bowed their heads in pain. Silently, they walked back to barracks #7, but they could not look each other in the face.

Leonidas recalled his dream of the shattered fig tree.

"Another winter ahead of us—cold and endless nights of fear and famine." His thoughts came out in a prolonged sigh. "Then spring and summer, O God, away from this Dantesque *Inferno!*"

In the harrowing weeks that followed, Leonidas withdrew to his corner in barracks #7, asking himself over and over again: "Why my son and not me, Lord?" He smoked continuously and surrendered his body to the grief and anger and love that assailed him. In the blackness of his despair, he eventually found the courage to join Takis and his friends every evening after the barracks were locked. In sorrowful tones they spoke about the unjust death of Takis's father and the premature death of Leonidas's son.

CHAPTER 18

Voices of Hope

Athens, 1943

December cold lashed faces and penetrated the bones; snow covered the mountaintops and gradually visited the city. Death continued to plow the earth and dig deeper graves as thousands of people died of starvation, illness, and enemy attacks. Kalavryta—Goodsprings—a city in northern Peloponese, which in 1826 had been destroyed by the Turks, was once again razed to the ground, this time by the Nazis on December 13. On that fateful day, the entire male population of the city—1,300 men and boys—were executed on Kape's hill by German machine guns.

Sentries guarded the immortal pathways of the Acropolis. The famous stadium had become a parking lot for tanks and cannons awaiting repair. Crippled and half-sunken ships crowded the port of Piraeus, making it dysfunctional.

On December 23, early in the morning, iron monsters darkened the sky above Haidari. Dying men uttered anathemas at the airborne terror, and the green-clad knee of the regimented goose-stepping soldiers marched against hundreds of insubordinate citizens in the streets of Athens. Reprisals had increased in severity; now the life of a German soldier taken by the resistance movement cost three hundred prisoners, and that of an officer, three hundred and fifty. The supply of prisoners in Haidari remained plentiful, for it was replenished weekly by those who defied orders.

Takis, his hands in his pockets and shoulders slumped, roamed around barracks #7 checking out orphaned bunk beds. He was gazing at the spot that Dalabaras the cripple had once occupied. Mitakos, the physician, patted him on the back. "Yesterday's smiles, today's sighs. We may be next for the execution line!"

163

"Doctor, you sound pessimistic. Until our time comes, there is hope!"

"I wonder!"

"We've survived so far! By the time the trees blossom again, we may be free!"

"You and your friends are young—you have a future to look forward to."

"You're not old! Look at Leonidas and Anestis—they're much older than you, and they're looking forward to the day of freedom."

Takis had grown to enjoy the doctor's company, for his conversations were interesting and informative. At first Takis had the impression that Mitakos was a cold, callous man, one who operated without feeling; but after spending time with him, he discovered he had the heart of a child. Before the war, the doctor had been husky and enjoyed good food; but since his entry into Haidari, his face had become emaciated, his skin had lost the luster of health, and he was now able to tighten his belt five notches. As he tightened his belt, he said, "Takis, you're a caring young man; you should become a doctor."

"Oh, no, not me."

"Why not?"

"I hate to give injections and medicine to people."

"But that's what makes patients well."

"Sorry, doctor. That's torture."

Dr. Mitakos cracked a smile. "You get used to it," he said.

"I can't torture people."

"Maybe you would like to be a priest . . . save souls?"

"Let's hope we can save ourselves in this tormented land."

Takis looked at his sorrowful eyes and bushy, prematurely gray mustache. Though Mitakos's character was strong, his conflicting thoughts about survival troubled him greatly.

The two came across Leonidas crouched in a corner, his head and shoulders bowed. Nothing remained of the big man. He looked like a tormented child with frightened eyes. His mind was constantly occupied with the unjust execution of his son, and he could not carry on a conversation without weeping. It seemed as if he had suddenly discovered the evil and injustice of the world. He realized Takis and the doctor were watching him. Slowly he raised his head, tacitly begging them with his gaze to leave him alone in his mourning.

* * * * *

In the dark of night, the cigarettes burned and the light dwindled. The men were silent, as night quietly embraced them. Takis said "Good night" to Leonidas and Dr. Mitakos and joined his sleeping friends. He was dozing when he heard the first collective scream that made him jump in fear; the Nazi terrorism and their ruthless attacks against defenseless prisoners was in progress. He braced himself, waiting, preparing himself for the ordeal. He called out for the hero within to take over, for pure instinct to take control and guide him safely through the night.

Like a sandstorm in the desert, Gruber swirled into their hushed silence, his mouthpiece Niketaras at his heels. The few remaining cigarettes were quickly extinguished and hidden. Gruber wanted a detail. "Line up! All of you!" he roared.

Startled out of his sleep by this unexpected visitation, Bouras complained that it was the holiday season, Christmas, a time of celebration. Gruber, interpreting the remark as one of defiance, raised his whip and flayed indiscriminately at the prisoners, making sure that the lash landed on flesh. His whip whistled through the air as he attacked Bouras, viciously hurling insults at him with every stroke. He opened the barrack doors and ordered the prisoners out into the cold, where four SS men awaited them, one with two German shepherds. Gruber kicked and pushed the stragglers through the door, and the prisoners were confronted with a huge heap of debris in a corner, two hundred yards from the barracks.

"You have two hours to clear all this away. Unless the job is completed in time, there will be no washing or breakfast in the morning." Niketaras translated Gruber's orders, strengthening his voice to add personal impact.

The four SS men stood by to ensure that the job was thoroughly executed. "Any sign of protest will prove futile," Gruber said. The soil and wreckage outside barracks #7 was to be carried about a quarter of a kilometer and dumped at another corner of the camp.

The only vessels available for carrying the refuse were ten wicker baskets and about fifteen old gasoline cans. Anestis, the oldest in the group, approached Gruber and Niketaras and asked if they could have more containers for holding the debris. Gruber scratched his chin with the end of his whip as if to ponder. "That is your problem," he said. "Now get to work, you serpent."

Some of the prisoners dared to glare at him. Takis nudged Leonidas and whispered, "Easy!" for he could see Leonidas's fist clenched like a steel hammer. Pantsaris, in an effort to find a solution, bent over the heap of slop and filled his pockets with dirt. The others followed his example.

"If your pockets don't hold enough, fill your shirts," Gruber ordered through the interpreter.

As daybreak approached, a light, cutting wind blew across the camp. The dark sky was laden with heavy clouds, and before long, snowflakes filled the gloomy morning.

"Remove your coats," ordered Gruber. "Tie the sleeves and the necks, and use them to haul the debris."

The cold was intense, and the prisoners needed no coaxing to increase their pace. The SS men, too, increased their speed; and no matter how fast the prisoners ran, their tormentors continued to hit them with their clubs. Leonidas's knees trembled with exhaustion and anger, and aloud he cursed Gruber's birth. A crack was heard as a club descended on his head. Blood rolled down Leonidas's cheeks. Takis, trying to defend his friend, received a blow across the face from Gruber, and his nose spurted blood. They were ordered back to work.

There was so much debris that the men had made little impression on it.

"You must increase your loads," screeched Gruber.

"We've nothing to carry it in," growled Bouras.

"Use your mouths," barked Gruber.

"How?" asked Pantsaris. His pockets were full, his shirt was bulging, and his coat was filled like a sack.

"I'll show you how!" yelled Gruber through Niketaras. "Open your mouth . . . wide!" And he stuffed a handful of dirt into Pantsaris's mouth.

Pantsaris spat the soil into Gruber's face. Gruber, trying to regain his composure, lost his balance and fell. Tsakiris picked him up, threw him on the pile as if he were a piece of garbage, and shoveled handfuls of dirt into his face. He would have buried him had not the SS jumped in to rescue their colleague. The labor continued.

With the taste of dirt on their tongues and rage in their hearts, the prisoners hurried, trying to beat the deadline. The snowfall became thicker, and everything was veiled in white. Feet and hands became numb.

"Return to the barracks!" Gruber suddenly barked, as he felt the cold penetrating his boots. No warmer words were ever uttered by a tyrant's mouth.

"Bless his grandfather's bones," said Anestis, whose blood felt frozen.

It was Christmas Eve. Later in the morning, a great commotion occurred at the entrance to the camp when a work crew, who had been dismissed because of the snow, waited at the gate to be re-admitted. Each worker was searched, as usual, and cigarettes, slipped to them by those in the free world, were found and confiscated. It was the discovery of four pieces of newspaper that brought about the disturbance. The news spread quickly.

"Germans retreat in France and Belgium . . . railway stations are overrun by terrified civilians. Dutch Nazis crowding the railroad station wait all day for a train bound for Germany. The Dutch Service of the BBC announces that the fortress city of Breda, seven miles from the Dutch-Belgian border, has been liberated. The supreme general of the Allied Forces, Dwight D. Eisenhower, confirms that freedom is imminent."

Even before Gruber could piece the newspaper together, the prisoners knew what was in it. Their singing echoed through the barracks, as the men joined each other in the square: *The hour of our liberation is approaching.*

"You dirty worms, there'll be no food today!" Niketaras yelled. Within a few minutes, six large vats were brought out from the kitchen and emptied in roll-call square.

"What a shame!" Anestis said. "They killed two of my six muttons to make a Christmas meal for us—and now look at it."

"And I helped to cut the meat into tiny bits so that there would be a piece for each of us," Tsakiris said.

"Gruber is a cobra!" said Bouras. "But his day will come sooner than he thinks."

"Okay, dogs, start licking your food," commanded Gruber.

The steam from the boiling mess filled their nostrils. Steckelhuber, who could not stand the sight, departed.

* * * * *

The next few days at Haidari were difficult. The news of the approaching Americans threw the Nazis into a frenzy, and the torture of prisoners increased.

"On your faces!" ordered Gruber. The men had no recourse but to follow his instructions. However, in the front line, Leonidas remained standing. "Hey, you! Do you expect a special call? On your face!"

Necks craned to see who dared to defy the command. Takis crawled over to him and tugged at his knee. "Leonidas, you are here and still alive. Bend down," pleaded Takis.

"Takis, my brother, it is you I was looking for."

Gruber dashed between them, his whip poised. "Civilities must cease at once. Orders must be obeyed by all. Is that clear?" He raised his whip.

Leonidas, now satisfied that he had found Takis, whom he loved as a son, laid his weak, thin body face-downward. Takis was prostrate at his side, and each derived comfort from the other.

Master of their bodies, Gruber strutted among the scattered men, exchanging one or two words with the SS soldiers who were ready for action.

"I want these rats to crawl in the snow on their elbows." Gruber's voice resounded.

The SS men followed orders blindly, and with screams of *Heraus!* they used their clubs to move the prisoners.

"Crawl to the end of the yard and back!" commanded Gruber. "Those who are slow to return will be whipped and will spend Christmas Eve naked in the snow."

Like a herd of crippled animals, the prisoners attempted to carry out the order.

"Courage, fellows! Our day of freedom is at hand."

Takis tried to be optimistic, but the pain was unbearable. The men crawled like animals. The north wind blew fiercely, bringing more snow and frostbite. It was strange though that no weariness or despair could be detected in their voices as they began to sing. They sang the words that Pantsaris had awkwardly arranged to fit the tune of the "Blue Danube." He sang each verse, and they echoed it.

> Make way, you Rock, for me to pass,
> Raging Wave, I'm speaking to you,
> The Boulder on the shore—the Tyrant,
> Your doom is nigh, you Rock, will topple.
>
> Whenever I stole up shyly, licking and lapping
> At your base, for I was still enslaved,
> In pride you did upon me stare,
> Piling on me dire mockery and shame.
>
> But I, in turn, by utter stealth,
> Night and day a fatal kiss I bestowed,
> Biting and chewing into your roots
> Tore wide open, the gaping pit I hollowed.
>
> Boulder, my name is Nemesis; Time in slavery,
> Nursed with gall, contempt, and anguish,
> A tiny tear-drop was I once; behold me now,
> An all-sweeping tide! Fall down, and vanquish.

The singing died down when Anestis, his face pale and withered, could crawl no further. He fought with passion to drag himself along, but his strength failed him. He lay like a black speck in the snow.

Gruber approached, kicking at the helpless form. "You miserable specimen, why don't you crawl?"

"I can go no farther," gasped Anestis.

"Speak to me humbly, you foul old peasant!"

"Not peasant, comrade. I'm a shepherd."

"Bow your head when you talk to me."

"I'll bow my head to my flag when the time is ready."

Gruber swung his whip and brought it down on the old man's back. The helpless prisoners stopped and watched.

"I am your master now, you loathsome worm. I will crush you in no time!"

"I expect no better fate from an accursed tyrant, a repugnant race. You are a cruel and wretched creature in a world that will shame your descendants."

"Shut your filth-festered mouth. That is my last warning!"

"One day, the worm will break chains and sprout wings. Then, who knows how high the low crawling worm will fly!"

"You stubborn rebel! Do you refuse to obey my orders?"

"I would rather hang! . . . else I would be a traitor. If I were to obey, may this soil crack open and swallow me alive."

Gruber, incensed, whipped Anestis mercilessly into unconsciousness.

A shrill whistle sounded from the administration building summoning the executioners to the general's office. Gruber gave Anestis a last look as he turned on his heel and, with the SS men behind him, headed for Steckelhuber's quarters. Now the prisoners had a chance to rest.

Leonidas and Dr. Mitakos went over to Anestis, and then one by one, the prisoners made a circle around him.

"Are you hurting much?"

"Not any more." He sighed.

"Have courage, and we will survive," said Leonidas. "Each day is a week of gain in the underground. Be patient! Our patriots may be near us at this very minute! The Allies are winning." Since the news of possible freedom had arrived, Leonidas seemed more hopeful.

"Empty promises of the Allies," remarked the doctor.

"I don't blame you for your feelings," replied Leonidas.

"Greece's worst enemy is her Allies," Bouras interjected.

"Such remarks are not necessary," said Takis. "Here we all share the same fate. We've accepted our share. Let's be grateful we're still alive."

The prisoners nodded with approval. Dr. Mitakos massaged Anestis's legs and arms, and the old bones showed signs of reviving.

"We're winning the battles at the front. The Nazis are retreating in Europe." A crowd gathered around Pantsaris, and his words brought them hope. "If they find no reason to kill us, our day of liberation can-not be far off."

A sigh of anguish escaped Anestis's parched lips. He whispered one word at a time as if he were drawing water out of a bottomless well to quench his thirst. "We are the seeds of a grape being crushed between the feet of two people fighting. . . ."

"But we have hopes . . . and they are many," said Takis, clearing a space in the snow to sit beside Anestis.

Anestis looked around earnestly, painfully—a reflection of splendor, a legendary father with his many sons, before the day of departure to the angelic world. The prisoners, like little children near their father to hear yet another story, moved closer to Anestis. For a few minutes their hearts were delivered, and they shared their small hopes, remedies for relaxing a tired soul.

"When we get out of this hell," Takis said, "we'll go to Athens on foot . . . to enjoy the trees and flowers on the way."

"The first thing I'll do when I get out of here . . . ," Leonidas paused, and they all looked at him, a question in their eyes. "I'll drink twelve cups of freshly ground Greek coffee. Ha . . . ha!"

"Where are you going to get the money?" asked Tsakiris.

"Never mind the money. I'll enter the first coffee shop I find on the way. 'I'm from the Haidari camp,' I'll say. And you'll see, they'll give me anything on credit."

"And a whole carton of cigarettes," added Anestis. The thought brightened his eyes. "American cigarettes! I'll smoke them all with one light, one after the other. A thousand cigarettes! And I'll watch the smoke curling upward like a prayer ascending."

"My first stop will be at my mother's," said Dr. Mitakos. "She's the best cook in the whole world. I'll have her prepare my favorite, *youvar-lakia*— ground beef meatballs, rice, and plenty of spices. I'll eat and drink for three days, and then I'll go see my wife."

"Dr. Mitakos," interrupted Leonidas, "I think you'll need a doctor!"

And Takis, embracing his friends with a smile of yearning, said, "All we need is a small motorboat to carry us back to Lesbos, where even the stones smile."

Entangled in the net of dreams and chimeras, they laughed, like little children who believe they can grasp the sun and play with that strange bright ball. They surrendered their cares to a rainbow of hope. In the hell of Haidari, optimism was always a virtue.

"Eh, Dr. Mitakos," Takis teased, "many people need our company. Let's visit them now. It's Christmas Eve so we'll bring them presents.

I'll give them American cigarettes, and you can give them a few tasty *youvarlakia*. Let them share our dreams."

"I have some work to do," replied the doctor.

"Here or in the free world?" asked Leonidas.

"Where are we now?" He seemed nonplussed.

Takis grabbed his hand and shook it. "Let's get to our work."

"Our work is here . . . with our companions who are distressed," added Leonidas.

Takis and his friends carried Anestis back to the barracks as Anestis mused in endless dreams. A long procession followed. Carefully, they stretched the old bones on a bunk vacated by a prisoner who had been selected for the execution line, and only the dead had been spared that sorrowful sight—the sight of Dalabaras, the cripple, proudly dragging his body to join the doomed.

"Dalabaras must be smiling down at us from his heavenly home, knowing that a brave man rests in his bunk," said Takis.

CHAPTER 19

Heroes Fight Like Greeks

Athens, 1944

Winter with its gruesome tortures breathed its last, leaving haunting memories. The newspaper that had been smuggled in the previous night showed a picture of two thirteen-year-old boys who had been singing carols when the Nazis killed them because they disturbed their peace. Another article reported that three thousand Jews were executed daily in Auschwitz. Takis read the headline in bold letters:

> GREEKS NO LONGER FIGHT LIKE HEROES;
> HEROES FIGHT LIKE GREEKS.
> England claims that someday Greece
> will dominate the whole Mediterranean world.

"Soap bubbles," Takis said, crumpling the paper and disposing the evidence in the latrine. Then he sat on the latrine, resting his head in his hands, and thought.

Night embraced the prisoners as a trusted friend. Some of them fell asleep from sheer exhaustion, while others, believing that the morrow would be a better day, slumbered in relative tranquility. When he returned to his cot, Takis could not get to sleep. In the very hour when every threat seemed about to vanish, when their hope of return to life ceased to be a crazy notion, he was overcome by a new and greater pain, the loss of his father, the possibility of never again being able to see Lesbos, of loneliness, and of death.

The Nazis, obedient to the higher command of their Führer, continued to construct shelters and dig trenches. They repaired damages; they built; they imprisoned; and they killed. What else could they do because they were Nazis? Their behavior was not mediated and deliberate but followed from their true nature and from the mission they had chosen.

As he turned over on his mattress and rested his head against his arms, an old myth came knocking at the door of his memory and insisted upon being let in. The myth spoke of Pandora, who opened the box of evil from which war, pestilence, disease, famine, and all their kin escaped to drown the world. Last to emerge was the greatest evil—Hope, the great postponer, the tempter to abdication, the death blow to initiative. Takis's body jerked as he lay curled up, his knees to his forehead. "Hope is a whore, a cheat, a deceiver," he whispered. His anger surged at his inability to grasp the idea of freedom which seemed so close. For a few minutes he had been seduced by Hope, certain that someone would rescue him from his hell, but now doubts tore his heart. As he gazed through the darkness, silhouettes of the prisoners moved, and he heard a prolonged groan. It sounded as if someone were choking and needed help. He tiptoed among the sleeping bodies, careful not to tread on anyone. The old shepherd was probably having a dream.

"Barba Anestis, are you in pain?"

"No, my son."

"I heard you moaning and came to see if . . ."

"It's my heart that aches, Takis." He propped his head up on a burlap sack, his eyes glittering in the dark. The agony of human bondage had left its cruel marks on his wrinkled face. He sighed and said, "Sit with me a minute." He removed some of the rags he slept on to make room for Takis. "Why is the day of liberation taking so long to come? Why are we so passive and silent?" Anestis sighed.

"Because we are trapped under the oppressor's heavy boot."

"Then, undermine his step," Anestis said, with a ferocious look in his eyes. "What are you waiting for?"

"I'm beginning to hear the bells of freedom," Takis said in a hushed voice. "Any day now it will happen."

"I'm tired of this ordeal," roared the shepherd.

When he returned to his place and looked at Pantsaris, who sat near the light, time lost its desperate clutch on him. Suddenly he no longer felt afraid. *One more spring—at most, one more summer,* he thought, his mind searching for that time of 1944 as if it were around the corner. *Three more months or even three more years. . . . We'll survive.*

"For us, this is surely the last act. Winter has ended and spring is at its peak. There's no longer any reason to doubt that this is our last spring in captivity," Pantsaris said. Next to them slept Bouras and Tsakiris. They seemed peaceful, but something woke them up—maybe a dream.

"Pantsaris, soon you will sit at your own desk with plenty of light, notebooks, and pencils, and you'll fill pages of memories. There'll be no interruptions from invaders," Takis said.

"Aren't you guys going to get some sleep?" asked Bouras.

"I can't sleep. Pantsaris and I are chatting."

Pantsaris looked at him, and time paused in its flow. The past mingled with what was to come and nothing existed but that instant—that single instant of life which envious time itself could not snatch away.

Pantsaris, blinking his eyes, caught a sluggish beacon from a light bulb in the far corner and tried to rewrite his poem. "It's called 'Sunset at Noon,' a poem about Fotis," he said, but I need to refine it."

"Do you think Leonidas could bear it?" Tsakiris asked.

"Leonidas is emotionally strong; he would probably want to hear it," Bouras said.

"Let's hear it," said Takis.

> Who could expect
> My son's sun to set at noon?
> Who could expect
> A youth to die so soon?
>
> Lofty ideas our Fotis thought,
> Spoke of love and liberty,
> A world of peace for everyone,
> Justice and harmony.
>
> But the mechanized vultures
> Visited our land one day,
> Devoured innocent people,
> Fotis, they did away.

"A poem is not enough to heal a father's pain," Tsakiris said.

"Keep it in your collection. Don't let Leonidas read it just yet," suggested Bouras.

"The poem is an appropriate tribute to anyone killed unjustly," said Takis. He squatted next to Bouras. "I'm sick and tired of this living hell," he whispered.

"They'll probably dispose of us like rats in a trap," Bouras said, and instantly regretting his ugly thought, he reached out and touched Takis on the arm. "But we'll fight the bastards to our last breath. Remember our oath?"

Tsakiris, upon hearing these words, felt a resurgence of revenge. "What are we waiting for?" he said.

Anestis, who had fallen into a deep sleep, let out a high-pitched snore. He was probably dreaming about grazing his sheep in the verdant valley of Thessaly. In his present state it made no difference to him whether or not the Germans ever left Greece. The snoring reached a crescendo and faded out.

Haidari vibrated as aircraft roared overhead. The prisoners stood apprehensively against the walls. The air creeping into the barracks was warm, and the sky was hazy. Earlier in the night, Allied airplanes had bombarded the harbor of Piraeus, turning it into an inferno, sending smoke and flames soaring high.

Firm steps cracked on the cement walkway bordering barracks #7. Miserable and sleepy, the night guard followed in Gruber's footsteps like a butcher's dog.

The door opened. The beam of a flashlight cutting through the darkness searched the room. Faces etched with lines of anguish gazed at the light. Did this herald Gruber's routine inspection?

Gruber remained in the doorway, scanning the sullen faces, and turning around to depart, he realized the guard was no longer behind him. The prisoners were also aware that Gruber had been left unprotected. As he tried to back out, he felt their fierce eyes upon him, and in a flash he was knocked to the floor.

"*Lassen Sie mich nicht sterben,*" he pleaded.

Tsakiris stuffed his mouth with a dirty shirtsleeve while Bouras held a dagger to his Adam's apple—Fotis's dagger, which Leonidas had given to Bouras on the day his son had been selected for the execution line.

"Don't kill him!" shouted Leonidas. "Grab his revolver and cut his belt off."

Takis would have liked Bouras to finish the job, but the consequences could be too dire.

Leonidas must have a reason for wanting him alive, Bouras thought. Quickly he removed Gruber's belt and handed the gun to Leonidas. Like a whirlwind, the prisoners dragged the guard back into the room and tied him back to back with Gruber. They laid them between two mattresses, covering them with a third. The two captives froze in fear.

Discovering the absence of guards on the grounds, Takis, his friends, Leonidas, and Dr. Mitakos made their way to headquarters. Since the previous evening, the Nazi retreat was finally in operation. It had been decided that Haidari should be demolished, but the sudden nighttime air raid and the rapidity of the guerrillas' advance threw the German plans into confusion and left the Nazis no choice but to flee before daybreak. Dark shadows flitted through the grounds and vanished.

Mitakos had Gruber's gun, and Leonidas carried the machine gun that belonged to the guard. Takis pushed open the door of headquarters. The air in the room was permeated with cigar smoke and fumes of alcohol. In a state of stupor, Steckelhuber was sprawled on a leather sofa. He stumbled to his feet and reached for his pistol, but Tsakiris had already relieved him of his belt. Trying to maintain his dignity, the general pompously arched over his desk.

"Every inch of Haidari is equipped with deadly weapons, dear Greek comrades. One blow of my whistle and you will be dead instantly," Steckelhuber announced, dialing the phone. He clicked it nervously. There was no sound. Slowly he put the receiver down. "Don't be foolish. Hauptmann Heins Gruber should be back any minute, and then . . . need I tell you what will happen?" He studied the faces full of determination and courage, and tried to keep his composure.

"Comrade, don't take another step," ordered Takis. Tsakiris came up behind him, pressing the muzzle of his gun into the general's spine. "General Steckelhuber, hands up!"

"Comrades, I have been a just man. What concerns me is that Hauptmann will be back soon, and then all of you will be *kaput*."

"That abominable creature is now our hostage. We have plans for you, too," said Takis.

"Son of the American, how far do you think you can go?"

"The day of retribution has come. You can answer your own question, Comrade Criminal."

"I didn't kill your father. I am not responsible for his death."

They placed the general in a small room, handcuffed him, and tied him to a water pipe.

Dr. Mitakos and Tsakiris kept guard. "Move quickly," shouted Tsakiris to his friends. His mouth felt dry; his eyes darted fear. "Don't leave us here too long. The butchers may return at any moment."

The others shuttled back to barracks #7. Against the darkness of the sky the unmanned watchtowers pillared high, and the prisoners scurried from ward to ward exchanging words of hope. "Comrades, get up! Let's go out and fight!"

Gruber and his guard were still bound back to back when they returned. The guard was dead. Bouras freed Gruber, and throwing the dagger on the floor, issued his challenge: "Okay, Master Butcher, let's you and me fight!"

Gruber picked up the knife, tested its sharpness, and looked at Bouras vehemently. With trembling hearts, the prisoners gathered around to witness the event.

"I don't believe in cold-blooded murder. I'll handle him alone," announced Bouras, and in a flash he attacked his enemy and floored him. Gruber squirmed and struggled, but Bouras's steely fingers were relentless as they squeezed. Gruber dropped the knife, gasping for the last breath.

The prisoners, satisfied with the retribution, applauded. "Death to the Nazis!" they shouted in chorus.

Gruber lay lifeless next to the guard on the dirty floor. To spare the others from the ugly sight, a prisoner covered them with a tattered blanket. A moment of silence filled the room.

Christoforos, who had spent the night praying in front of an icon, began to repeat his familiar message: "Humans! O humans! Blood-thirsty brutes and sanguinary snakes . . . why so much hate?"

Takis grabbed Bouras by the arm and said, "We've got to move fast. Tsakiris is waiting in the lion's den." But in front of them paused Christoforos with uplifted arms: "Deeds of great daring do not belong to the weak. Death is our end by fate's decree . . . we are creatures of a day."

"Christoforos, we're a step away from the free world. Let's get out of this hell," Takis shouted.

Christoforos would not yield. Then Pantsaris and Takis grabbed him by the arms and hastened out of barracks #7 as he continued his monologue: "What is man? What is he not? Man is the shadow of a dream. But when the light, the gift of God, comes to him, bright is his way and sweet is his life."

"Those are Pindar's profound words," said Dr. Mitakos, a beacon of hope flashing through his tortured mind.

"Gruber should not have been killed," said Leonidas to Bouras.

"It was a fair fight . . . gave him my dagger to protect himself. I fought with my bare hands . . . not a drop of blood was spilled."

"But you know there will be reprisals. Do you know what Gruber will cost us?" said Leonidas.

Demos removed Gruber's boots and searched his pockets. "Don't feel sorry for him! He was a monster!"

"I had an inner urge to kill him," replied Bouras. "I made that promise to myself on the day I first witnessed his cruelty."

"You did him a favor, Bouras. He was a miserable creature. The crimes he committed were slowly choking him to death." Demos saw no reason for pity.

"Now that I've done it, Demos, I feel at peace with myself. They can cut me up into a thousand pieces, if they catch me."

The sound of a jeep approaching silenced the prisoners. Pantsaris made the sign of the cross.

"Keep me covered," said Takis to Leonidas, who still held the machine gun against his breast. "I want to see what that jeep is all about."

With Leonidas at his heels, Takis tiptoed outside and watched the jeep approach. Against the low and gloomy sky waved the Greek flag attached to the jeep's antenna. The driver stopped, and four armed men jumped out of the jeep, moving quickly. "*Paidia Eleftheria*," they shouted.

"*Eleftheria*—freedom at last!" cried Takis. He saw their dark features and khaki uniforms—and knew the weapons slung across their shoulders were not a threat.

He felt protected. "Come, compatriots, take a look at barracks #7." Leonidas pointed the way. The prisoners with a bittersweet smile could not quite understand what was going on.

Anestis was curled up in his corner in a desperate position, his knees to his chest, his elbows squeezed against his sides, and his hands like wedges clutching his shoulders.

"No more sighs, Anestis," Takis said, standing over him. "Stand up, my friend; the time of freedom is here."

A shrill cry escaped Anestis's lips as he rose from his corner.

The hour of liberty rang out grave and muffled and filled the souls of the prisoners with joy. Yet the pain of the horrors they had seen and endured permeated them, so that they wished they could wash their consciences and memories clean from the foulness of the Haidari camp.

"Fellow prisoners . . . freedom at last!" shouted Takis to the crowd.

Dozens of jeeps carrying more liberators sped through the gates of purgatory, breaking the chains of slavery and degradation.

Most of the prisoners were ecstatic and ran to greet the messengers of freedom; some fell on their knees in prayer and kissed the soil; others could not comprehend that the Nazi occupation had truly come to an end.

"You must go to headquarters. We have two men there holding General Erwin Steckelhuber captive," Takis explained.

"Let's barbecue the general," yelled Demos, and many joined him in jeering, "Let's barbecue the barbarian in a slow fire!"

But a familiar figure stood up and, jutting out his huge jaw, proclaimed, "Humans! O humans! Bloodthirsty brutes and sanguinary snakes . . . why so much hate? Why so much self-destruction?"

Takis led the way to headquarters and pointed to the general, bound hand and foot and guarded by Tsakiris and the doctor.

"No chance of him escaping," said a bearded liberator.

* * * * *

At the crack of dawn, restless sleepers woke as light filtered through the shuttered windows. Hitler's mechanized army had emerged from all directions and was pouring down Stadiou Street to Salonica highway on their way to the Yugoslavian border. It was rumored that powerful Allied armored units were blocking the major highways. Because of the curfew, the populace had been unable to leave their houses during the night to investigate the truth of the rumors. They watched incredulously as the shattered remnants of the Nazi army from Athens and central Greece streamed past their doors.

By the time the sun's rays were embracing the old Parthenon, excitement among the Athenians was intense. The city itself was quieter than usual, although the familiar commotion of military jeeps could be heard. General Steckelhuber and several officers of lower rank had already been escorted to the liberators' headquarters in Constitution Square and held as captives.

By 10:00 A.M., hundreds of handsome youths and brave Evzons, mounted on their steeds in symmetrical lines, were in control. They were a glorious sight in deep-blue velvet jackets embroidered with gold and spangled with golden florins. Their shining scimitars glinted in the bright sunlight, and huge ebony pistols hung on either side of their leather saddles. Their short *fustanella*—pleated tunics—white woolen socks and shoes with pom-poms completed the picture.

As the strutting steeds catapulted around Constitution Square, their manes gleamed like a cloud of blazing hay. Following them in twos and threes was the army of liberation. Long mustaches intertwined with their beards, and they wore sashes of ammunition across their broad breasts and shoulders. Their swords were fastened to a thick belt around their waists, and their bayonets hung on their right side.

In shredded clothes, hundreds of prisoners who had survived the Haidari holocaust formed an awkward line and joined the parade. The four friends marched with the men from barracks #7 and initiated their anthem, "One More Spring," and gradually all the freed captives sang in chorus.

The whole populace joined the march of victory as the ringing church bells filled the air. Cannons bellowed from the slope of Lycabettus, and the blue and white flag was once again raised on the hill of the Acropolis. Priests and bishops, ceremoniously dressed in gold vestments, marched in the procession, chanting doxologies and thanksgiving prayers. Altar boys, holding precious sacred tapers, slowly wended their way with the pressing crowds toward the monument of the "Unknown Soldier." The streets were strewn with palms and myrtles, filling the air with a fragrant scent. Wave upon wave of people emerged from their doors, now decorated with flowers, and joined in the festivity of freedom.

Four magnificent horses in silver-studded harness and saddle, approached the monument of the "Unknown Soldier." Their riders, decorated with medals and ribbons, held in their white-gloved hands the flags of the Allies—America, Britain, Greece, and Russia. Damascenos, archbishop of Athens and of all Greece, vested in ecclesiastical raiment, was escorted to the old and new altar of liberty. Surrounded by priests and deacons, the archbishop lifted his voice in fervent supplication. The crowd was hushed. Suddenly a fleet of American aircraft furrowed the Attica sky, breaking the silence and leaving symbols of victory. When the roaring planes vanished over the Aegean islands, the words of the archbishop re-echoed:

> O sacred shadows of the brave
> Who have felt captivity's pain,
> Who have tasted the bitterness of slavery,
> Who have given us an example—
> Bless our struggle.
> Give us strength to prove ourselves worthy
>   of your noble achievements.
> Help us to banish any barbaric and contemptuous
>   conqueror from our glorious land,
> And let Freedom, the much sought-after treasure,
>   be ours again.

Takis and his friends climbed to the top of the marble steps of the parliament and watched the mayor of Athens placing a wreath at the foot of the "Unknown Soldier." Then the military band played:

> Greece will never die,
> She is afraid of none,
> A few moments she needed to revive,
> And again a new glory she's won.

Activities in the square continued. The leaders of the liberators held up their heads proudly. Earlier in the morning they had put to death many of the Greek traitors, Stavros Niketaras being the last to spill his fetid blood. At gun point, they led their German captives to the Chamber of Deputies, a colonnaded building that had preserved its ancient appeal, and was now occupied by the EAM—the National Liberation Front. There the war criminals were held for sentencing.

Takis and his friends took Nike Street, a preferred shortcut, and found themselves scrambling over the rubble of collapsed walls, broken electric columns, entangled wires, debris, rubbish, and buried wagons—apparently the result of a recent bombing.

A crowd of spectators waited in front of the Chamber of Deputies.

The four friends inched their way into the courtyard and stood on a bench to witness the sentencing. When an EAM chief approached them and ordered them to move, Takis stepped down and tapped his chest. He felt as tall as the chief and unafraid.

"Sir," he said boldly, "those three up there and myself are survivors of the Haidari holocaust."

"Really?" said the chief in disbelief.

"Really," said Takis, and looking him straight in the eye, he proposed to unbutton his shirt. "Under this tattered shirt, I have scars to prove it."

"Comrade, you're one of us." The chief saluted, raising his fist.

A stone's throw away, the German captives waited their lot. Steckel-huber and his constituency witnessed the fury of the liberators and shrank instinctively against the high wall of the courtyard. The once roaring lion of a general was now chained in fear. The devil's band of subalterns had turned on him. His time was fast running out. The armed chiefs demanded vengeance on the German captives. Standing in a semicircle in front of the general, they hurled insults and worked themselves into a frenzy. Certain of impunity, they rushed forward, bold and snarling.

Two bearded mountaineers wearing their sash of ammunition descended the marble stairway of the main building and marched toward the mob. One held the accusation, and the other waved a sheet of yellow paper containing the sentence: slow death.

The crowd, eager to play a part in the punishment, became more unruly, a pandemonium of insults, screaming, uncontrolled emotions. The general, sweating and pleading, was unable to make any impression.

"Stop it, you fools! Listen for a moment."

Everyone turned to see who had dared to interrupt the execution of the sentence.

An old man with a venerable face emerged from the crowd to project a word of caution. Behind him followed Takis and his friends, and next to them, Leonidas and Dr. Mitakos. Silence prevailed as hundreds of listeners felt the magnetic power of a voice.

"My children, there isn't much life left in me. I have seen many deaths. I have lived through the ordeal of Haidari," Anestis said. "I know this man. He is a vicious beast. No punishment can atone for the numberless crimes he has committed. But we will not kill him." Anestis shook his head. "No."

"Yes, we will. He deserves death . . . slow death," screamed the liberators, and their words were echoed by a vindictive crowd.

Anestis, catching his breath, and with the help of his cane, trudged to a spot in front of the general. "If we must avenge blood with blood, then kill me. There's still some blood in my veins." He raised his cane high and shook it. Then his voice turned soft, mellow, and prophetic. "Today is the day we have all hoped and prayed for, the day of independence. A new page starts in our glorious Greek history. Let's not sully it with the blood of vengeance. Now, take this man and show him the Greek spirit. But guard him."

Takis and his friends, with mixed emotions, followed the two guards escorting the general to headquarters. Anestis pushed his way through the dispersing crowd, managing to exchange a handshake with Leonidas and Dr. Mitakos. The four friends encircled Anestis, hugging and kissing him. It was difficult to part.

"Barba Anestis, are we going to see each other again?" Takis asked.

"My sons, I'm old and weary. I must return to the mountains of Thessaly and rest these old bones."

"We'll visit you, then," proposed the other three.

"You're too young to climb." He shook his head in wonder. In the bleary eyes of the old shepherd, the young men saw an end to a painful story.

Dr. Mitakos, witnessing an exchange of sadness, reached out and grabbed Leonidas by the arm. "Come," he said, "let's make some plans. We must meet again and celebrate. Lighten up, comrades." He tapped everyone's shoulder gently. "And you, young man," he said, pointing an admonishing finger at Takis, "I still believe you should become a doctor."

"A doctor?" The three friends glanced at Takis, a smirk spliced on the corners of their mouths.

"Yes, a doctor," said Mitakos, and addressing the four of them, he added, "All of you, comrades, return to the classroom and get some education."

"Thanks, Dr. Mitakos," they said.

"It's time to return to our roots," Takis said. "Some day you might come to our island."

As the feelings about their separation surfaced, Takis and his friends became impatient. They agreed to get to the harbor of Piraeus as soon as possible and board the first available boat for Lesbos.

That same September evening on the silvery Aegean, a small motorboat mounted the waves. Among the passengers was the undivided quartet, Takis, Bouras, Pantsaris, and Tsakiris. They were excited, and yet feelings of sadness lingered over experiences at Haidari, the price of freedom, and their survival, a reward for their struggle.

CHAPTER 20

A Day of Resurrection

Lesbos, September 9, 1944, Midnight

The Nazis unexpectedly besieged Moria in their determination to annihilate the liberators. Innocent populations could not be spared. Papavasile secretly contacted thirty-six families, and by 12:30 A.M., many men had joined his barefooted battalion. They crossed their rifles, swore "Freedom or death," and attacked.

Feeling compelled by another-worldly force, Papavasile, sure footed as a mountain goat, leaped over the rocks, faced the enemy and fought, sprang over ditches, and played with death, his bayonet piercing the guts of those who would have destroyed his people. Terror formed a mound of heroes.

A company of Nazis was ensconced on the top of St. Demetrios's hill. Papavasile maneuvered his men swiftly, and with strategic dexterity took the adversary from the rear. The bayonet battle, which began at one o'clock in the morning, raged for more than an hour.

Nailed like arrows of fate to the earth, bodies shook spasmodically. Moans from the lacerated fighters filled the air.

The butchering between the Greek liberators and the enemy ended with the surrender of the remaining soldiers, after a harrowing blood bath.

Papavasile, the bearded priest in the khaki uniform, emerging from the shadows of death, looked poignantly at the leaders of the liberators and thundered, "I want you to promise God, here in my presence, that there will be no more killing."

"What if they try to escape?" protested Antonis and Paraskos, two ferocious, mustached mountaineers.

"I said 'No more killing,'" the priest said.

"I saw you in action—you killed," argued Antonis, pointing to the priest's blood-stained bayonet.

183

"It's written: 'There is a time to kill and a time to heal.'" He placed his hand on the shoulder of the champion and added, "It's time for healing."

He watched as the liberators, at the point of a bayonet, rounded up their prisoners, a quarter of a company.

Still holding his rifle, he trudged downhill. Mind and heart set on his homeward journey, he marched forward in sleepless anguish, taking each step with effort. His feet, tired and sore inside a pair of old boots, stumbled among corpses.

He had gone about a hundred yards when he saw the two cypress trees where he had buried the two brothers, and there he took a moment's rest. His face tense, eyes brimming, and beard bristling in the late-night breeze. Dense clouds unfurled a nightmarish shadow over the western mountains, chilling his spine. The treetops seemed to lean toward each other, whispering what his priestly heart longed to sing: *Dead brothers of the mountain, the sea, and the field, lend me your fiery spirit to shape a new life under the light of your sacrifice.*

Inner conflict had been cutting through his heart since he had left the battle scene. *Fortunate is the man who has been spared the distress of this dreadful night,* he thought. The nearer he came to the foot of the hill, the heavier his weapon seemed to grow. He removed his old cotton belt and was about to clean his bayonet when he realized that the steel blade was inviolate, shining as if it were new. He felt an aura of relief in his heart at the mysterious disappearance of the blood stains and trudged along repentant, asking God for his forgiveness.

The September sun, like a divine chisel, etched colors in St. Basil's Church. Papavasile entered with a trembling heart, feeling the weight of his rifle. Step by step, with eyes raised toward the icon of Christ, he walked toward the altar and rested his rifle on the holy table. In the oak trees outside, a few sparrows twittered in harmony a Byzantine chant: *Glory to God. . . . Peace on earth!* A sigh escaped him, destroying every dismal thought. Softly he uttered: "Christ is risen . . . the enemy is conquered." In the ghostly silence he moved and then lit the censer. The fragrance spread throughout the church. Gratefully, he breathed in the scent of the incense. "Christ is risen . . . the enemy is conquered," he chanted, and the church echoed his words.

"This is the second resurrection!" he exclaimed. He wanted to run and proclaim his message of freedom to the world, but his feet seemed nailed to the floor. In front of the icon of Archangel Michael, he shuddered in trepidation, seeing the face of the Archangel turning red and the silver sword seeming to drip blood. "It must have been the Archangel Michael who fought through me last night," he said. In his mind, he relived the scene: the flashing of the bayonets, the confusion of faces, the Greeks and Germans, and the fury as they shed each other's blood. He was sobbing uncontrollably now and begging God for forgiveness. He heard his own voice pleading with God, a voice asking for mercy.

In the vaulted dome, the icon of Christ, Sustainer of the Universe, came alive and appeared to approach him. The church was flooded with resplendent light. "Christ is risen!" The priest leaned against a marble pillar to support his shaking limbs. Awe-struck, he lifted his head and inhaled a sweet aroma.

"I have returned, Archangel of God. Pray for my forgiveness; I have killed in the name of freedom."

Eyes blurred with mixed emotions, he could still see and hear the clanging of bayonets and the roaring thunder of the machine gun as bodies were stabbed and hacked to death. It was a harrowing event when he embedded his bayonet in the chest of the enemy. Jesus had commanded him to love his enemies, a commandment he had defied.

Now in the church, he heard the echo of a choir of a hundred saints singing: *Christ is risen. Death is destroyed!* A vapor of guilt that clouded his soul lifted. He threw himself at the feet of the Archangel and wept. He sighed, "O Divine Land, drenched with blood . . . !" And sobbing, he stretched out his arms to embrace the Infinite. No music, no voices ever sounded as harmoniously as that celestial melody which now pervaded his heart. The melody filled the church like the fragrance of autumn, sweet and ineffable. A window blew open, and a gentle breeze caressed the priest's weathered face, reassuring him that *life is sweet, and death is darkness.* He lifted his rifle from the altar and raised his eyes in awe, focusing on the ancient icons. The faces of the saints radiated colors of warmth.

"Lord God, I place this weapon at your feet, with faith and gratitude," prayed the priest. "I don't want to touch it again as long as I live." He made the sign of the cross. "Our land has been drenched with blood. In an uneven combat, each Greek son fought with confidence and determination. I, too, bent low and exchanged your cross for a rifle; I fought; I killed, defending freedom." He gazed at the icon of Jesus, who returned the gaze. "Since your stern will, O God, has ordered that I survive, I pray that you give me the strength to comfort my mourning people. Today our freedom is your first gift to us." Crying, he collapsed on the floor, and when he woke up, it was morning.

* * * * *

Proud sea gulls glided through the morning mist, moving with one mind in reverie and occasionally diving for a fresh catch. After sixteen endless hours on a boat crossing the Aegean, Takis and his friends, herded together with other passengers, like a flock of wild goats, returned to liberated Lesbos, officially freed on September 10, 1944. As they approached the harbor, their hearts beat faster, and they clenched each other's hands, reassuring themselves that they were home at last—a haven where they could hear the voices of those they loved.

Dawn swept across the harbor, barely wetting its heels in the gold-tipped waves. As their sea legs gradually accustomed themselves to the land, Takis knelt and kissed the ground. Silently, his friends followed suit. "Home at last!" Takis whispered.

"Thank God," said Bouras, and in the same breath he blurted out, "I wonder if Merope remembers me . . . would I like to smell her sheets tonight!"

"You've a one-track mind," said Pantsaris, pushing him gently aside.

"She's probably married by now," said Tsakiris.

"I don't think anybody in Moria will recognize us," Takis said. Then he stretched his arms and embraced the others. "Can you believe it? We're back home alive!"

Pantsaris began to sing and the rest joined in:

> One more spring,
> Another season,
> No more treason.
> End of oppression, end of cruelty,
> We paid with blood for our liberty.

The four friends had changed dramatically. Although emaciated, their bodies had lost the boyish gangly appearance and had taken on adult dimensions; they had grown taller and their bony shoulders were broad. Bouras and Takis nurtured a mustache. They were dressed like army veterans in clothes provided by the American War Relief program on the day they were released from Haidari—new brown shirts, khaki pants, and army boots. They were particularly fond of the boots, which added a few inches to their height.

Takis said, "Your mustache could do with some fertilizer, Bouras. It looks kind of bald in spots."

"How about a dose of manure?" said Pantsaris. "We've got plenty of chicken manure for you at our place."

Their voices, now deep and manly, rang through the air as they followed the coast road to Moria, a road they had traveled together many times in the years gone by. Their singing and chattering ended abruptly when they saw a group of girls returning from work in the fields. The girls giggled among themselves and made eyes at the boys as they came toward them.

"Good morning," said Bouras, the fascinating group making his blood circulate freely.

"Good morning," replied the girls, laughing and quickening their pace.

The four friends gaped at them, their eyes following the movement of the girls' buttocks. It had been a long time since girls had crossed their path.

"Someone slap me," said Tsakiris. "Am I dreaming?"

"I don't think so," replied Takis. "Look! Up on the castle!"

The Greek flag with its blue and white cross had replaced the accursed swastika and was flapping in the morning breeze of freedom. Takis felt his joy ebbing. He gazed at the flag, walking silently. Memories rippled in his mind: the day of the Nazi invasion, his bike—his precious bike—and the ugly Nazi who had snatched it away, the day he dared to steal the swastika. He wondered, too, about Eleni. *Will she recognize me after all this time?* he wondered. Pantsaris, noticing Takis's withdrawal, said, "It's time to sing. No more sadness."

"When we get to Moria, let's celebrate for a whole week," said Tsakiris. He looked at Bouras. He, too, seemed preoccupied. "What's with you men? You'd think we were at a funeral!"

Bouras was concerned about Eleni. What condition was she in? Was she still in the convent? Or had the Germans taken her away? Was Aunt Pelagia still alive? Worrisome thoughts tormented him.

The September sun provided Moria with an abundance of warmth. The houses looked refreshed, and the windows were open wide to let in the fresh air. Feathery floats of pigeons strutted in the streets, and flocks of swallows soared over the town announcing the return of the four friends. Moria had recovered from the Nazi ordeal and looked different—the houses, smaller, the streets narrower—and as they walked across the town, even the sky appeared lower.

"Everything seems to have changed," said Takis.

As they went by the marketplace, people greeted the four friends and circled around them.

"Welcome back!" a group of by-standers shouted.

"Welcome back!" shouted the merchants.

"How tall you've all grown!" said Apostolos, the butcher.

"How handsome you've grown!" Stratya said. "Do I have some beautiful brides for you!"

"Where have you been all this time? It's years since I saw you," Niko, Merope's son, screamed. He, too, had shot up like a cypress tree.

Takis picked him up and held him high in the air. "Niko, I sure have missed you."

"Oh, just look at you! Such good looks! If only I were a few years younger," said Merope, pursing her lips as if she were kissing them with passion.

"People of Moria, step aside." Alexis dashed out of his tavern. The news that Takis and his friends were on their way had traveled fast. He hugged and kissed them and gave each an affectionate slap on the face. "You had me worried to death. I thought you had died in Haidari's hell."

"And that's what I thought had happened to you," said Takis.

Averof prison was not that bad for me—but what they did to the two Americans is beyond talking about." Alexis bit his lip as he recollected the torture. "And they compelled me to watch their cruelty."

"Are you talking about the two merchant marines who brought the weapons to Lesbos?" asked Takis.

"Yep. You remember Dan Cohen, the American who fell in love with Nitsa, Cambas's daughter? And the other tall, chubby, guy—I forget his name?"

"How did the Nazis get hold of them?" Bouras asked.

"Listen, big pricks, I'll tell you that story some other day," Alexis said. "It's such a sad one. . . ."

"Are they alive?" asked Takis.

"Dan Cohen and I came to Lesbos on the same boat a week ago. He's staying with the priest."

"Is he going to marry Nitsa Cambas?" Pantsaris asked.

"I don't think he knows that she became a nun," said Alexis.

"That's sad," Takis said, knowing that his Eleni had also found refuge in the Convent of St. Mary.

"All of you go home and get some rest. We have a big celebration ahead of us," Alexis said.

"I'll bring some fried potato peels," Tsakiris said, shaking his head with a joyful smile, and to his friends, he added, "The wolf sheds his coat once a year; his disposition, never. Alexis never changes either."

As they tarried proudly at the edge of the marketplace the villagers shook their hands, but Bouras sensed a coldness. The men, in particular, were hostile to him, although they were friendly with his three friends. Dismissing a tinge of jealousy, Bouras hurried to Aunt Pelagia's hut. The greetings he received at home were joyfully intense but short lived. Bouras suspected something was wrong when he noticed a bittersweet expression in the eyes of the two women. Eleni had grown into a very attractive, mature woman with a beautiful face and full breasts. She wore a black dress that accentuated her figure. Aunt Pelagia had developed the habit of repeating herself, but she was aging gracefully. She cried with happiness, but both she and Eleni appeared apprehensive. He was about to ask them what was wrong when his eyes caught a glimpse of a picture on the mantelpiece—a picture of a Nazi soldier standing outside their hut.

"Who's that?" asked Bouras, annoyance in his voice.

Eleni blushed but said nothing. Pelagia gathered her thoughts together and stood beside Bouras. She was amazed at how much taller and stronger he had grown.

"I'll explain. Come with me," she said as she led the way to the loft. "Eleni, get fresh water from the well; your brother must be thirsty."

When Bouras was told that his sister was engaged to a German, he was wild with rage and threatened to kill them both. He believed his sister would be better off dead than married to a Nazi. The memories of Haidari haunted him. In his madness, he ran out into the field and along the tracks that brought him to St. Basil's Church. *Papavasile will intervene,* he thought. *He will understand that the wedding must be stopped.*

Papavasile's penetrating eyes could see Bouras's turmoil, unraveling the mass of pain in a survivor's soul. He embraced Bouras and said, "Son, Christ gave us a unique commandment: 'It's good to love those that love you. But I want you to love your enemies.' Our whole nation has suffered. And I'll tell you something else: Fritz Bittrich saved Moria from a total holocaust. God works even through our weaknesses."

"I don't understand."

"A day before their retreat, the Nazis wired the electric factory with explosives, set to go off and blow up all the important facilities of the island the following morning at five o'clock, the hour when the workers begin their day. Fritz, who knew of the secret plan, went to the factory and ordered it closed until noon. Meanwhile, the Germans retreated."

"Where is Fritz now?" Bouras's curiosity rose.

"The liberators are taking him around the villages and telling the people of his heroic deed."

"How did Eleni get involved with him?"

"Bouras, you're a man now. Don't ask too many questions."

"What shall I tell my friends? That Eleni is marrying an enemy who is now a hero?"

"Eleni is a heroine." The priest smiled with compassion. He knew more about human needs than Bouras would ever learn. He did not tell him that Eleni had found Fritz three days after a battle between Greek guerrillas and a German garrison. Three German soldiers had been killed, and Fritz had been counted among the twenty-one wounded.

"Why is she marrying a Nazi?" Bouras persisted.

"Because love conquers our human weaknesses. Eleni loves him."

"An enemy?"

"He loves her."

"Why?"

"Love, like God, cannot be asked 'Why?' They have reasons of their own. Try to understand."

"I understand nothing," Bouras complained as he made a movement to leave.

"I understand your anger, but in time. . . ." The priest put his arm around Bouras's shoulder. "In time, we will all understand life and its adversities."

Bouras was too distraught to understand anything. He left the priest and, in his despair, sought his friends.

Katerina had taken Takis's brother and sister on a pilgrimage to St. Mary's Convent. Takis took off his boots and waited. The smell of flowers—the geraniums, the peach trees—brought back the sweet memories of his childhood: delicious dinners steaming on the table, Katerina's passion for perfection, his father's pride in America, Kiki's innocent fears, Jimmy's mischief making, and a delicate moth always fluttering around the lamp when his father was reading the newspaper.

The bare floors creaked as he walked from room to room. The Nazis had removed even the carpets and left little of significance—a wooden sofa and a few straw chairs. On the wall at the entrance to the living room hung two framed pictures—one of Asimakis as a young man in America. This was his father's cherished photograph, taken when he was serving Franklin D. Roosevelt, president of the United States. Asimakis had been a proud maitre d' at the Washington Hotel in the state capital. The echo of his father's voice reverberated: *America, the land of freedom and opportunity. Abundance of everything—food, clothes, warm houses, recreation, and freedom. There you can go to school and become a doctor!*

I don't want to be a doctor. I don't even want to go to your America.

Why not? Bacon and eggs for breakfast, prime ribs and potatoes for dinner. . . . America, here we come!

Takis had made no comment. *I prefer olives and beans and my Eleni,* he thought.

But since his father's death, America seemed like a promise to be fulfilled—a promise to his father.

In the other picture, Kiki and Jimmy stood on either side of their father—they were much younger then. Kiki was pale and skinny with blunt curls and hazel eyes; Jimmy's head looked too big for his body, his short pants displayed his spindly legs, and his eyes gleamed with high spirits. Takis smiled. *I doubt I'll recognize them now*, he thought, wondering where they were.

Melancholy overcame him. No life, no furniture, nothing much except memories remained in their wretched house. In his mind's ears echoed the family laughter, a harmony of seraphic tunes. Slowly he descended the creaking staircase. His legs felt like lead. He slipped out of the door into the street. With long steady strides, he took the road going west, leading to Pantsaris's house. A little girl about seven years old in a white dress smiled at him, and he forced himself to return her smile.

"I see you're all dressed up. Where're you going?" he asked.

"Today I'm going to a party, and on the Day of the Holy Cross, I'm going to a wedding!"

"To a wedding? Who's getting married?

"Haven't you heard? I guess you aren't from Moria," she said. "A girl who used to be a nun is marrying a German."

"Marrying a German?" Takis felt a blow in his lower abdomen. He took a deep breath and offered a silent prayer: *Oh God, prevent from happening the ugly thought that crosses my mind.* "What's her name?"

"She's called Eleni," said the girl as she waved good-bye.

Takis's vision darkened. He cried, and with each tear, his pain increased. *It can't be true!* he thought. *And if it is, I must prevent the wedding. Besides, Bouras would never permit such a thing.* He kicked at the stones along the way and broke off a few branches of a lemon tree. His personal pain over the loss of his father and the hardships he had endured were not as hard to bear as was Eleni's betrayal. *Perhaps the little girl in white was mistaken. Eleni would never do such a thing!*

Bouras had just finished talking to Papavasile and was also on his way to Pantsaris's house when Takis met him. Bouras's eyes were swollen and red.

"Is it true?" asked Takis.

"I guess you've heard the news," Bouras sighed.

"So it is true!"

"Yes, what can I tell you, my friend?"

"Tell me that you're not going to allow it."

"Do you really think I can stop it?"

"Yes."

"She has been engaged to him for six months."

"I can't believe it!"

"It's true."

"If she were my sister, I'd barbecue her alive!"

"Takis, I understand how you feel, believe me."

"No, you don't!" responded Takis, breaking down in tears.

"I do. I know you love my sister. I feel for you. It hurts me, too." He put his arm around Takis. "I can't erase from my memory what happened to my sister almost four years ago. Perhaps, as Papavasile said, this is God's way to vindicate the crime. A Nazi officer destroyed her honor; a Nazi soldier seeks to restore it by marrying her. What can I say?"

"And you understand that to be a solution?"

"There's very little that I understand these days. As Papavasile said: 'What a mystery is a human being!'"

The two friends, their arms around each other's shoulders, walked along silently, avoiding each other's eyes. Instead of going to Pantsaris's home, they went to the Roman aqueduct, where they sat on a big boulder and gazed at the marvel of twenty-three hundred years.

"These stones have been lying on each other for centuries. They have no feelings as we humans do." Bouras pulled away from his friend and faced him, eye to eye.

"I can't face living in Moria any longer. After my sister's wedding maybe I'll go away—live in another country or somewhere else in Greece."

"Me too. I want to fulfill my father's dream and go to America. There's nothing left for me here."

"You're lucky; you know what you want. I don't have any idea where the hell I want to go. Maybe I'll end up in Germany."

"Perish the thought," said Takis.

After a few deep sighs, Bouras said, "You know something—you and I are going to Eleni's wedding."

"Not me. No way." Takis bit his tongue.

"It's time for us to grow up and not be so childish. We nearly died together. It won't hurt us to go to the wedding. I want the four of us to be there."

On the way back to Moria, Takis couldn't control his ambivalent feelings, but when the Church of St. Basil came into view, sudden uninvited thoughts gave him some relief. *I'm not ready for marriage. I need a career. As a matter of fact, I don't want to get married. Perhaps I'll become a monk or a priest and live in a monastery. This world stinks. It's crazy. I don't want any part of it.*

Although they had had nothing to drink, Bouras and Takis felt intoxicated. Their thoughts about Eleni marrying a Nazi—"savior of the island," as Papavasile emphasized—caused a numbness. They wished that the earth would crack open and swallow them. In ten minutes they reached the town well where they parted ways.

"Friends till death!" Takis saw a ray of hope in Bouras's eyes.

"Friends till death!" Bouras said, unable to force a smile.

"I'll see you at St. Basil's?" Takis said with evident dejection in his heart.

At the sight of Takis, Kiki and Jimmy ran to him and jumped up, clasping him around the neck. "Welcome! Welcome! We'll never let you go again," they shouted joyfully. "Takis, promise you'll never leave us again!" Kiki said.

Kiki had grown into a tall, slender, pretty girl. There was not much change in Jimmy. He was still running around in short pants, and his head still seemed too large for his body. After hugging and kissing him, they went around the neighborhood announcing that their big brother Takis had come home.

Concealing the sadness she had experienced while he was gone, Katerina said in a trembling voice, "I've missed you so much and I worried about you all the time. Every day I offered prayers for your safe return. And here you are! My prayers have been answered. And you are a handsome young man, as tall as your fath . . ." She choked, unable to complete the word "father." Mother and son fell into each other's arms and wept. In their tight embrace, they both held back a bundle of emotions too painful to reveal. The loss was still too painful. Takis saw profound grief in her face.

"Something is eating at you from within," she said. "What is it?"

She sat him down on the sofa where his father used to take his after-dinner snooze and settled herself beside him. "It's your father's passing, isn't it?"

"Yes, but not only that," Takis said softly. "I saw so many unjust deaths. Mother, my feelings almost became dulled. I saw my own death coming several times."

"But you're alive! You ought to be happy!"

"I'm happy to be alive. It's the betrayal I can't stomach."

"What betrayal, my son?"

"Eleni—marrying a Nazi."

"Oh my God, yes, I heard that. I didn't realize you still loved her."

"I still do."

"My dear, dearest one, listen carefully. Nothing could erase what that poor girl has suffered. Where the Germans left off, evil tongues took over and ruined her reputation. I think this marriage is God's will. I call it a miracle that a German soldier found enough love in his heart to make amends for the crime against her." After a few minutes, Katerina stood up. "Your fresh underwear and pressed pants are in your room.

I'll make you a bowl of *trahana* soup while you're washing up." She smiled. Under her loving smile was a thought that brought some consolation: *Takis is now the man of the house.*

Having put on his clean clothes, Takis sat down to his meal.

"Why did father risk his life by going to Haidari? He knew what the Germans did to Lefteris."

"Your father believed that as an American with an inviolate record, he could save you. He thought that if he appealed to the German authorities for your release, it was quite possible they would keep him as a hostage. He was even willing to risk his life in exchange for yours. When Alexis sent the message through a German soldier that you were in the Haidari camp, your father could not keep still—he could neither eat nor sleep—until the idea of a bribe came to him. 'Germans like gold,' he said."

"And you gave him your dowry—gold coins!"

"How did you know that?"

"He told me."

"I wanted to go to Haidari with him, but I had nowhere to leave Kiki and Jimmy." She cried.

Takis saw that familiar gleam in her eyes and felt apprehensive.

"Since his return to Moria, Alexis has come here every day to ask about you," Katerina said.

"I saw him in the marketplace. He looks great. His hair has gone gray, but he's very much alive."

"He returned about a week ago. He said the prison of Averof was liberated by the guerrillas."

"I'm so glad he's safe! I thought they'd executed him."

"Stop in and see him later," Katerina said. "Thank him for his concern."

"He's having a big celebration for us tonight," said Takis. "I'll make sure to tell him."

Katerina nodded. "It's time for joy."

* * * * *

Several men and a couple of women were helping to set up tables. Behind the counter, Alexis was busy frying meatballs. When he saw Takis coming into his tavern, he left the pan on the fire, and with hands covered with flour, he ran to Takis and gave him a big hug. "Where are the other three?" he asked.

"They should be here any minute,"

"Let's have a drink."

"Let's have a strong one!" said Takis

Alexis ran behind the counter, placed half a dozen meatballs on a plate, and poured two glasses of ouzo. "I promised myself that I wouldn't touch a drop of ouzo until I had seen the four big pricks back in Moria." He downed the ouzo in one gulp and said, "We've a lot to talk about, but first we need to celebrate."

Takis savored his ouzo, his eyes resting on Alexis's face, and with the smile of a son to a loving father, he said, "Alexis, don't ever change."

"Change? Only when the sun rises in the west will I change."

"Haidari was hell on earth. How was Averof?"

"I was lucky." Alexis refilled his glass, and with a mischievous look in his eyes, whispered, "Remember that blond soldier who used to come here for cognac—and other things, you know what I mean? He saved me. He got me a job as a cook in the officers' club in Averof prison. But let's not talk about concentration camps and prisons." Alexis did not want to mention that it was through the same soldier that he had managed to send the message to Takis's father. *Had I left things alone,* he thought, *Asimakis would never have gone to Haidari.*

"Alexis and his magic wand," said Takis.

"There's a look of sadness in your eyes, Takis. What's eating your liver?"

"Eleni."

"I understand. It must hurt. But, on the other hand, you're destined to go to America. Hey! Beautiful women in America." Alexis tried to humor Takis, but he did not succeed. "Maybe you'll send me an *Americana* some day, and she can take me to America."

* * * * *

September 14, the Day of the Holy Cross, was heralded by the ringing of the church bells. Stores and houses were decorated with myrtle branches and flowers. Mountaineers in tattered clothing descended from the heights; islanders in their Sunday clothes emerged from their white dovecote houses; children and teenagers in colorful apparel joined the throng that headed for St. Basil's. The placid morning brought forth thousands of swallows to welcome a brilliant day. Everyone knew it was the day of the second resurrection. No more fears. No more tears. No more bondage. The Nazis had been vanished. The mountains, rivers, rocks, gorges—all proclaimed victory:

> Risen from the bones, a hallowed Greek trail,
> And valiant as of old, Hail, O Liberty, Hail!

Mingled with the ordinary folk of Moria were Takis, Pantsaris, and Tsakiris, who went along with the flow. Bouras was nowhere to be seen.

The Byzantine melody echoed in St. Basil's Church, and the hearts of the faithful vibrated with joy. The divine liturgy was ending, and the three friends joined the choir. Papavasile, in red vestments embroidered with golden crosses, stood elegantly at the altar and read the Communion prayers. As he lifted the cup to receive the precious Blood, he saw the icon of Christ, robed in a blue and red mantle, his face radiant, his right hand raised, and his left hand holding the New Testament open. Across the page was the inscription: "Peace be unto you." Papavasile shivered, and closing his eyes he whispered,

> Son of the Living God, receive me today as a partaker of your mystic feast; I will not question the mystery, I will not kiss you as did Judas, but as the thief on the cross I will pray, "Lord, remember me when you come into your kingdom."

The cantor, accompanied by many male voices, chanted the Communion anthem:

> Receive the Body of Christ,
> Taste the Fountain of Immortality.
> Alleluia.

Papavasile brought the cup to his lips and drank. "This has touched my lips, and my iniquities shall be taken away, my sins shall be forgiven," he said.

Then emerging from the altar, in a melodic voice he intoned: "With reverence, faith, and love, draw near."

The members of the congregation, one by one, made the sign of the cross and approached the holy cup. Young and old prayed softly: "Remember me, O Lord, when you come into your kingdom."

The last to receive Communion were Takis, Tsakiris, and Pantsaris. Papavasile smiled. Years had passed since the dreadful day of their departure from the island. He wanted to empty the love from his heart into theirs as he gave them Communion:

> "Christ is risen," he said.
> "Indeed, he is risen, Father," they replied.
> "The enemy is banished. . . ."
> "The precious Body and Blood of
> our Lord and Savior, Jesus Christ,
> is given to you, worthy soldiers
> of our land, for remission of your
> sins, and unto Eternal Life."

When the recipients returned to the choir, Papavasile saw a familiar figure kneeling at the far end of the church. He blinked. "Bless, O God, these people," he said and invited the kneeling man to come forward, for he was the only one of the congregation present who had not received.

Everyone turned to look at the stranger who stood before the priest, head bowed. Some knew by his features that he was a foreigner.

"My son, Christ is risen. Sorrow is over. You must raise up your head."

"I cannot."

"Look at me!"

"My eyes hurt when I look at you," the stranger said.

"Don't be afraid. You are one of us."

"I am not even of your faith."

"But you helped save our island. Now you may share with us the cup of joy and salvation."

The priest bent forward. Although the rest of the congregation had received Communion from the familiar spoon, in the Orthodox manner, Papavasile gave the stranger communion directly from the cup. The people made a commotion.

"Fritz Bittrich, thank God for his infinite love. We have survived. He is with us."

Takis and his friends saw the German soldier making the sign of the cross awkwardly and rolled their eyes in wonder as the priest chanted:

> Save, O Lord, your people and bless your inheritance.
> Give them the peace of Christ which surpasses all
> understanding.

* * * * *

In the evening, the marketplace and the taverns were decorated with flags and lights. Alexis looked around his tavern. On the walls hung colorful ribbons, the leather sofas were polished, and glasses sparkled against the white marble table. Smaller tables held plates of fried eggplant, stewed leeks, and stuffed tomatoes. Ceramic dishes of *skordalia*—garlic sauce—and eggplant dips were displayed in niches. The buffet was arrayed with salad bowls filled with fresh tomatoes, lettuce, radishes, and black olives. The wedding fare was graciously improvised by the women of Moria.

Papavasile finished the office of vespers and joyfully unfolded his vestments—a soft blue satin *sticharion* and gold-embroidered chasuble and *epitrahilion*. Adroitly, he vested himself again, this time for the wedding. The groom, Fritz Bittrich, nervously waited for his bride. Takis, having a problem in witnessing Eleni's marriage to a Nazi, chose to watch from a distance. Tsakiris and Pantsaris, who were serving as ushers, teased Fritz.

"Brides are always late," said Pantsaris.

"Yes, and often they change their minds at the last minute," chimed in Tsakiris.

He had barely finished the sentence when they heard an uproar in the street. A crowd had gathered. Pushing their way through the crowd were two callous liberators, Antonis and Paraskos, dragging Eleni in her bridal gown. Bouras was shouting at them angrily, telling them to leave Eleni alone.

The mob broke out into hostile cries and howling demands. Papavasile tried to calm them, but several rebels dared to defy him. "The voice of the mob, the wrath of God," the priest whispered to himself. A dense circle of jeering men stretched out their arms toward him, yelling, "You gave Communion to a Nazi, and now you plan to give him a wedding service! Are you one of them? A traitor?"

"What do you think you are?" shouted the priest. "Who made you judges?"

"Traitors must die!"

"Eleni is not a traitor."

"She is a whore!"

The bride looked tearfully at the priest. She had confessed her sins the previous day.

"If you call my sister a whore once more, I'll kill you with my bare hands." Bouras pushed aside the liberators with a steel arm and then said to the priest.

"Whatever you must do, do it quickly."

The priest, giving Bouras a candle, invited him to light it and join the bridal circle.

Takis, in an agonizing haze, stood sadly beside the cantor. Through his mind paraded tormenting scenes from Haidari.

Fritz stood beside Eleni, but the serenity of their souls was stirred by the tumult of scoffing and incensed, angry faces. Even Bouras could not understand their viciousness.

Then, in a flash, the sleeves of Eleni's white gown were ripped off. She felt herself swimming in air as she was roughly passed from hand to hand above the crowd. The church turned into a mob scene. A chorus of angry voices shouted: "Death to the traitor!"

Papavasile beckoned the remainder of the wedding party to follow him, and he hurried after the bridal pair. The mob headed toward the town square about two hundred yards away, determined to destroy Eleni. Fritz held on to her for dear life. An execution at the town square would eradicate any stigma attached to the Moriani. The priest pressed his way through the mob and persuaded some of the people to disperse, but Antonis and Paraskos, the two stubborn patriots, advised him to stay out of ethnic issues.

"I mind the spiritual affairs of my people, for I am a Greek priest not a political puppet, and in times of danger, I can place the cross on the altar and pick up the rifle! I did this once before, as you well know—and I can do it again!"

Takis could no longer endure the machinations of the supposed liberators. His blood throbbed in his temples. Seeing the venom in their eyes, he moved close to the priest. "Forgive me, Father," he said, "I'm going to do something to those devils."

"Don't go near them. They are killers," the priest said. "Let me handle the situation."

Standing beside the priest, Fritz watched as Eleni was swallowed up by the beasts in the arena. He jumped in front of the crowd and lifted his hands up in total surrender.

"Greek patriots!" His statement brought silence. "I'm the one you should punish. My people brought catastrophe to your homeland. It is because of Eleni that you and I are alive today. It was Eleni who saved my life a few months ago, and I, in turn, was able to return the favor to your island. Since you have spared my life thus far, I beg of you to reconsider. I want Eleni to become my wife. Wrong was done to her, but she has done no wrong."

During a moment of suspenseful anticipation, Takis and Bouras snatched the rifles from Antonis and Paraskos. Tsakiris and Pantsaris helped remove the ammunition.

"Maybe it's her fate to marry an enemy," said Apostolos, the butcher.

"Not all the Germans were rotten," protested Alexis who came running from his tavern.

"At least this one is attempting to restore Eleni's honor," shouted Stratya, and everyone turned to look at her, marvelling at her wisdom.

"Papavasile, get your equipment," pleaded Alexis, and while he ran back to his tavern to see that all was in order, the priest, his beard and robe flying in the breeze, hastened for the ceremony. In the town square, under the oak trees, the office of matrimony was performed. Eleni, pulling her torn gown around her, stood beside Fritz with tears in her eyes. Tsakiris exchanged the wedding crowns; Takis and Bouras held lighted white candles, and Pantsaris assisted the priest in singing: "Isaiah, rejoice . . . !"

Papavasile, overwhelmed by the complexities of life, raised his voice in a solo, unprecedented in tone:

> Holy Martyrs who have fought well the good fight
> and received the crown,
> Pray to the Lord to grant us mercy.

Later in the evening, the whole town of Moria was in an uproar of merriment. Music, dancing, food, and wine brought new spirit to the residents. One more glass of wine, one more dance. . . . Young and old felt joy participating in the *festivity of freedom.*

* * * * *

The nightmare of the Nazi occupation was over. For the inhabitants of Moria, once again, everyday life began to take its normal course. The following spring, in the year 1945, the United States government sent telegram announcements inviting all American citizens of Greece to America. Takis felt it was a sign for him to return to his birthplace, Philadelphia in Pennsylvania.

Early one morning, his friends arrived at his house to escort him to the harbor in Lesbos. On the way, they chatted teasingly to camouflage their sad feeling over their separation.

"Why don't you take us with you?" said Bouras.

"What a great idea!" Tsakiris exclaimed. "We could work hard and make a fortune and then come back to Lesbos and marry wealthy girls."

"No, I wouldn't want to come back to this place," Bouras said. "Takis, if you took us to America, I could marry an *Americana*—a blonde with blue eyes."

"Take me to America," Tsakiris said. "I'll open up a factory producing fried potato peels. We'll make a fortune." Everybody laughed.

"You're coming back some day?" asked Bouras.

"Of course he is!" Pantsaris said. "He'll be dressed like a Greek-American, with a golden chain hanging over his big belly attached to a golden watch."

"I still think you should take us with you," Tsakiris interrupted. "I want to own a factory."

In utter sadness that their comradery was dissolving, Takis pulled himself together. He pinched their cheeks individually and sighed. "You and I have always lived together, soul in soul, and walked through paths of life and death. You and I expanded our strengths to pursue our freedom. We paid a high price, but we are now free!"

His friends listened, and each word shuttled their minds back to those ugly days. Pantsaris, concealing his feelings with great difficulty, began to sing:

> The time to part is drawing near,
> We cannot accept our separation,
> And our hearts shed a silent tear,
> But life unfolds a new direction.

Papavasile, walking with Katerina and the two children, Kiki and Jimmy, joined the group of friends. Reaching the harbor together, they exchanged hugs and kisses, tears and promises. Takis's eyes welled up with tears as he said his good-byes. Last to wish him well was Papavasile. He reached into his breast pocket under his robe and handed Takis a small vial.

"Take this with you, Takis. It is a little vial of earth—Greek earth. You can look upon it as an amulet to ward off evil and grief. There is nothing more precious, my son, than this little piece of Greece, cooled by nocturnal winds, baptized in the blood of the brave, and scented by the Aegean breezes.

Takis kissed his hand. "I'll keep it close to my heart and draw strength from it."

"And some day, come back to see us."

"It is my earnest hope that I'll be able to come back."

"Yes, Takis, you must," chimed the others. "We'll be waiting."

But if fate or circumstances prevent me, Takis thought, *I'll find solace in touching this earth.* He held the little vial tightly in his hands and kissed it, a little piece of earth from the land he had grown to love so much. Then, with the utmost reverence, Takis kissed Papavasile's hand once more, and hugged his friends and family. Katerina and the two children wiped their tears. "Write to us often," Katerina said, weeping.

"And come back soon," said Kiki and Jimmy.

"Takis! Takis!" It was Alexis pushing his way through the crowd. "Sorry I'm late. I nearly missed you. I had to stop and get a bottle of the best ouzo in Lesbos."

"Thank you," Takis said, trying to suppress his sadness.

"Take this also." He handed Takis a small box, tightly packed. "This is dried octopus—don't worry, it won't spoil."

Takis smiled. It was not just a friend he was leaving behind, Alexis was truly a loving father figure. *History will write a page for this man,* Takis thought. He put his arm around Alexis and said, "When I reach America, I'll broil the octopus, open the ouzo, and drink to your health."

"*Kali antamosi*—until we meet again!" shouted his friends.

Takis crossed the gangplank, and turning to salute his friends, his eyes caught sight of the flag on the castle. He gave a farewell wave to the group on the pier as the boat sailed out of the harbor. Through tearful eyes, he watched until his friends faded from view. It was a sad and beautiful day. It was the long-awaited spring.

Epilogue

"It's real hard to believe! It's like a Twilight Zone movie! You and your friends went through all that hell and lived to tell the tale!" With adoration in his eyes, David handed me back the last chapter. "It sure is cool!"

"Yes," I said.

"Guess you're like a hero. Like the troops coming home from the Gulf War. Big heroes."

"No. Just grateful to be alive." I smiled. I felt I had made a lasting dent in his life.

"You know, Doc, I'm in a sort of concentration camp right now. Life with my parents stinks. They're always at each other's throats. My dad is Hitler all over again; I'd like to dismember him. And my mom is nasty all the time, bitching even over little things that don't matter a damn. School's like a prison. The teachers nag, nag, nag: *Where's your homework? Is this the best you can do? I need to talk to your parents,* he mimicked the teacher's voice. Talk about compulsory labor! And the S.O.B. of a principal is like Commander Steckelhuber—Great and Mighty Boss Man throwing his weight around. And do you know what the coach expects? He expects us to report at 7:30 in the morning to run around the track. Another Lieutenant Gruber type. Pompous assholes, both of them. They'd better get out of my face."

"So, you do remember Gruber and Steckelhuber?"

"How could I forget creeps like that when I see them every day—live with them right here in this town. I know something of your Nazi occupation! It's enough to send me over the brink."

"That bad, eh?" I felt empathy for him. His eyes reflected adolescent frustration.

As we sat in silence for a few minutes, I saw his expression changing and a glow of redemption blossomed in his face. He smiled.

"You gave me your book for a particular reason, didn't you?"

"A sort of uncommon therapy," I said.

"Guess I need to have the patience you and your friends had in Haidari." And then, shaking his head decisively, he whispered, "You know, I really don't want to wipe myself out—at least, not yet."

"Life can be painful, David . . . often unfair. But it can also be very exciting."

"For you, it was. You people had exciting stuff going on every day. Not that I would want that kind of thing—but I find everything so dull and so boring. There's nothing happening. I feel literally bored to death."

"Bored? Maybe you haven't been born yet."

"That's a typical remark of a shrink."

"I mean born into the *real* world."

"Seems to me I *am* in the real world, and that's the trouble. I need to escape from it, or it needs to improve," said David sadly.

"Well, of course it can be miserable. It's costly to be alive. That's why so many people nowadays take to drugs and alcohol. They don't want to feel pain. They don't realize that what they are suffering exists within creation itself."

"That's easy for you to say, Doc."

"Easy?"

"Yes. You survived. It blows my mind how you pulled through that hell, but you did, so now it's easy for you to talk about living."

"Are you afraid you may not?"

"May not what?

"You are going through your personal Haidari now. Are you afraid you may not pull through?"

"Sometimes I want to go to sleep and never wake up. That would solve this whole problem of living. Of course, if it were that easy, you'd be out of a job. But it'd be a good solution, wouldn't it?"

"Not at all. Be loyal to life. Accept what life is giving you at this time. Make yourself worthy. Whatever you're good at, do it well—your writing, for example. Be proud of your talent. Ponder what you're working on now, imagine its potential, and enjoy it. This is the way to remain alive."

A week later, David came to my office full of excitement.

"You seem pretty happy today," I greeted him.

"I feel good. I did well in my midterm exams—not in geometry though. Geometry's not my thing," he blurted out.

"Oh, to hell with geometry," I replied with a comrade's enthusiasm. "I failed it all through high school."

"The other subjects were a breeze."

"That must be a relief."

"Yep, but that's not all I feel good about. I have a fantastic plot for Diane's story," he announced. "Remember my story of Diane in prison?"

"Yes, am I allowed to hear the plot?"

"It came to me in a dream last night. While in the prison, Diane meets Herbie, a friend who's a bit older than she is. His face and arms are covered with scabs. He's been tortured by the Nazis. She makes herbal tea from sage plants that grow beside the barbed wire. She washes his sores with the liquid that acts like a miracle medicine. The scabs dry up, he returns to good health, and as time unfolds they fall in love. They build a tent, which they call *Ruach,* and many of the wounded prisoners come to the tent for medical aid. Diane and Herbie gain a reputation throughout the concentration camp. Everybody needs them. That's what motivates them to stay alive. How's that for a plot?"

"Herbie and Diane were your grandparents' names, weren't they? What's the meaning of *Ruach?*"

"It's a Hebrew word. I got it from an article that my grandfather wrote. It means 'the all-pervasive presence of God.'"

"What do you think the dream means?" I asked as my mind scanned what I knew about the influential people in David's life that his unconscious had woven into a dream.

"It gave me material for my story."

"That it did," I responded, "but what message is the dream giving you?" This was a good question to pose to end the session. "I want you to think about this dream and any other dreams you may have."

A week later, David came back with another dream to relate.

"A crowd of mourners was standing around a grave site in a cemetery. You were a priest or a minister or a rabbi—I don't remember which. You lifted your hands toward the sky and mumbled prayers I couldn't understand.

"As the coffin was lowered into the grave, the cement vault cracked at the seams and crumbled into the sodden ground, which belched and threw up the coffin. The crowd pulled back in fear at the sight. Hitler, rising from the dead, jumped out of the coffin, stood on the lid, and shouted in his familiar fury, 'Germany has now prepared another Hitler mightier than I.' The mourners ran in shock, and my girlfriend and I, hand in hand, followed them."

"Quite a dream!" I said.

"I hope it's not a prophecy. The world doesn't need another Hitler."

"Dreams are psychic energy. They reveal deeper needs," I explained.

"This time, you were included."

"While you're in therapy, I'll creep into your dreams somewhere. Can you figure out what the dream is telling you?"

"My girlfriend and I are writing about young people in a concentration camp. Actually it's a play, and we've called it *Beyond Brains and Barbed Wires*."

"Quite a title," I said.

"The drama teacher says she'll help us stage it toward the end of the school year."

"That's really something to be proud of. I bet your girlfriend is pleased, too. What's her name?"

"Diane." He smiled.

"Diane?"

"Yes, my grandmother's name. Strange?"

"Not strange. In therapy everything has meaning."

David became silent. He stared at my diploma on the wall and then at me, yet he didn't even see me and was startled when I again asked, "What's the meaning of your dream?"

"It frightened me." David closed his eyes while he contemplated and then in a pleading voice said, "I need someone to help me figure it out. I can't make any sense out of it."

"It's your dream. It's just like a story that you write. However, this time the story comes from your soul and is trying to give you a message."

David shrugged his shoulders, his face nonplussed as he agonized. "Why a funeral? And why Hitler? And why were you a religious figure at the graveside?"

"Well, you must work out the answers to your own questions."

I was not about to involve myself in the interpretation. It would be to his benefit to arrive at his own insights.

"Is Hitler the part of me that wanted to kill?"

"That's a good start," I said.

"So I want the Hitler in me to be dead and buried?"

"Right on target."

"But he comes back to life and threatens us."

"Are you afraid?"

"Afraid of what?"

"Of the Hitler in you."

"No way! I've no desire to kill anybody. There was a time I wouldn't have minded bumping off a few—but not anymore."

"You may have to convince the angry part of you."

"Apparently I need to work on my feelings."

"I think that all of us need to work on our feelings."

David's dream left me unsettled for a long time after he left my office. I pondered on the needs and the wisdom of the unconscious. I could see how ingeniously the unconscious worked for David's struggle to survive and be liberated from his problems. What I could not understand was David's unconscious insight which portrayed me as a priest. For the first twenty-two years of my professional life I was a priest, but I never make this information public to my clients—in this I take heed of Dr. Tate's words: "They pay you to hear their stories . . . they don't want to hear yours."

In my next session, David seemed preoccupied with the events of my early life—a sort of normal resistance, I thought.

"So you came to America. What about your friends? Are they still alive?"

"David, this therapy is for you. Why do you want to know details about my friends?"

"I'd like to know what happened to them."

"If you find it so interesting, then I'll tell you."

"Good," he said as he perused the pictures on the walls.

"That's Alexis's tavern you're looking at, and the man sitting by the door is Alexis himself."

"Still alive?"

"Alive and vibrant and pushing eighty. I took that photo last year."

"You went over there last year? You're really something!"

"Well there are no Nazis to fear now. I go back every year and visit my friends. We spend the first week of August together, celebrating and reminiscing."

"That's a neat idea. Whose picture is that?"

"That's Bouras."

"The big prick!" he shouted, laughing heartily.

"He has aged . . . but not mentally," I remarked.

"Let me guess this one. It must be the poet Pantsaris!"

"That's right! How did you know?"

"Easy . . . just look at his bald head and sunken eyes and sad face. Poets always look like that."

"And this is Tsakiris," I said. "He's the only one who became a millionaire."

"The potato peeler?"

"Yes, now he's Tsakiris the Potato-Chip King of Greece and of other countries in Europe."

"You guys led a fantastic life. It would make a great movie."

"And you would be the producer?"

"Sure thing . . . and I could have my girlfriend to help me write the screen play."

"Of course," I said. "Now let's get to work and talk about you."

"Okay, but before we do that, I want to hear more about the Moria quartet."

"I thought I had told you."

"Well, I know all about you—you're a shrink and a damn good one, at that. You told me about the Potato King, but what became of the poet and the big prick?" he persisted.

"Pantsaris the poet is still on the island of Lesbos, still writing poetry. Bouras lives in Germany. He married a German woman and established himself there. He owns a paint factory."

"Are you going visiting this year again?"

"Yes, in August."

"I'd love to go with you."

"Why?"

"I really don't know why. Maybe I want to see all four of you together celebrating—whatever that means."

"Well, we'll think about it."

Several sessions went by without David mentioning anything more about my early years or about the plans he had when he originally came to see me.

"Do me a favor," he said. "Get rid of the gun and the execution list I left with you." He handed me the keys to my office and the cabinet. I shook his hand.

During the session, he talked at great length about his involvement in the drama class, and he was particularly delighted with a scholarship award he received to study Shakespearean theater in England.

The following August in the inner room of his noisy tavern, Alexis set the table for five. He referred to us all as Americans since he claimed that "anyone who comes to Lesbos from another land must be an American." He was always excited at this time of the year when his old comrades gathered together in Moria. He thought of how quickly fifty years had flown and crossed himself in gratitude that he still had the strength to serve his friends. He felt old age in his bones and knew that his time for departure was not far off. "Death, the curer of all ills, is nigh," he said as he bent over the table. "One more spring or one more summer will see the end of our reunions."

Tsakiris protested, for he didn't want to hear such talk, and Bouras reassured Alexis that the Americans had found the elixir of youth.

"I have all the money it takes," announced Tsakiris.

"So you'll pay for this new potion?"

"Anything your heart desires."

"God bless America," Bouras said, enjoying the light-hearted chat.

"Takis, you must send us a bottle of this miraculous liquid. In fact, better send a dozen bottles," Tsakiris said in a blustery voice."

"Alexis has just poured us a glass of it," Pantsaris said with a laugh.

Alexis offered the toast. "Welcome back to Moria!" he said with gusto. They clinked their glasses and drank to their friendship.

Pantsaris's eyes filled with joyful tears. "Where did the years go?" he wondered aloud.

"This is a forty-year-old wine. I brought it all the way from Cyprus." Alexis licked his lips with pleasurable pride.

As I sat and savored the wine, I remembered old times fifty years ago. My mind shuttled from event to event, from my teenage years to current life and to David who wanted to visit Alexis's tavern . . . and I contemplated the brevity of life. *Dear Lord Jesus, where have the years gone?* My friends as teenagers, once fearful and frustrated under Nazi domination, were now once again together.

The time for separation is near, and my heart is whimpering. How often I heard those words from Alexis.

On our day of departure as I waited at the airport of Lesbos surrounded by my childhood friends and hundreds of my countrymen, I comforted myself—as I did each year—by saying that it was the best visit ever. It was difficult to abandon the place where I had experienced my first love and the joys and sorrows of the first twenty years of my life. Although it was fifty years later, the terror of departure was still upon me, insinuating itself in the tenuous gesture of farewell to my stepmother, Katerina, who was steadily declining, to Alexis, my aging and ageless friend, whom I adored as a father figure, and to Papavasile, the brave soldier of Christ, the astute patriot who had fought with cross and bayonet for the welfare of his people, and who was now succumbing to a dreadful disease of the lungs which would allow him but a few more months of life.

In Katerina's eyes I saw a shadow that I interpreted as fear of approaching death; the words she whispered in my ear conveyed a loss of purpose in her life: "My son, be well and healthy that you may come back again. You need not worry about my presence or absence, for my life is complete." I felt uneasy leaving her to a life of aloneness. I wanted to cry out with all the wildness and tenderness of the boy I had been when I first left Lesbos, but I remained silent in the midst of a noisy crowd, holding her in my arms, smelling the walnut leaves of sweetness in her hair. The loquacious therapist could not find the comforting words that his heart yearned to say. A fifty-year banquet of memories—of joy, pain, and survival—was coming to an end, and I couldn't express to my friends what I felt.

Bouras was returning to his paint factory in Germany; Tsakiris was going to Athens and then Paris to promote the sale of his potato chips; and I had the longest trip ahead, to the United States of America. But all three of us had to touch down in Athens and change to larger planes for our separate destinations. Simultaneously we looked at the poet; he would stay on the island and continue to write, for he belonged to Lesbos. Friendship for us was not one of life's solubles—it did not dissolve like sugar in water.

Another reunion had come to an end, and we were already anticipating the one next year. Our few nervous words were suddenly drowned out by the loudspeaker announcing our departure. We exchanged wordless hugs, kisses, tears, and smiles with those we were leaving behind.

The roar of the jet engines was deafening. We looked out of the little windows of the plane and could barely see the four sad figures waving their hands in farewell.

I made an effort to glean some fragments of wisdom from my experiences over the fifty years since my original departure from Lesbos. They were as amber beads—a long string of worry beads dissolving in my hands. The following day I would be in my office in Westfield, New Jersey, involved with work once again in providing therapy. Soothingly, I would be telling David about my visit to the island that I love with a passion. But why would my story have any real meaning for David, I wondered.

That day as the plane soared over the Aegean with its dozens of white islands strewn like pearls over blue velvet, I felt my whole life filled up with the grandeur of completion. On my right sat Bouras, and beside him was Tsakiris, nursing a glass of ouzo. We did not need to speak; we saw in each other's eyes a flame, a trust, a ceremony of divine affirmation: We shall meet again!